CAMBRIDGE STUDIES IN PHILOSOPHY

Deeper into pictures

CAMBRIDGE STUDIES IN PHILOSOPHY

General editor SYDNEY SHOEMAKER

Advisory editors J. E. J. ALTHAM, SIMON BLACKBURN,
GILBERT HARMAN, MARTIN HOLLIS, FRANK JACKSON,
JONATHAN LEAR, JOHN PERRY, T. J. SMILEY, BARRY STROUD

Deeper into pictures

An essay on pictorial representation

Flint Schier

Department of Philosophy
University of Glasgow

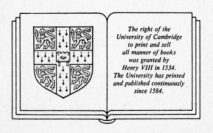

The right of the
University of Cambridge
to print and sell
all manner of books
was granted by
Henry VIII in 1534.
The University has printed
and published continuously
since 1584.

Cambridge University Press

Cambridge

London   New York   New Rochelle
Melbourne   Sydney

Published by the Press Syndicate of the University of Cambridge
The Pitt Building, Trumpington Street, Cambridge CB2 1RP
32 East 57th Street, New York, NY 10022, USA
10 Stamford Road, Oakleigh, Melbourne 3166, Australia

First published 1986

Printed in Great Britain by
Redwood Burn Limited,
Trowbridge, Wiltshire

British Library cataloguing in publication data
Schier, Flint
Deeper into pictures: an essay on pictorial representation.
– (Cambridge studies in philosophy)
1. Art – Philosophy
I. Title
701   N66

Library of Congress cataloguing in publication data
Schier, Flint.
Deeper into pictures.
(Cambridge studies in philosophy)
Bibliography.
Includes indexes.
1. Art – Philosophy. 2. Visualization. 3. Visual
perception. I. Title. II. Series.
N71.S355 1986   701'.1'5   86–6874

ISBN 0 521 32042 9

For my parents,
JOAN AND EARL SCHIER

Contents

vii

Preface

This book evolved out of a paper given to the Moral Sciences Club in Cambridge in 1979. The ideas in that paper were later developed in talks given in Glasgow, Edinburgh and St Andrews, until they swelled into the immediate precursor of this book: my Oxford D.Phil. thesis, submitted in 1982. It is a pleasure to thank my thesis supervisor, Malcolm Budd, for his extremely exhaustive and illuminating comments on every aspect of my project. I also profited from the reactions of my examiners, Richard Wollheim and David Wiggins. Many people have tried to make this a better book by advancing suggestions and criticisms at various moments of truth: I thank especially John Skorupski, Dudley Knowles, Frank Sibley, Eva Schaper, Warren Goldfarb and Tom Ricketts. The comments of the referees for Cambridge University Press have been most valuable. Any shockers that remain are of my own doing.

F.S.

1

The enigma of depiction

Pictures are my theme, what they are and how we understand them. Anyone who reflects on pictorial experience cannot fail to sense that pictures are both like and unlike literary works. A Dutch landscape painter and a travel writer can give us, each in his own way, an idea of what a town or river looks like, but while the painter makes us see his town, the writer can at best inspire us to imagine our seeing it. Vermeer's *View of Delft* is just that: a view of Delft: we seem to see through his canvas to a small Dutch town, its dark reflection shimmering in the river. No doubt the gifted writer can 'paint' such a scene with a few deft words, but reading her will not remotely resemble a Vermeerian view of Delft.

To get a feel for the importance of this distinction, imagine replacing various depictions by descriptions. Take down the portrait of grandfather judge and replace it by a description of his appearance; replace the altarpiece by a passage that describes the crucifixion; take down the poster of Bakunin or Colette and put a description in its place. Pictures, one finds, are more apt than descriptions to stand in for what they symbolise or denote. Nor is the representational virtue of depiction due to any aesthetic inferiority of description, for not even the most moving description of the crucifixion could take over the function of the meanest provincial altarpiece. Icons and not prose arouse the ire of purist and puritan, Christian and Muslim. Pictures, not descriptions, steal away the soul of the depicted one. Jonas Barish has documented a two-thousand-year anti-theatrical streak in Western thought.[1] It is impossible to imagine such a campaign of vilification directed against sonnets, villanelles or short stories as such. Books have been burnt, but almost never simply on account of their being books. It is the dream of the philosopher of art to account for the magic of pictorial experience,[2] but unfortunately, despite the distinctiveness of the experience, analysis has proved diabolically difficult. Do depictions

[1] Barish 1981. See also Kenneth Clark's *Moments of Vision*, London, 1981.
[2] Cf. Kris and Kurz 1979 and Gombrich and Kris 1940 on the magical aspects of depiction. Panofsky 1964 is also highly suggestive.

give us illusions as of seeing what they depict, as the numerous fables about Zeuxis et alii suggest? No: only a rude mechanical would reach for the ripe peaches ensconced in Sebastian Stosskopf's *Allegory of the Five Senses*. Then again, perhaps a picture resembles what it depicts. But it is hard to see how a cracked painted surface could look like a ripe, round, succulent peach. The failure of the resemblance model has encouraged some to infer that depiction is not so much distinct from language as a peculiar form of it, while others have concluded that the very idea of depiction as a clearly definable sort of symbol is just so much marshgas.

It is evident that pictures strictly so called have affinities with other symbols. Consider, for example, an actor's gesture in stabbing the King, or an impersonator's version of Humphrey Bogart's voice, or a bust of Louis XIV. Aristotle (*Poetics* 1448a) drew a distinction between the mimetic action of the actor and the narrative description of an action. I am tempted to say that whereas the narrator describes action, the actor depicts it. C. S. Peirce, the first to perceive the uniqueness, integrity and extent of this class of symbols, gave them the name that has stuck: they are 'icons'. In this essay I shall concentrate on visual icons and on pictures in particular. A successful account of depiction should set us on the right path to a theory for all icons.

Although the present work is intended to offer an account of depiction and not a survey of the wreckage of previous accounts, it will help the reader to get his bearings if first we sketch the main theories of depiction now on the market, warts and all. Philosophical excitement starts when the best accounts fail and we have to go back to the drawing board. I should warn the reader that the theories which come in for criticism in this chapter are being rusticated and not excommunicated. The concept of natural generativity proposed in chapter 3 will help us see more clearly which pieces of each rejected theory can be summoned back from the flames and which must be consigned to them for ever.

I RESEMBLANCE

The view that pictures resemble what they depict is enshrined in vulgar aesthetics; it is common to compliment a picture for being a good or striking likeness of its subject, and what could this mean but that the canvas or drawing or photograph resembles its subject in some good and striking way? But the resemblance model of depiction has migrated from folklore into theory, thanks especially to the associationist psychologists of the eighteenth and nineteenth centuries, and it is as theory rather than proverbial commonplace that we must assess it.

The resemblance model says that depiction is mediated by resemblance, or, to put matters on a formal footing:

(R)   S depicts O just if S represents O in virtue of visually resembling O.

We can break this down into two claims:

(Ri)   If S depicts O, then S visually resembles O.
(Rii)   If S represents O in virtue of visually resembling O, S depicts O.

The visual resemblance model contains or presupposes some such theory of pictorial understanding as

(RU)   If S depicts O, the viewer's understanding that S depicts O is mediated by his noticing that S resembles O.

At the moment I am playing fast and loose with the dummy letter 'O' which in these formulae can stand for anything from an individual object to a state of affairs. To avoid the clumsy locution 'what S depicts' I shall often resort to the dummy letter 'O' or to the locution 'iconic content' to refer to a picture's depictum. It is too early to refine the notion of pictorial content (see chapters 5 and 6), but the resemblance model suggests some such theory as

(RC)   If O resembles S, where S is a symbol, then S depicts O.

As it stands the resemblance model is obviously incomplete. Many writers have pointed out that in saying that X resembles Y one gives very little away: everything resembles everything else in some respects.[3] The prime responsibility of a model of depiction is to tell us how pictures differ from other sorts of symbols; in simply telling us that pictures resemble their depicta the resemblance model does not discharge this responsibility, since it is also true that many non-iconic symbols resemble what they symbolise.

But of course the resemblance model does claim a little more than a resemblance between picture and depictum when it says that the resemblance mediates or explains the picture's representing what it does. Thus, if I write the word 'black' in black ink, the resulting inscription resembles what it denotes, but its doing so is accidental

[3] See Davidson 1979 for similar thoughts. The same point is stressed in Max Black's 'How do pictures represent?' in Gombrich, Hochberg and Black, 1972.

and unnecessary; the word 'black' continues to mean black whatever colour of ink it is inscribed in. By contrast, the resemblance model claims, alterations in what a picture resembles would change what it depicts.

However, this qualification is insufficient, for it is obvious that resemblance-mediated representation need not be iconic. A child may choose a red block to be his fire engine because it has the colour of a fire engine without thereby transfiguring his toy into a pictorial representation. So resemblance-mediated representation need not be iconic. People will say: 'The trouble with the child's toy fire engine is that it does not resemble real fire engines in the right number of respects. Iconic representation is mediated by a reasonably rich resemblance between icon and iconified.' But this proposal suggests, at first blush, that iconicity is positively correlated with resemblance, so that the greater the resemblance between symbol and symbolised, the more the symbol will tend to depict or iconify what it symbolises. However, this expectation is doomed to frustration. Consider a sample of Liberty fabric that tells you what the Bauhaus design is like; this sample stands for the fabric which it perfectly resembles, of which indeed it is an instance, yet it does not so much depict as 'exemplify' this fabric.[4] So we must conclude that representation mediated by rich resemblance need not be pictorial.

If there is some doubt that the resemblance model offers conditions sufficient for pictoricity, there is also room for doubting that its conditions are necessary. It is no easy task to chivvy out the respects in which a picture of David Bowie resembles the man himself. Of course, there are trivial respects in which the picture resembles Mr Bowie – they are both physical objects – but there seem to be no interesting such respects. Certainly the 'rich resemblances' called for in the last paragraph seem a long way off.

It is tempting to try to put across the resemblance model's message by saying, very emphatically, with furrowed brow and much pounding of the table, that Mr Bowie's photograph *looks like* Mr Bowie. Of course, it is admitted, Mr Bowie does not really share any properties in common with his photograph, since he is human and his photograph not, etc.; but even so, his photograph *appears* to resemble him.

On reflection, the introduction of appearances and looks into the discussion does little to advance the case for resemblance, for it is simply not true that Mr Bowie's photograph appears human. It is at this point that the advocate of resemblance imputes a technical

[4] For the term and concept of exemplification see Goodman 1968, chapter 2, section 3.

meaning to the notion of appearance. Of course, to everyday, conceptually impregnated visual consciousness, Mr Bowie's photograph does not appear to have any of the more interesting attributes of Mr Bowie. However, it is not appearances of this everyday sort which concern the resemblance theorist. He hankers after a more exotic brand of appearance which we might call 'raw appearance'. An object's raw appearance at a moment consists of those properties it would seem to have were the perceiver to regard it simply as an item in his current visual field, quite apart from such knowledge as he may have gleaned from sources outwith his current visual field.

How strange are these raw appearances which are apparent to no one![5] So far from their being immediately evident to visual consciousness, they are rarely if ever sighted. It is not as if we could at will perform the conceptual striptease required to whittle Mr Bowie down to his raw appearance, nor do we know what he would look like at the end of this enterprise of conceptual defoliation. Indeed, how do we know that anything at all will remain of either Mr Bowie or his photograph once the last conceptual fig leaf has been peeled back? If Mr Bowie's raw appearance is postulated as a theoretical entity, the better to explain certain facts about visual consciousness, it is not obvious why it should be expected to give much joy to the resemblance theorist, who, I presume, must claim that photograph and subject are identical or at least very alike at the level of raw appearance, despite their being so very dissimilar at the level of everyday visual consciousness. Some very funny things must happen on the way from raw appearance to everyday appearance.

Let me expand on this last point. If the raw appearance model is to work its magic, it requires us to suppose that the everyday aspects of Mr Bowie, in virtue of which we decline to allow that his photograph resembles him, are either suppressed or transferred to his photograph at the level of raw appearance. For example, one obvious fact is that Mr Bowie is humanoid while his photograph isn't. This difference would not be registered at the level of raw appearance.

What does it mean to say that the difference between S and O in respect of O's being human is not registered at the level of raw appearance? I think it can mean but one of two things: either (a) that neither S nor O rawly appear human; or (b) that both S and O rawly appear human.

[5] On the vagaries of the innocent eye see Gombrich 1960 (especially the introduction), Goodman 1968 (pp. 7–9) and Wilfrid Sellar's famous demolition of 'the myth of the given' in 'Empiricism and the Philosophy of Mind' in Sellars 1963.

Taking the first possibility, that neither S nor O rawly appear human, we are left with the problem of explaining how the picture can depict Mr Bowie as human if it does not rawly appear human. I take it as given that our picture of Mr Bowie depicts him as human. But then, on the resemblance model of depiction, our picture must resemble Mr Bowie in point of his being human. And on the raw appearance version of the resemblance model, this is tantamount to saying that our picture of Mr Bowie presents the raw appearance of being human. Consequently, if the picture does not rawly appear human it cannot depict Mr Bowie as human. But, *ex hypothesi*, it does depict Mr Bowie as human, so it does rawly appear human. Thus, option (a) is not compatible with the raw appearance model of depiction.

This leaves us with the second possibility, which claims that when S depicts Mr Bowie as human, S presents the raw appearance of a human being. But if S presents the appearance of being human, it presents a false appearance. In other words, S causes (at some level) an illusion as of S's being human. Hence, on the second version of the raw appearance model, we no longer have a version of the resemblance model *per se* but of that particular brand of it known as the illusion theory, a brand dealt with in the next section.

There is an additional ambiguity instinct in the notion of raw appearances. Originally I simply said that an object's raw appearance was constituted by how it would appear to me were I to subtract all knowledge gleaned from outwith my current visual field. The question then arises whether such raw appearances are purely hypothetical or are actual components of normal visual experience. That is, when I see Mr Bowie, do I actually perceive, among other things, his raw appearance or is this something I would only perceive under rather unusual conditions?

Let us suppose that I would only perceive Mr Bowie's raw appearance under those abnormal conditions of cognitive suspension already adumbrated. Under normal conditions I perceive neither Mr Bowie's raw appearance nor his photograph's. Yet surely there is something about Mr Bowie's photograph that distinguishes it *qua* picture from other symbols even in normal conditions. There must be some cue, other than the photograph's rawly appearing to resemble Mr Bowie, that triggers my recognition that it is a picture of Mr Bowie. What is this mystery cue? The hypothetical version of the raw appearance model is in no position to say.

In order to explain how pictorial interpretation is available to everyday visual consciousness, and how the peculiarity of pictorial representation registers itself upon even the conceptually jaded eye, the raw appearance model must claim that, somehow, the fact that picture and depictum would present similar appearances to a conceptually innocent eye is registered by normal perceivers in normal circumstances. *Ex hypothesi* the normal perceiver does not consciously experience an object's raw appearance, so how then does he know what an object's raw appearance would be? Remember: an object's raw appearance is what the object would look like to a drastically truncated perceiver. We are asking how a normal perceiver could ascertain what S and O, picture and depictum, would look like to a truncated perceiver. From the argument of the last paragraph, we have seen that the raw appearance model of depiction is committed to ascribing such knowledge to the normal perceiver. Now the question is how the normal perceiver gets such knowledge.

I can think of only three answers to this question: (1) someone, an internal homunculus, tells the perceiver what O's appearance is; (2) the perceiver remembers O's raw appearance; or, (3) the perceiver subliminally perceives O's raw appearance.

The homuncular theory claims that within every normal perceiver there resides a subnormal, conceptually innocent perceiver, who nevertheless has the advantage of the normal perceiver in being able to see the raw appearances of things. The subnormal homunculus condescends to pass on the fruits of his negative capability to his more intelligent host. Baroque as this theory seems, elements of it are suggestive of the illusion theory of depiction, and I suggest that we bracket it for later consideration (see chapter 9).[6]

The second theory claims that once upon a time we perceived the raw appearances of things; we no longer perceive them, but our mature perception continues to be informed by the experiences of our innocent past. Aside from the lack of any evidence to support it, this theory overlooks one glaring fact: novelty. There are many objects whose raw appearances I have, *ex hypothesi*, never seen: these are the novel sorts of objects I meet with regularly. Since I have never experienced their raw appearances these appearances cannot form part of my memory. For any such novel object O and novel picture S, there is surely nothing to prevent my recognising that S depicts O, yet it cannot be my remembering their raw appearances that effects this recognition.

The final possibility is that I perceive the raw appearances of

[6] See Gregory 1966 and Gregory 1970; on homunculi see Dennett 1978, pp. 85–7.

things, but only subliminally, as one might register the floral pattern in a carpet without noticing it. But one can switch one's attention to the subliminally registered figure in the carpet. Try switching your attention to the raw appearance of the carpet. Try to look at Mr Bowie and his photograph in such a way that they appear identical to you. I dare say you won't have much luck. You will discover that you have not subliminally perceived their raw appearances.

Perhaps there are things we know even though we do not in any sense perceive them, and perhaps raw appearances are just this sort of trackable but unperceivable entity. I suppose that we can know about atoms and molecules even though, strictly, we should not wish to say that we can see such things. Nonetheless, we perceive their effects; they are the hidden order behind the apparent order of the world. Of course, it may not be exactly impossible to perceive an object's raw appearance – it is just extremely unlikely that one has ever done so – but the crucial point is that we can know about something's raw appearance without our ever having perceived it. So we posit raw appearances rather as we posit atoms and molecules.

Note that the raw appearance theorist is not just saying that *he* wants to postulate raw appearances; he is making the more interesting claim that we know about raw appearances in rather the way we know about atoms: by their explaining the order of experience. The raw appearance theory, in other words, must ascribe itself to all perceivers. But it must, incredibly, do more than that: it must suppose more than just that the normal perceiver entertains or believes the hypothesis that there are raw appearances. The raw appearance theory, as we have seen, must suppose that we actually know what an object's raw appearance is. To see that S depicts Mr Bowie, it isn't enough just to know that S and Mr Bowie have some raw appearance and that they are similar in point of this raw appearance. One most also know just what this raw appearance which Mr Bowie and his photograph both share is. As I think most perceivers are unaware of entertaining all these hypotheses, there could be grounds for ascribing all this knowledge to them. Moreover, *what* in our experience is explained by such hypotheses? What could be their function?

It appears that we have reduced the resemblance theory to near absurdity. We first nudged the resemblance theorist into admitting that Mr Bowie and his photograph did not have many properties in common; we then got him to admit that, to the conceptually informed eye at least, Mr Bowie and his photograph did not even *appear* to have much of interest in common. With his back against the wall, our theorist imputed a rather extravagant meaning to appearance. We have now worked out the implications of the raw appearance model and found it wanting in several respects.

There are further problems for the resemblance model of iconicity. For example, the resemblance model's account of depicting particulars seems to be a comedy of errors. Indeed, the claim that resemblance plus representation begets depiction has already been confounded by the examples of the child's toy fire engine and the samples of Bauhaus prints. But even if we grant that S is, say, a picture of a lemon and that it resembles a lemon, we are not entitled to conclude that S depicts any particular lemon it resembles: it may depict one lemon while resembling many. Likewise, a picture of one twin brother is not necessarily a picture of the other. So perhaps the problem of the double provides a swift refutation of the resemblance theory, its *coup de grâce*.

2 ILLUSION

The crudest form of the illusion theory is just the resemblance model *in excelsis*. Pictorial experience of a peach depiction is modelled on an illusion as of seeing a peach; in other words, a picture of a peach is so like a peach that we are liable to mistake it for one. While few if any writers have held so crude a doctrine, many have held views that are little better. On at least one reading of Gombrich's early views of depiction, our experience of a picture is said to alternate between a perception as of the depicted object and a perception as of a flat, rectangular, painted object. Gombrich's model for the pictorial experience is the famous duck-rabbit figure that can be seen as either rabbit or duck but not both.[7] Wollheim has had some justly critical things to say about this facet of Gombrich's story, noting, among other things, how unaccountable it makes the value of pictorial experience.[8] Presumably, our seeing a picture of a peach may give us some aesthetic thrill that does not attach to the mere contemplation of a peach; what then could be the aesthetic mileage to be got out of seeing a peach picture if this experience consisted in a mere alternation between seeing the peach and seeing a flat, rectangular, painted object?

The simplest refutation of the alternating illusion view of depic-

[7] Gombrich 1960, pp. 5–7.
[8] Wollheim 1968, Wollheim 1974, and Wollheim 1980.

tion is that it makes no contact with pictorial experience. Of course, it is true that I can see a Canaletto as a rectangular phantasmagoria of coloured blobs of paint instead of as a picture of the Grand Canal, and it is important to characterise this difference. However, as Wollheim has emphasised, the duck-rabbit analogy cannot illuminate the difference, because while it is only possible to see the duck-rabbit figure as duck or rabbit but never both, it is certainly possible to see the Canaletto as at once a picture of Venice and a flat, rectangular, painted surface. Moreover, it is clear that there is nothing obviously illusory about any part of my encounter with the Canaletto.

One can put the illusion theory in a hypothetical form that goes: S depicts O only if there are circumstances under which the perceiver would mistake S for O. I take it that the hypothesis is not that if we sufficiently dement the viewer he will take the Canaletto for a canal in Venice. I suppose if we make someone sufficiently mad he might mistake Hugh Honour's *Guide to Venice* for a gondola on the Grand Canal. The idea of the hypothetical illusionist must rather be that a normal, intelligent, pictorially competent viewer might be in circumstances where he mistakes the Canaletto for the Grand Canal. We need not waste any time trying to devise such circumstances,[9] for the hypothetical illusion model exhibits two outstanding and incorrigible faults.

First, recall that a theory of depiction must be general enough to explain the iconicity of everything from the meanest pictorial scrawl on the wall of a tenement close to a ceiling by Tiepolo. But there is no chance that a sane, pictorially competent person could be placed in a position in which he might mistake, for example, a Scarfe caricature of Mrs Thatcher for the Prime Minister. The hypothetical illusion theory has fallen into the snare of supposing it need only account for realistic depictions. Of course, it is a good question just what distinguishes realistic from other sorts of depiction, so it might be thought that hypothetical illusionism can aspire at least to some subsidiary role in the overall theory of depiction. 'A realistic icon is one which would give an appropriately placed viewer an illusion as of seeing the depictum', the claim might go. However, I doubt that we would withdraw an ascription of realism from a picture solely on account of its having failed all the relevant illusion-inducement tests.

On the hypothetical version of the illusion model it is not supposed that normally one mistakes the Canaletto for the Grand

<hr />

9 Cf. Goodman 1968, pp. 11–13.

Canal. Consequently, if there is something distinctive about normal pictorial interpretation, and about pictures in normal circumstances, the hypothetical illusion model is powerless to tell us what it is: for evidently, I can exhibit pictorial understanding of the Canaletto without sustaining the appropriate illusion.

The most highly evolved form of illusionism abandons the pretence that we necessarily undergo illusory experiences when deciphering visual icons; instead, some writers, such as Richard Gregory[10] and I think sometimes Gombrich,[11] adhere to the weaker claim that processes similar to those which could produce an illusion as of seeing a peach are essentially involved in our seeing a picture as being of a peach. Depictions could then be defined as those symbols whose understanding is mediated by these illusion-like processes. I shall not now discuss this interesting conjecture, but I return to it in chapter 9, where I argue that something like it is intimated by my conceptual analysis of depiction.

3 DEPICTION AS IMAGINATIVE VISUAL ATTENTION

In *The Psychology of the Imagination*[12] Sartre pursues an interesting analogy between visual experience and depiction. Though Sartre's account is not a variation on the illusion model it nevertheless shares some of that theory's drawbacks.

On Sartre's analysis of consciousness, the visual experience of my attending to a red poppy cannot itself be the object of my conscious attention. I may, of course, be aware that I'm attending to a poppy; but when my attention is focused on the poppy, I cannot also make the focusing of my attention an object of my attention. It should not be supposed that Sartre's argument here must rely on the very doubtful proposition that I cannot simultaneously attend to several things. Instead, Sartre seems to be presupposing the more credible thesis that modes of attention cannot themselves be objects of a simultaneous second-order attention.

It is interesting that Sartre deduces from the impossibility of second-order attention the impossibility of our attending to our states of consciousness. He here seems to repeat the mistake made by Auguste Comte in his argument against the possibility of introspection, the mistake, that is, of supposing all states of consciousness to be intentional, object-directed states. But not all states of

---

[10] Gregory and Gombrich 1973.   [11] *Ibid.*   [12] Sartre 1948

consciousness are intentional; certainly not all states of consciousness are modes of attending to other things. For example, my pain does not seem to be a mode of attending to anything else and hence it can be the object of my very devout attention.

Sartre made the further deduction that consciousness is nothing. Since it can't be an object of my attention, it cannot be an object in my world. It is nothing for me. However, even granting the supposition that all states of consciousness are modes of attention and hence not possible objects of attention, Sartre's deduction that consciousness is nothing for me is flawed, for as we have already seen, I can be aware of something even if I cannot attend to it. When I am absorbed in contemplating a peach, I may be aware of my contemplation, of what it is like to contemplate that peach, even though I could never make that contemplation itself the object of my attention. Still, Sartre has put his finger on an interesting problem. Usually, when I am subliminally aware of something without attending to it, I could attend to it if I chose. If Sartre were right about consciousness, I would never be able to attend to my consciousness. So, just what is the mechanism whereby I am aware that I am in a state of attending to a peach?

Sartre's view of depiction is that a picture *is* a mode of visual attention. From this he infers that when we look at a picture we so identify our perspective with the picture's that instead of looking at a picture we end up looking at the object depicted. If I have understood Sartre's view correctly, it is open to the objection that, quite often, a picture must be an object of attention before we can appreciate its aesthetic merits. A pair of old boots is not in itself an object of lively suggestion; but when I look at Van Gogh's famous painting *Boots with Laces* this experience has a greater value than my contemplating a pair of boots could have, and at least part of this surplus value consists in attending to the way Van Gogh has painted the picture. This extra value can be extracted from pictorial experience only if, *pace* Sartre, we can attend simultaneously to the boots in the picture and to Van Gogh's way of depicting them.

It may be wondered whether Sartre's view does not collapse into the illusion theory. If I am merely attending to O when I look at a picture of O, surely this is tantamount to being under the illusion that I am seeing O. This doesn't follow, as the case of self-awareness shows. If I am attending to the movements of a bird, I cannot also attend to my visual state, but I am nevertheless aware of it. Likewise, on Sartre's view, when I attend to the depicted object I cannot attend to the pictorial surface, though I can be aware of it. I suppose it is even possible that this awareness leaks into my attention so that while I cannot attend to the pictorial vehicle *per se*, I can nonetheless attend to the depicted object *as* a depicted object. I might appreciate a landscape in a painting rather as I might appreciate a picturesque landscape: by attending to it is as though it were in a painting. What Sartre's view does not allow for is my simultaneously attending to Van Gogh's pair of boots and to his brushwork. Yet I must accomplish this feat of simultaneous attention if I am to have an optimal appreciation of Van Gogh's achievement.

Sartre's view of depictions as transparent modes of visual attention is more suitable for those images, such as photographs, that have in themselves little or no physical presence. The photograph is self-effacing, its physical surface rarely if ever a source of aesthetic delight. A photograph's aesthetic interest consists in our looking (as it were) at the depicted object and remarking how it has been depicted, from what angle, in what light and so on. The focus of interest is on the depicted object *qua* depicted object, not on the physicality of the photographic vehicle, a fact which perhaps led Erwin Panofsky to make his provocative claim that the medium of motion pictures is physical reality itself.[13] I take him to have meant that the literal, physical presence of the photograph has no intrinsic value; it is merely an instrument which facilitates our awareness of the object depicted. It is our awareness of the depictum, Clark Gable or Greta Garbo, and not our awareness of the photograph itself, which has an intrinsic value for us. But even though the actual surface of a photograph is of no aesthetic interest, it is still possible, *pace* Sartre, to attend to it while also attending to the object depicted.

However imperfect his analysis, Sartre's sensitive phenomenological antennae registered an important fact about pictorial experience: that in some sense it consists in an imaginative vision of the depicted object. He was wrong, however, to suppose that the pictorial image is purely diaphanous. The rest of the theories I shall discuss in this chapter attempt to bring out more clearly the role of imagination in pictorial perception.

4 SEEING-AS AND SEEING-IN

In a famous passage Leonardo encouraged aspiring painters to avail themselves of every opportunity to cultivate their visual imagination. In particular, he warmly recommended the practice of peer-

---

[13] Panofsky 1959.

ing at damp stained walls until battles, faces and ferocious animals emerge from the stains.[14] Every child knows that there are faces in the passing clouds. Nowadays we are likely to regard the physiognomies of inanimate objects as the emanations of visual fancy rather than as occult signs of the hidden nature of things.[15] However, there is a realm in which physiognomic or aspective seeing is still a medium of knowledge and not just an idle pastime (or imaginative propaedeutic). Sartre, Gombrich and Wollheim have all urged that imaginative perception is essential to the understanding of works of pictorial art. Pictorial interpretation is like seeing faces in the clouds, but whereas the face in a cloud tells us nothing about the cloud, the face in a picture reveals its very essence.

Richard Wollheim in particular has canvassed the idea that seeing-as is the key to pictorial perception;[16] a pictorial symbol can be seen as what it symbolises and such seeing-as tells us precisely what the symbol is, since to interpret a symbol is to know its essence. So pictorial seeing-as is that kind of seeing-as which yields knowledge of the object we imaginatively see as something else. It is, prima facie, an odd kind of knowledge that consists in seeing one kind of thing (a picture) as another kind of thing (e.g. a face). But Wollheim is very careful to emphasise that in seeing a picture of a peach as a peach I do not cease to be aware that it is a picture and not a peach. Indeed, *pace* Sartre, I can concentrate on a peach by Stosskopf while at the same time admiring the brushwork that brings out the fur on the peach with an intensity that is unmistakably erotic. Wollheim's theory, therefore, allows not only for the vulgar photographic 'What is it?' approach to depiction, but also for that loving attention to the handling of the physical medium which is the delight of the true aesthete.

Seeing a picture of Meg as Meg or, to use the locution Wollheim now prefers, seeing Meg in the picture, yields knowledge of the meaning of the picture because the picture is intended to be seen as Meg. But since 'the disenchantment of the world'[17] that has been handed down to us by reformers, puritans and such philosophers as

---

[14] See Holt 1957, p. 283

[15] See Foucault 1970 and Thomas 1971 and Thomas 1983 for discussions of the premodern doctrine of signs.

[16] Wollheim 1968 and Wollheim 1977. Wollheim 1980 replaces the notion of 'seeing-as' with the notion of 'seeing-in'. In this discussion I have retained the familiar terminology but insinuated the pertinent modifications.

[17] This phrase of Schiller's has gained currency through Max Weber's celebrated lecture 'Science as a Vocation' (collected in Gerth and Mills, *From Max Weber*, New York, 1958).

Bacon, Descartes and Galileo, we no longer believe that our seeing a face in a flower (for instance) reveals any secret about it. The most such an experience reveals is our 'propensity to spread ourselves upon the world'. So we have a clear division between interpretative seeing-as and merely fanciful seeing-as. The question is whether pictorial interpretation can be defined as interpretative seeing-as; if it can, then pictures can simply be defined as those objects that can be understood by seeing other objects in them. It is worth noting that 'can' and not 'must' is the right modal here, since it is possible to know what a picture depicts without seeing it as that thing.

At first blush, Wollheim's account of seeing-as seems to explain the distinction between the imaginative perception of a face described in a novel and the imaginative perception of a face inscribed in a drawing. To vary the example, the skilful, imaginative prose of a travel writer may conjure up so vivid a 'picture' of some obscure corner of Venice that I imagine seeing a fountain in the middle of a deserted square. However, I do not see a fountain *in* the writer's prose. My actually reading her prose and my imaginatively seeing what she describes are distinct experiences. By contrast, when I look at one of Guardi's *veduti*, I see a fountain in the picture; my actually seeing Guardi's picture and my imaginatively seeing the fountain depicted are aspects of one experience. To borrow a turn of phrase from J. L. Austin, I see the Guardi and *therein* I imaginatively see a fountain.

We can define Wollheim-style pictorial seeing-as roughly as follows: P's seeing S as O is pictorial seeing-as just if (1) P believes that S is not O and he is able to attend unrestrictedly to aspects of S which he does not see as belonging to O at the same time as he is imaginatively attending to O, (2) P thinks it is part of S's purpose to be seen as O, and (3) P's seeing S as an O that is F makes P believe that S is true just if O is F.

It is obvious that P's seeing S pictorially does not entail that S actually is a picture. However, having defined pictorial seeing-as we can go on to define depiction as follows: S is a depiction just if one can see S pictorially as some O and S was intended to be pictorially seen as something other than S and S was intended to ascribe properties to the object that it was intended to be pictorially seen as.

Someone might object to Wollheim's account as follows: 'It is a consequence of Wollheim's view that I can see X as Y without my believing X to be Y. This appears to contravene a popular account of perception according to which to see X as Y necessarily involves being disposed to believe that X is Y (in virtue of one's visual input).[18] But Wollheim nowhere suggests that we have any tendency to mistake a picture of a face for a face. Consequently, there must be something wrong with either Wollheim's view or the cognitive theory of perception. Since Wollheim is committed to postulating episodes of seeing X as Y which do not induce tendencies to believe that X is Y, Wollheim is committed to postulating non-conceptual perception, since to conceptualise X as Y is precisely to be disposed to believe that X is Y. So Wollheim's theory, committed as it is to there being a pre-conceptual given in experience, must be false.'

The supposition that conceptualising X as Y necessarily involves a tendency to believe that X is Y is a gross superstition, and Wollheim merely needs to invoke the distinction between predication and assertion. It is possible to entertain the thought that X is Y without being disposed to assert that X is Y. When we see X as Y, we no doubt think of X as Y, but this does not entail our believing X to be Y. Seeing-as is merely an instance of that free play of our conceptual faculties which Kant thought distinctive of (or at least essential to) aesthetic experience.[19]

The mere fact that we entertain the unasserted thought 'X is Y' does not entail that our cognitive capacities are engaged in free play, since we may be entertaining this proposition as a hypothesis to be tested. However, in the case of pictorial perception we are entertaining the thought that X is Y with no such purpose whatever. On the contrary, we know that X is not Y, so it would be pointless to entertain 'X is Y' with a view to testing it.

However, in the case of pictorial perception our entertaining the known-to-be-false thought that 'X is Y' has a cognitive aim, since if X is a picture its being seen as Y tells us something about it, even though it is not actually Y: it tells us that X is a picture and a picture of Y to boot.

Some of Kant's views about aesthetic experience consort happily with Wollheim's account of seeing-as. First, when I see a picture as a face, my interest is not in whether or not it is a face, since I know it not to be, but in the subjective question whether it can be seen as a face. One may compare Kant's view that an aesthetic judgement is essentially subjective or reflective.[20] Second, the best way to find out whether we can see a picture as a face may be to pretend that we

[18] A good example of a causal theory of perception is George Pitcher's *Theory of Perception*, Princeton, 1971.
[19] See Kant's *Critique of Judgement*, section 9.
[20] *Ibid.*

are trying to confirm that it is a face. Our perceptual and cognitive enterprise may be as if directed to the aim of discovering whether this flat surface is a face without its really having that aim.[21] In other words, pictorial seeing-as exhibits what Kant called 'the form of purposiveness without purpose'.[22] Third, although we are not interested in whether X is really Y, but in whether X can be seen as Y, we nevertheless believe that other perceivers with similar cognitive and perceptual faculties will also see X as Y. While our concern is directed at the subject's experience of X as Y, we nevertheless suppose similar subjects will react alike. Consequently, when we say 'There is a Y' pointing to a picture we see as Y, our statement is objective in the sense of claiming to be intersubjectively valid even though it is not strictly true of the object. In other words, we are objectively warranted in the imaginative assertion 'That is a Y' provided people with similar perceptual and conceptual faculties are likewise spontaneously prompted to the same judgement when they allow their faculties to be in 'free play'. Imaginative seeing-as provides an important paradigm for objectively warrantable assertions (or quasi-assertions) that are not grounded in claims to truth.[23]

Despite the undeniable attractiveness of Wollheim's account, it can fairly be doubted that he has enumerated conditions sufficient for pictorial seeing-as and depiction. Here is an imaginary case in point. Imagine a tribe in which ancestor worship takes a strange form. When a man dies, his grandson goes through a process of training that will enable him to see his grandfather in a certain stone. He is taught to project the image of his grandfather on to the stone. Just as one can see an after-image on a wall, so he is able to see his dead grandfather in a stone. For each grandfather there is only one stone that can properly be seen as his and this stone is marked with his runic name. Someone with the appropriate training will see the appropriately marked stone as his grandfather. The whole point of this rigamarole is to keep the evil eye off the image of the dead, so only someone who can be trusted to mean well towards the dead man can see him in his stone. When a young man sees the stone as his grandfather he is aware that it is a stone. This is no illusion. He is able to attend simultaneously to the appearances of the dead man and the runic stone. Nor is this seeing-as or seeing-in merely a form of free association; on the contrary, it is systematically brought on

[21] For the view that seeing S as depicting O involves trying out the O-hypothesis on S, see Gregory 1966 and Gregory 1970.
[22] See the 'third moment' of Kant's *Critique of Judgement*.
[23] Kant, *Critique of Judgement*, section 9.

by the appropriate objects – though of course error is possible – and in being brought on by an object reveals that object's purpose. Moreover, it is believed that a malicious witch can so alter a dead man's runic stone that his grandson will receive a false image of him, so it is appropriate to speak of the accuracy or inaccuracy of the image which the initiate sees in the stone.

Thus, Wollheim's conditions for pictorial seeing-as and depiction are met by the runic stones, yet the grandson's experience of looking at his grandfather's runic stone clearly need not be an experience as of seeing a picture, nor are the stones themselves depictions of dead men or anything else. The initiate sees his grandfather in the stone; he is well aware that the stone is not his grandfather and is able to attend to qualities of the stone he does not see as belonging to his grandfather while also attending to his grandfather's appearance; finally, he has various opinions on whether or not the stone is relaying accurate information about his grandfather. Yet he is not having an experience as of seeing a picture of his grandfather, nor is he seeing such a picture.

Let me quickly scotch one reply to this counter-example. Someone might say that the stones in my story are not visually appropriate to the seeing-as of which they are the vehicle. This is false. Each stone is emblazoned with certain runes which induce the appropriate episodes of seeing-as in the initiates. It is in virtue of seeing these runes that the initiate sees the stone as the appropriate vehicle for a particular episode of seeing-as. It would be viciously circular to exclude these runes as being conventional or non-iconic symbols since it is precisely the concept of iconicity that we are trying to understand. Nor will it do any good to say that the runic designs do not make the stones appropriate in 'the right way'. What is the right form of appropriateness? Surely it is just this: the stones would be visually appropriate to these episodes of seeing-as if they depicted what the initiates see them as. Clearly the attempt to spell out the right form of appropriateness involves the very notion we are seeking to analyse.

I have tried to incorporate in my account of Wollheim-style seeing-as the most recent modifications of it in the second edition of *Art and its Objects*. In particular, Wollheim there draws a distinction between seeing-as and seeing-in.[24] He felt that in saying one sees a picture of a peach as a peach one is not excluding the possibility that one switches between seeing it as a peach and seeing it as a peach pic-

[24] Wollheim 1980, Essay V.

18

ture; but this is just the possibility that he wanted to exclude. The essence of seeing-in, as I understand it, is that when one sees O in S, one is able to attend simultaneously to both the O-aspects and the S-aspects of S. It will be obvious that my definition of pictorial seeing-as above incorporates this point, and so in Wollheim's new vocabulary I should have spoken of 'seeing-in'. While I admire the nuances Wollheim has added to his account, I do not believe they substantially affect my counter-example.

Wollheim makes one particularly suggestive remark about the relation between seeing-in and perceiving the intended purpose of the symbolic object that may be thought to answer the objection I have just offered. He notes that it is characteristic of seeing-in that one does not have to know in advance what one is supposed to see in a picture; rather, one sees something in a picture and this seeing-in forms a basis for one's suppositions about the intended interpretation of the object. We may draw a parallel with interpreting novel sentences; when one meets a new sentence one does not have to have prior information regarding its meaning. One interprets the sentence – ascribes a meaning or truth-condition to it – on the basis of prior lexical and grammatical knowledge, and assumes that one's interpretation is the intended one. Now it may be thought that my example of the runic stones must necessarily flout this constraint on seeing-in, for it appears that the initiates must know what the runes are intended to be seen-as prior to their being able to enjoy the appropriate episode of seeing-as. I believe the example could be modified without much difficulty to take account of this point. One need only imagine that the initiates are first trained on elements of the rune; in seeing these elements, they are eventually able to see parts of the grandfather image. One day they confront the whole rune and – hey presto! – without any further ado they see the whole as their grandfather. For whatever reason, they had not known what the whole rune would look like until the great day. So they see the whole rune for the first time and in seeing it see their grandfathers. They deduce, correctly, that these runes are meant to be seen as their grandfathers. Here the seeing-as precedes or grounds assumptions about the object's intended interpretation, yet the rune stone still fails to be a picture, nor is it seen as a picture (I presume). So despite the suggestiveness of Wollheim's additional remarks in the new edition of his book, I still cannot see that his analysis of depiction is adequate.

Of course, I have at most shown that Wollheim's delineation of depiction is a *nonfinito*. It is a matter for later judgement whether the notion of seeing-as or seeing-in will keep its place in the complete theory of iconicity. We must distinguish three possibilities. First, the analysis of depiction will provide an analysis of seeing-as, or at least a basis for such an analysis. Seeing-as so analysed will be seen to be a necessary component of pictorial experience. Second, the concept of seeing-as will remain unanalysed. In its unanalysed form the concept of seeing-as will form a necessary component in any account of depiction and pictorial experience. Finally, it may turn out that we can analyse depiction and pictorial experience without resorting to the notion of seeing-as and that seeing-as is strictly unnecessary for pictorial experience. In this case, the notion of seeing-as would simply be relegated to conceptual limbo.

5 DEPICTION AS VISUAL MAKE-BELIEVE

Inspired by Ernst Gombrich's idea that (for example) a picture of a peach is, among other things, a surrogate peach,[25] Kendall Walton has suggested that it is definitive of a peach picture that in seeing it one make-believedly sees a peach.[26] By contrast, when I read a description of a blanched peach in Jane Grigson's *Fruit Book*, I may indeed make-believedly see a peach, but my seeing the words on the page does not itself constitute my make-believedly seeing the peach. When one looks at a picture of a peach, the experience of the picture *is* the make-believe perception of a peach; when one reads a description of a peach, the experience of seeing the descriptive words and the make-believe perception of the peach are distinct.

Walton takes as his model of make-believe a game in which globs of pebble-studded mud count as raisin pies. Make-believe truths are a species of non-literal truth, a non-literal truth being a proposition such that there is a context in which a group of people agree to accept the proposition as warrantably assertible even though they all know (and know that all others know) either that the proposition is false or that its truth is not what makes it warrantably assertible in that context. The objectivity of such an assertion, or quasi-assertion, consists in the agreement of a group of people to accept it.

Not all non-literal statements are make-believe. There are two crucial distinctions among the set of non-literal truths. Walton distinguishes fictive from metaphorical truths and distinguishes those fictive truths which are make-believe from those which are not.

If someone utters a metaphorical statement, he is interested in

[25] See 'Meditations on a Hobby Horse' in Gombrich 1963.
[26] Walton 1973.

characterising the real world in non-literal terms. Thus, if someone says 'Jones's campaign set the prairies alight' he utters something which is true or acceptable in virtue of the truth of certain non-literal paraphrases of it. For example, one might paraphrase 'Jones's campaign set the prairies alight' by saying 'Jones's campaign caused widespread enthusiasm among the populations of the prairies.' This paraphrase is non-literal – it is not literally a paraphrase of the burning prairies metaphor – but the truth of such non-literal paraphrases is what warrants a metaphorical assertion.

By contrast, if someone utters a fictive statement such as 'This is a raisin pie' (pointing to a glob of pebble-studded mud) he is not chiefly interested in conveying information about a bit of the world, in this case his glob of pebble-studded mud, though indeed if he is playing a game of make-believe there may be rules about what actual states of the world make his make-believe utterances true. Thus, there may be a rule that something is a pie if it is a glob of mud and a raisin if it is a pebble. So 'This is a raisin pie' said of O is made true by O's being a pebble-studded mud glob. However 'O is a pebble-studded mud glob' is not an acceptable paraphrase of 'O is a raisin pie' within the game of make-believe, for that game is not at all intended to convey information about O's actual composition. The only paraphrase of a make-believe statement which is itself acceptable within the game of make-believe is a statement which is literally a paraphrase of the make-believe statement. So if 'raisin' means 'dried grape', 'O is a dried-grape pie' might be an acceptable paraphrase of 'O is a raisin pie' within the relevant game of make-believe.

The contrast between metaphorical and fictive statements should now be clear. A metaphorical statement is chiefly intended to convey information about the real world; it does so in virtue of the truth of certain non-literal paraphrases of the metaphorical utterance which are often – but not always – themselves literally true. A fictive statement is not concerned with the real world; it may be true in virtue of facts about the real world, but the statements expressing these real-world facts are not themselves paraphrases of the fictive statement. Within a game of make-believe the only acceptable paraphrase of a make-believe statement is a literal paraphrase.

Walton distinguishes two kinds of fictive truths, the make-believe and the merely fictive. A make-believe truth is a non-literal, non-metaphorical truth which is not true just because someone imagines or stipulates that it is true. A make-believe truth involves something like 'correspondence rules' and an implicit grammar. Thus, the rules that X is a pie if it is a mud glob and that Y is a raisin if it is a pebble, when taken together with some implicit grammar, generate the conclusion that O is a raisin pie if it is a pebble-studded mud glob. Note that we need rules of grammar if we are to distinguish the non-sensical 'O is a pie raisin' from the grammatical 'O is a raisin pie.' I presume that in most cases of make-believe, the grammatical rules will be those of the natural language of the speakers taking part in the game, the fictive or make-believe component of their language game being the correspondence rules which map 'raisins' on to pebbles and so on.

It is clear that Walton envisages games of make-believe as conservative fictive extensions of the players' natural language. In distinguishing make-believe truths from merely fictive ones Walton is relying on an important feature of language, namely its compositionality. Roughly, the point of compositionality is that the elements of a sentence may receive their significance through arbitrary stipulation; but that does not entail that the sentence itself receives a truth-condition through an additional act of stipulation. On the contrary, once the rules of grammar and the meanings of the elements have been fixed, the truth-condition of the whole has been fixed. Consequently, the whole sentence has a truth-value, determined by its truth-condition (if any) and the state of the world, that is independent of anyone's thinking that it has that truth value.[27]

It is the compositionality of the make-believe fragments of a natural language that allows Walton to distinguish make-believe truths from merely fictive or imagined truths. Given the fictive correspondence rules or satisfaction conditions 'X satisfies "pie" just if X is a mud glob' and 'Y satisfies "raisin" just if Y is a pebble' and the grammar of English, 'O is a raisin pie' can be make-believedly true independently of anyone's imagining it to be true. Consequently, players in a game of make-believe may discover new make-believe truths.

Walton's theory of depiction is just that when I look at a picture S of O, my seeing S counts make-believedly as my seeing O. Given what Walton has told us about make-believe, we know that our pointing to a picture of a peach and saying 'Look at the peach' is not a metaphorical utterance but a fictive one. In applying the label 'peach' to a picture we do not characterise the picture's literal qualities, nor are we interested in doing so. Of course, 'peach' applies to

---

[27] Authors who stress this Fregean point include Lewis 1969, Davidson 1968–9 and Craig 1975.

the picture in virtue of some marks on the canvas, but saying that these marks constitute a peach is in no way to characterise them. In particular, in labelling S a peach we are not adverting to some similitude between it and a peach. Moreover, if E is a visual experience of a peach picture S, then saying that E counts as seeing a peach is not in any way to characterise E; in particular, one is not saying that E is an experience which resembles seeing a peach.

On Walton's view we apply the label 'peach' to a peach picture because of the marks on the canvas and because of rules which entail that these marks shall make-believedly count as a peach. Or, to put Walton's thesis in terms of vision, there are rules about the significance of the marks within a game of visual make-believe which entail that seeing these marks shall in itself count as seeing a peach. In other words, if E is an experience of looking at a peach picture S, E could make-believedly count as an experience as of a peach even if the subject did not know that her experience E was make-believedly an experience as of a peach.

Walton's analysis is open to several objections. For a start, I do not know what reason Walton has for supposing that there are rules in the game of pictorial make-believe corresponding to those in the game of raisin pies. On Walton's analogy, we would expect there to be rules correlating marks on a surface with labels make-believedly attaching to those marks. Yet it does not seem right to suggest that we generate pictorial interpretations in the way Walton imagines, by our first imbibing (or coining) make-believe satisfaction conditions for 'peach', 'round' and so on and then cranking out such make-believe statements as 'This is a round peach.'

Quite apart from the lack of evidence for such rules, we can imagine games which meet Walton's criteria for pictorial make-believe but are clearly not practices of pictorial interpretations. Imagine a game in which seeing some totally arbitrary marks counts as seeing what those marks denote. Perhaps 'X' represents a raisin and 'Y' represents a pie. Seeing 'X' counts as seeing a raisin and seeing 'Y' as seeing a pie. Consequently, seeing 'XY' counts as seeing a raisin pie. On Walton's analysis, it follows that 'XY' is a picture of a raisin pie. If Walton wants to avoid this absurd consequence he is going to have to add some further constraints on make-believe seeing. To be sure, it is both pointless and bizarre to make believe that seeing XY is seeing a raisin pie, while it would be quite natural to think of seeing a picture of a raisin pie as seeing a raisin pie. But it is precisely the task of a theory of depiction to explain the unnaturalness of the first game and the naturalness of the second.

It will be evident that Walton's analysis differs fundamentally from Wollheim's in not putting any phenomenological constraints on the subject's experience of a picture. On Walton's view, its being make-believedly true that E is the seeing of a peach does not entail either that E is subjectively similar to an experience as of a peach or that the subject of E is aware that her experience E is make-believedly the seeing of a peach. Indeed, it is one of Walton's requirements on a proposition's being make-believedly true that it could be true independently of anyone's supposing it to be true. If I am playing a game of make-believe in which I don't know all the rules, then for all I know my looking at 'XY' might count as having an experience as of a raisin pie even though I am not myself aware of this.

By contrast, Wollheim does require that in seeing a picture of a peach I have an experience as of a peach which blends with my experience of the picture so that one and the same experience is both an experience as of a peach and an experience as of the picture (of course, as we have seen, Wollheim places additional constraints on pictorial experience). So, for Wollheim, S is a picture of O only if S can give rise to an experience E which is simultaneously an experience as of O and an experience as of S. Walton, on the contrary, does not require that a picture S of O should give rise to an experience as of O; instead, S gives rise to an experience, as of marks on a surface, which counts as seeing O within a certain game of make-believe. Wollheim's account of pictorial experience is primarily phenomenological; it says that there is something it is like to experience a picture as being of O, namely, it is like seeing one thing as or in another, and this involves a blend of an experience as of a flat, painted surface with an experience as of, as it might be, a peach. Walton's account of pictorial experience and depiction is functional or, more specifically, institutional; an experience E of certain pictorial marks counts as seeing the depicted object because of E's role within a game or practice of make-believe. For Wollheim, then, when E is an experience of a picture S as being of a peach, E *literally* includes an experience as of a peach, while for Walton E only make-believedly counts as an experience as of a peach. To summarise, when I see a peach picture Walton thinks I merely imagine my experience as being of a peach, whereas Wollheim thinks that I imaginatively see a peach.[28]

An advocate of seeing-as or seeing-in is bound to think that

[28] The points I make in this paragraph were informed by an unpublished paper by Malcolm Budd on music and the expression of emotion.

Walton's make-believe seeing misses out the heart of pictorial experience, and in this I am inclined to agree with him or her.[29] But let us remember that in the last section we found that the notion of seeing-as or seeing-in is not by itself adequate to the task either of characterising what makes E an experience as of a picture or of analysing what makes S a picture.

Moreover, it is blazingly obvious that our simply adding Walton's account to Wollheim's would get us no closer to an adequate understanding of depiction. For example, it would be easy – if bizarre – to transform the runic stone example, as deployed against Wollheim in the last section, into a game of make-believe along Waltonian lines. There would be rules governing whether a certain combination of runic marks were to be seen as a certain dead man or not; the initiates would have the authentic experience as of seeing the dead man in his runic stone and they would see themselves as playing a game of make-believe in which seeing the runic stones counted make-believedly as seeing dead ancestors. Since the runic stones would not, *ex hypothesi*, depict anything, we must infer that the grafting of make-believe seeing on to seeing-as will not achieve the desired analysis of depiction.

Incidentally, the hybrid of make-believe seeing and seeing-as in the last paragraph raises the question of whether such a combination is either coherent or useful. I suggest that we can get clear on this if, rather crudely, we break down a standard episode of P's seeing O as F into three causally linked components: (a) O's being F which causes (b) P's having an experience as of O as F which causes (c) P's belief in O is F. Now on Wollheim's view, when I see S as O this often involves my having an experience as of S's having properties F and G which I know to be incompatible (e.g. 'being a face' and 'being a painting on canvas'). So on Wollheim's view, components (a) and (c) of literal seeing are absent from seeing-as. On Walton's view pictorial seeing involves the absence of all three components. Now given Walton's analysis of make-believe it would be incoherent to claim both that it is literally true that P has an experience as of O as F and that it is make-believedly true that P has an experience as of O as F. So in this sense, Wollheim and Walton give incompatible accounts. However, even if we grant that pictorial experience involves seeing-as, Walton's notion of make-believe might have some use with respect to components (a) and (c). Thus, someone might have an experience as of S's being O and also make believe (a)

---

[29] Though I would not give a seeing-as account of pictorial experience; see chapter 10.

that S is O and (c) that he believes that S is O. So there may be some room for Waltonian make-believe pictorial seeing with respect to components (a) and (c) of seeing even if we accept Wollheim's seeing-as. Moreover, of course, the case I mentioned earlier, in which seeing 'XY' counted as seeing a raisin pie, did not involve the participant's seeing 'XY' as a raisin pie (in Wollheim's sense), and in this case we would have an instance of 'seeing' which was make-believe in all three respects: it is make-believe that 'XY' is a raisin pie, make-believe that seeing 'XY' involves an experience as of seeing a raisin pie and make-believe that the participants in the game believe that 'XY' is a raisin pie. Of course, I need hardly add that even though hybrids of seeing-as and make-believe seeing are possible, such combinations do not help us to get closer to an analysis of depiction which overcomes the runic stone sort of counter-example.

6 GOODMAN ON DEPICTION

In *Languages of Art* (*LA*), Nelson Goodman stresses the 'analogy between pictorial representation and verbal description because it seems ... both corrective and suggestive'.[30] Although he stops short of calling a system of pictorial representation a language, he is nonetheless convinced that previous accounts of depiction have calamitously failed to capture important symmetries between depiction and description. In particular, Goodman emphasises four points of resemblance:[31] (1) description and depiction alike necessarily involve 'reference to an object', (2) no degree of similarity to this object is necessary or sufficient for either depiction or description, (3) neither descriptions nor depictions refer to such imaginary 'entities' as unicorns, but are instead 'unicorn-descriptions' or 'unicorn-depictions' and (4) just as whether a newly encountered sentence of English describes a horse is a function of the conventions of the system of English, so whether a newly encountered pictorial symbol depicts a horse depends on the particular conventional rules for correlating surface marks with (other) objects.

However, Goodman is also intent on characterising the *distinctive* features of pictorial representation. His first suggestion is that what a picture denotes depends on its pictorial properties.[32] He then says that a picture's pictorial properties are given by a pictorial character-

---

[30] Goodman 1968, p. 40. [31] *Ibid.* [32] *Ibid.*, pp. 41–2.

isation of it and that a pictorial characterisation of *s* specifies the arrangement of colours in regions of *s*. In short, S is a picture if what S denotes depends upon the specific arrangement of colours on its surface.

It should be evident that this account is not very satisfactory. Clearly Goodman does not think that a picture denoting O can be entirely a function of that picture's colouring. But then, he must be making the claim that a picture is something whose denotation is sensitive to its colour-properties. But it is easy to imagine many sorts of symbol system, not in the least pictorial, in which the meaning of a symbol in the system is influenced by its colours. Moreover, it is clear that many intuitively pictorial symbols – drawings in black ink – do not easily fit Goodman's criterion of pictoricity. What a simple drawing in black ink denotes is not so much affected by the colour of the ink – another colour might have done as well – as by the shape of the lines. Similarly shaped lines, of *whatever* colour, could have an identical denotation. This shows that sometimes differences in colour make no difference to a picture denotation. This is intuitively clear if you imagine a drawing in black ink fading into a lighter colour – say purple – with the passage of time. Neither the identity of the work nor its denotation changes, but its colour does.

Goodman's first remarks on pictorial representation are informal, and in subsequent chapters of *LA* he offers a more rigorous theory of depiction in counterpoint to a theory of notation which he develops in response to an interesting puzzle about the fakable and the unfakable in art.[33] Goodman asks why certain art objects – paintings, prints, sculptures, and so on – can be forged or faked, while others – literary texts, symphonies, and so on – cannot. Goodman marks the distinction by saying that painting is an autographic art whereas music is allographic. For example, whether S is the *Flagellation* by Piero depends upon whether Piero had a hand in producing it, whereas whether P is a performance of the *Symphonie Fantastique* depends solely on its conformity to Berlioz's score. Similarly, whether this marble object is Bernini's *David* turns on Bernini's role in shaping it, while a book is an instance of Joyce's *Ulysses* so long as it is letter-for-letter identical to the original.

Music is two-stage, literature, one-stage. In the case of music, you establish that a score is that of the *Symphonie Fantastique* by showing its note-for-note identity with Berlioz's score, and then

---

[33] *Ibid.*, chapter 3.

whether P is a performance of that symphony depends on whether P conforms to some score that bears the same-spelling relation to Berlioz's original score. On Goodman's view, the authenticity or identity of a painting is established by its history of production, and the status of a text, score or performance by sameness of spelling (or, in the case of performance, compliance with a correctly spelt score). The rules of a notational scheme determine the criteria for same-spelling (and the rules of a notational system also determine the criteria for compliance). So music is a notational art and painting isn't: we need a notational system to determine whether P is a performance of the *Symphonie Fantastique*, but it is history of production, not any notational conformity, that determines the authenticity of Piero's *Flagellation*. A painting neither is a member of a notational scheme (like a score or a text), nor does its identity hang upon compliance with some notational utterance.

Two questions arise: has Goodman successfully explained the autographic–allographic distinction? and does Goodman's discussion of notation shed any light on the nature of pictoricity?

Goodman's account of allographic art is not correct as it stands. Same-spelling is not a necessary and sufficient condition for being the same-allographic-work-of-art. Borges has told the story of Pierre Menard, an imaginary symbolist poet, who aspires to create a work which will be the same, word for word, as Cervantes' *Don Quixote*. As Arthur Danto points out,[34] if Menard had succeeded in his mad ambition, his work would not *be Don Quixote* by Cervantes, but rather the emanation of a peculiar symbolist poet of the early twentieth century. Similarly, it is logically possible that a musical performance which complies with a score of Berlioz's isn't a performance of a work by Berlioz: perhaps it is a performance of a work by a Twin Earth Berlioz. It would seem that aetiology is also important in allographic art. Whether P is an instance of the *Symphonie Fantastique* depends on its complying with and originating from Berlioz's score.

Perhaps we should state Goodman's claim more circumspectly: in autographic art, if S is a work of A's, S itself must have been directly made by A. However, Goodman himself would clearly eschew any such claim, since he acknowledges many forms of autographic art which clearly do not always involve direct contact between artist and finished work of autographic art (bronze-casting and print-making come to mind here).

It may seem that the modification I have suggested in Goodman's

[34] Danto 1981, pp. 34–5.

28

account of the allographic–autographic distinction is a trivial one, but I don't think it is, since we are forced to reject Goodman's elegantly simple answer to the question of why allographic art is unfakable. Goodman's simple answer was: it is unfakable because its criterion of identity is given in terms of structure that can be reproduced with the aid of a notation; its history of production is irrelevant. This structuralist claim is false. History of production is important for determining the meaning, and hence the identity, of allographic as well as autographic works. How then are we to mark the distinction Goodman is doubtless right to make?

We must see that faking involves a *claim*. Obviously, an academic copy which just happens to be very like a Vermeer is not automatically a fake or a forgery: it must be passed off as a Vermeer before it becomes a fake or a forgery. So this strongly suggests that there is something about allographic art which precludes an object's being *falsely* said to be a work by a given artist if that work exists and if indeed the object in question – a copied text or score, or a performance – is indeed notationally equivalent to the original. It is indeed inconceivable that someone could copy out *Ulysses* word for word and then *falsely* claim that the copy was the text of a work by Joyce. By contrast, if you copy the *Mona Lisa,* you cannot truly claim that the result is a work by Leonardo.

It is instructive to contrast the question of the fakable with the puzzle of the plagiarisable. It seems that just as you cannot fake or forge *Ulysses*, so you cannot plagiarise the *Mona Lisa*. Plagiarism involves copying something and falsely claiming that the result is your own work. But if you copy the *Mona Lisa*, however poor the result, the copy is then your work, not Leonardo's. Of course, you could falsely claim to have created the *Mona Lisa* – but simply falsely claiming to have done a work isn't the same as plagiarising it. Plagiarising involves both copying someone else's work and falsely claiming that the result is your own.

You cannot fake a notational work because if the first requirement of faking is satisfied – namely, copying an original – the second requirement of faking cannot be satisfied – namely, *falsely* claiming that the resulting work is by the artist who created the original from which you made the copy. You cannot plagiarise a painting, or autographic work, because if the first half of the requirement on plagiarism is satisfied – by your copying someone else's work – the second requirement cannot be met – since in the case of painting, you cannot *falsely* claim of your copy of a work that your copy is your own work: it *is* your own work.

I think Goodman is right to think that the notationality of a work makes it unfakable. It makes it unfakable because it makes it so easy to appropriate. Intuitively, the fact that *Ulysses* is in a notation means that copying it involves no work of the sort that goes into creating a work of fiction. But there are no similarly mechanical procedures for duplicating particular pictures, or the style of a particular artist, so any attempt at duplication, however unsuccessful, will count as producing something new and novel in the relevant domain (whether the novelties are worth while is a moot question). Similarly, when an idea is encoded in a notation, that makes it easy to reproduce, so copiers get no credit for originality, and if they claim it, they deserve censure. It is interesting to note that the photographic image, which is mechanically produced in the first place, does not easily admit the notions of either forgery or plagiarism.

Can we define pictorial art as visual art which is necessarily fakable? I don't think we can. Given that our target is an account of visual iconicity, it is evident that there are many fakable works which are not visual icons. A canvas by Jackson Pollock is just as fakable as a Piero, but Pollocks remain abstract, non-pictorial works of art for all their forgability.

Because Goodman's interests are orthogonal to mine – he inveighs several times against the folly of the iconic–non-iconic distinction[35] – there is no need to make a meal of his syntactic characterisation of pictoricity. He claims that there are two key syntactic features of pictorial symbol schemes, density and repleteness.[36] Basically, the density of the pictorial symbol scheme entails that any difference, however minute, in the pictorial properties of a picture make a difference to the identity of the resulting work. Consequently, any given work would always admit of a plurality of syntactic characterisations between which it would be impossible to adjudicate. Syntactic density is not sufficient for pictoricity; two additional requirements must be met.

The picture must be an object in a symbol system: that is, there must be rules correlating marks of the pictorial surface with objects of the world. Learning these rules, on Goodman's view, is not unlike learning the meanings of the vocabulary in a new language.

But syntactic density and semantic rules are only necessary conditions of depiction; they are not the whole story, since an ungraduated thermometer or the line on an electrocardiogram satisfies these

---

[35] Goodman 1968, p. 231.   [36] *Ibid.*, chapter 6, p. 1.

conditions without having any tendency to depict what it represents. Such analogue symbol schemes are characterised by Goodman as being less replete than pictorial symbol systems. Repleteness involves the number of sorts of features of the symbolic object which are relevant to giving a full characterisation of it. According to Goodman, we can say that for any P that is a picture and any symbol S that is non-pictorial (even assuming that S is in a syntactically dense system), P will be more replete than S. That is, more of P's properties will be relevant to classifying it as this or that sort of symbol.

I think it is evident that relative repleteness cannot be the mark of pictoricity. There are all sorts of graphs where more than the shape of the line matters: the colour may have a significance as well. By contrast, there are, as we have seen, ink drawings and pencil sketches, where the colour of the line doesn't matter at all: yet these are pictures. I don't see how we are to avoid the conclusion that a multicoloured graph is more replete than such a pencil sketch, and hence (on Goodman's view) more pictorial as well. Clearly an abstract expressionist painting may be more replete than a sketch by Rembrandt: but surely it is not therefore more pictorial. Repleteness is not the key to pictoricity.

Incidentally, it would seem that if my remark about the multicoloured graph being more replete than a Rembrandt sketch is right, repleteness cannot be the key to fakability either, since I don't consider the graph to be the potential object of the forger's art. Indeed, there appear to me many such non-notational symbols that are not obviously fakable or plagiarisable – precisely because there is no particular art in generating them in the first place. Goodman's foray into the theory of notation has left our two major questions unanswered. We still don't really have a full account of faking and forging and we certainly don't have an answer to the question, the one I address in this book, of what makes a symbol a picture.

7 A CONJECTURE

We have looked at theories of depiction which suggest that pictures look like their depicta, cause illusions as of seeing their depicta, are modes of attending to their depicta, are seen as their depicta, and are make-believedly identical with their depicta; and we have encountered one theorist who is disillusioned with the very distinction between iconic and non-iconic visual symbols. None of these theories sufficiently concentrates our attention on how pictorial interpretations are generated. The illusion and resemblance models highlight the appearance of pictures, while the Sartrean and seeing-as models delineate the phenomenology of pictorial experience. Walton devotes attention to how his make-believe truths about pictures are generated, but (following Goodman) he has modelled the generation of pictorial interpretations too closely on the generation of interpretations for novel sentences.

I suggest that we temporarily abandon the project of trying to say what pictures look like. I think we should also suspend for the time being our interest in what it is like to see a picture and not directly concern ourselves with whether and how pictorial experience differs intrinsically from experiences of other sorts of symbolic objects. Rather, we should focus on the causal or functional role of pictorial interpretation and experience. I think we can give an account of how all and only pictorial interpretations are generated that will enable us to produce a cogent theory of depiction and pictorial experience.

Let me lay down two propositions about pictorial interpretation. First, an interpretation of a picture is an assignment of meaning or content to it. My interest is in the distinctive way in which meaning gets assigned to pictures as distinct from other symbols. Generally, I shall suppose that knowing a picture's content consists of knowing under just what conditions the picture would be true. This notion of content will be refined in chapter 6 but until then it will serve my turn. When I speak of interpreting a picture, I refer to any process – however behaviourally manifested – of assigning truth- or accuracy-conditions to it. I believe that there is a peculiar way of assigning meaning to pictures that defines depiction.

The second proposition is this: to interpret a picture it is not necessary to experience it in a given way. It is therefore a further, but crucial, task to account for the nature of pictorial experience. Once the account of pictorial interpretation has been worked out, I believe it will be possible to give a functional account of what it is to have an experience as of a picture. (N.B.: an experience of a picture is not necessarily an experience as of a picture, as one may see a picture without realising that it is a picture one is seeing. Likewise, an experience as of a picture is not necessarily an experience of one, as you may think you are seeing a picture when you are not.)

So here, in a nutshell, is my conjecture: there is a peculiar mode of coming to know the meaning or semantic content of pictures in terms of which it will prove possible to define depiction and pictorial experience. In the next chapter, the reader will be offered reasons for accepting this conjecture, along with a puzzle that will inform and challenge the development of my theory. In chapter 3 that development gets under way.

2

The natural and the unnatural

Imagine that Churchill and the other Allied leaders are going to get together for a meeting. It is crucial to get the seating right so the conference table is being arranged ahead of time by 'seating' dots around a rectangular piece of paper. It would be perfectly natural, given the convention, to point to these dots and say 'That's Churchill on Roosevelt's right' or 'Churchill should be moved closer to Uncle Joe' and so on. The 'advance men' have anticipated and arranged the meeting by constructing a model of it. Yet the pieces of the model are not icons of the participants or anyone else and the whole model is not an icon of the conference. The model is, in some sense, a natural way of simulating the conference and for this purpose it is probably more useful than a series of drawings. Of course if one is staging a spectacle – a play, a masque or a film – one becomes interested in visual detail. But for the purposes of the organisers this model is what they want.

But the mere addition of information concerning visual detail would not in itself transform our model into an icon. It depends upon how the information is expressed. Suppose we use dots. That one is Churchill's nose, that one is his mouth, these are his eyes, and these are his ears. This will be his cigar, this one will be his furrowed brow and that one a frown. I arrange them in a row, attaching a number to each dot and the corresponding predicate to each number. Such a row of dots is no more than a list of Churchill's features. To make 'statements' with these dots we need some compositional rules. If we take the dot which stands for Churchill – the Churchillian dot – we might develop rules like these: if one of the feature dots (say the mouth dot) stands to the right of the Churchillian dot then the result is either a statement ('Churchill has a mouth') or a definite description ('Churchill's mouth'). If Churchill has a cigar in his mouth, then the cigar dot is placed to the right of the mouth dot which is to the right of the Churchillian dot. We create negations by placing dots to the left of the Churchillian dot. Thus the dot sequence (from left to right) 'cigar–Churchill–mouth' means 'There is no cigar in Churchill's mouth.' Let us call this dot system the Churchillian dot system and the original system (un-enriched by all these Churchillian minutiae) the Conference dot system.

It is clear, first, that the representations or models we construct using these systems are not pictorial. The model of the conference is not a sketch or a picture of it; an ensemble of Churchillian dots is not a portrait. The Conference system seems to be more natural than the Churchillian system even though neither system is iconic. In what does the greater naturalness of the Conference system consist? Clearly it cannot be a matter of the meanings attached to the dots themselves, for in both systems the meaning of the dots is stipulated arbitrarily. But if the distinction is not a matter of the significance of the parts, it must have to do with how they are arranged. The 'grammar' of the first system is somehow more natural than the grammar of the second system. Once we understand the purpose of the Conference system (to represent conference seating) and once we have stipulated the significance of the individual pieces (as-signing dots to participants), we are able to converge on ways of constructing and interpreting models in the system *without further explicit stipulation or agreement*. One could test this in either of two ways.

First test: Explain the purpose of the models to be constructed with the system and explain the significance of each part. Then verbally describe an arrangement of the conference that could be represented using the parts whose significance has been explained. If different people, without communicating, come up by and large with the same model-construction, we can say the 'grammar' of the system is natural. For without further communication or stipu-lation regarding rules of composition, they naturally converge on the same principles.

Second test: Again one explains the purpose of the models of the Conference system and explains the significance of each part. This time one asks the experimental subjects to interpret given models on the basis of this information alone. If similar models are given similar interpretations, then again we can say that the 'grammar' of the conference system is natural.

I have performed neither of these experiments, but I would pre-dict convergence in both cases. However, one would not predict a similar convergence in the case of the Churchillian system. If I explain just the purpose of the system – to represent Churchill's face – and the significance of individual dots, without specifying a grammar, I shall expect a wide divergence of constructions and interpretations. The grammar for this system seems not to be natural. What does the naturalness of this grammar consist in? Merely the fact that people converge on it without prior consultation? Or is this convergence merely a *sign* of naturalness?

I don't think the naturalness of the representation can just *consist* in a spontaneous convergence of certain constructions and interpretations in the first and second tests. The reasons for my thinking this are somewhat involved and will actually not surface until chapter 3. However, now it suffices to note that if one had set the system up on one's own, for the stated purpose and with the given stipulations for the pieces, one would have found certain arrangements of the dots more natural than others for conveying given arrangements of the conference. I want to say that it is because the imaginary experimental subjects severally found certain arrangements natural that they jointly converged, on those arrangements and not vice versa. While the fact that a given arrangement seems natural to people might explain the convergence, the converse simply could not hold; the convergence could not explain the fact that, prior to consultation with any other subjects, each subject feels that a certain arrangement is natural.

What keeps the Conference system from being pictorial? What distinguishes a depiction of the conference from a dot-model of it? Clearly not just the fact that a depiction contains extraneous visual details which the dot system ignores. For the Churchillian system contained much information about visual details and it was even less natural than the Conference system. And if 'less natural' means 'less like an icon', that would seem to rule out the suggestion that the distinction between the dot-model and an icon is simply a matter of the amount of visual information contained in an icon. We shall see, however, that there is something to this point. It just isn't the whole story.

What about the role of *stipulation* in the dot systems? Perhaps the point about icons is that they can be understood without stipulation of any kind. When I set up the dot system for representing the conference, I set up a series of conventions about which dot signifies or exemplifies which participant. Which participant any given dot represents is purely arbitrary. You need a manual telling you that the dot with number N goes with, say, Stalin. That is, if I succeed in manifesting an intention that dot number 4 shall stand for Stalin, then stand for Stalin it does. It is clearly not true of an icon, however, that manifesting an intention that it shall iconically represent Stalin is sufficient for it to do so. A child may manifest his intention that a certain blob of red paint shall represent a fire engine, but this hardly makes it an icon of a fire engine, for him or anyone else. Of course, both the deviser of the dot system and the child can succeed in communicating with us provided they make their intentions clear. But this just shows that something over and above using S to communicate that *p* is involved in S's being an icon of the state of affairs that *p*. An icon must, as it were naturally, elicit its interpretation from the viewer.

It does not follow from this that conventions and communicative intentions play *no role* at all in iconic representation. There is, however, a clear limit to the role of convention. Convention alone cannot an icon make. (Convention alone can reallocate the meaning of the word 'icon', but given the meaning 'icon' now has, conventions alone do not make icons.) This gives us a characterisation of iconicity in negative terms: it isn't purely conventional. Can we fill out this sketch in more detail? Can we say in what the naturalness of the icon consists?

There are two other points worth mentioning. If one were to perform with pictures an experiment like the one envisaged with the dot system, how would one go about it and what would one expect? As I have already suggested, the first difference would be that one would not need to stipulate the meanings of the parts of the picture or to stipulate modes of composition. This, however, is merely suggestive, since the same point would apply to a natural language. For all we know the reason one does not have to stipulate the meanings in a picture is that the subjects are already dab hands at pictorial interpretation. This would establish no asymmetry between depiction and linguistic description. Those who are in thrall to the linguistic model of depiction could say: 'Just because you don't need to make special stipulations about the meanings of novel pictures proves nothing; you don't have to make special stipulations about the meanings of novel sentences either, provided you have addressed them to someone with the necessary lexical and grammatical virtuosity.'

There is, however, a tantalising asymmetry when it comes to the constructive rather than the interpretative side of the experiment. In the case of the dot system, after spelling out the significance of the dots and describing a conference arrangement, I conjectured that my subjects would come back with more or less identical arrangements even though nothing had been specified about how they were to arrange the dots and no communication between the subjects was permitted during their task. But suppose we read the same description and ask our subjects to draw the described arrangement. What a diversity we should expect! The dot system is like a juggernaut. There are just so many dots, and given a description there is (we expect) just one natural way to represent the conference so described with the dot system. Not so with the depiction. It might be thought that to make the comparison fair we should have to specify that a given system of depiction should be used by the subjects. But I doubt that one could, in the case of depiction, specify a system of depiction. How does one individuate pictorial systems? And even to the extent that one could restrict the experimental subjects' degrees of freedom, I doubt that one could specify a system that would result in convergence on a unique outcome. The dot system allows one to make only a finite number of statements; a pictorial system worthy of the name has no limit set to it. But again, interesting though this may be, it merely points to a respect in which depiction is more like natural language than like the dot system. With the dot system, there is a set number of states of affairs it can represent; with a pictorial system or a linguistic system, there may be things the system cannot do or do well, but there is no non-arbitrary limit to the number of states of affairs a system can represent.

I have argued that the Conference system is more natural than the Churchillian system in respect of its 'grammar'. There is another sense in which it is more natural, and that is that it seems well suited to its purpose. Given the purpose of designing a conference seating arrangement, the dot system is ideal. It allows one to think out the arrangement beforehand; it is easy to shift pieces around to experiment with various outcomes; and the grammar is natural. It also allows one to take in arrangements at a glance rather than in serial order. Finally, of course, it may be impossible to keep all the details in mind at once; best, then, to represent them externally.

By contrast, the Churchillian system is extremely cumbersome. As a way of representing Churchill's visual aspect, it is hardly a winner. The rules of the grammar would probably be awesomely complex if one wanted to represent all the details of Churchill's face.

Furthermore, one can't take in the information contained in it all at once. One would have to work laboriously through each row of dots. Someone ought to invent depiction!

Some people have had the bright idea that icons distinguish themselves from the more conventional denizens of the symbol kingdom in virtue of being peculiarly easy to 'read' or 'decode'. Goodman has rightly pointed out that we are all virtuosi in our mother tongue and that understanding a language is probably no more difficult than understanding icons. Wollheim has protested that it is perverse to think that we decode pictures at all, though perhaps he would acknowledge that there is a class of cases, eccentric to be sure, to which the viewer must bring as much hermeneutic virtuosity as he might bring to the reading of a poem by a particularly obscure metaphysical poet. For example, Galileo compares the allegorical programme of Tasso's *Gerusalemme Liberata* with an anamorph which shows 'a human figure when looked at sideways and from a uniquely determined point of view but, when observed frontally as we naturally and normally do with other pictures, display[s] nothing but a welter of lines and colors from which we can make out, if we try hard, semblances of rivers, bare beaches, clouds or strange chimerical shapes' (*Opere* IX, p. 129).[1] Let us for the moment, however, leave to one side such apparent exceptions to Wollheim's 'no-decoding' claim as anamorphs, pictorial allegories and rebuses. Does the fact that we don't decode pictures give us a clue to their essence?

The 'no-decoding' claim would appear to apply to natural languages as well as to depiction. Perhaps if one is confronted with Etruscan script one will be at sea, and it took the ingenuity of Michael Ventris to unravel Linear B. But for a speaker at home in his own language it would be perverse to assert that he decodes the utterances of his fellow virtuosi. It would be downright insulting to tell someone that his utterances required decoding (like the compliments arduously contrived by Proust's aunts). Perhaps verbal understanding involves unconscious decoding (whatever that means), but so might pictorial understanding for all we know. This is simply an empirical question of choosing the best framework for explaining the mechanism of language.

[1] Panofsky 1954.

Wollheim has sharpened the issue by pointing out that there is a difference between understanding a colour-reversed icon and understanding a colour-normal icon.[2] A colour-reversed icon is one in which colours represent their complements rather than themselves. For example, in a red–green colour reversed system, green in the picture stands for red in the depicted object and red in the picture stands for green in the depicted object. Understanding the colour-reversed icon requires decoding; understanding the colour-normal icon, by contrast, seems not to involve any decoding operation (if we restrict ourselves just to colour representation for the moment).

Now I think most of us share Wollheim's intuition that the colour-reversed icon is not iconic with respect to colour. For example, in the colour-reversed system, a painting of a tree represents the tree as having green leaves by using red colours. It seems right to say that such a painting does not *depict* the tree as green. It *represents* the tree as green (given the reversal conventions), but that is a horse of a different colour.

But does this in itself shed any light on the nature of iconicity? In particular, can we say that what distinguishes iconic systems is that we do not have to decode them in the way we have to decode the colour-reversed icon? The crucial point is that this story about colour-reversal has no tendency to distinguish iconic systems from linguistic systems of representation. Indeed, I believe it doesn't even distinguish iconic systems from codes.

Let's begin by comparing iconic and linguistic systems of representation. Just as reversing colours – e.g. green standing for red and vice versa – might make a picture harder to interpret in point of colour, so reversing colour vocabulary – e.g. exchanging the meaning of 'red' and 'green' – might make colour descriptions harder to understand. So the difficulty of such reversals is hardly peculiar to iconic systems and in itself sheds no light on their nature. Indeed, if you actually *begin* with a pictorial scheme in which it is known that red stands for green and this is a tradition of long standing, then a particular picture in which, perversely, red stands for red and green for green will present more interpretative problems than the normal (colour-reversed) picture. So Wollheim cannot use this example to establish that the colour-reversed scheme is, as a scheme, more conventional or arbitrary than the normal or putatively natural scheme. The difficulty we experience in trying to interpret a colour-reversed scheme might, for all anyone has shown, have nothing to do with

[2] Wollheim 1974, p. 25.

40

the fact that it is a colour-reversed scheme. It might have to do, rather, with the fact that the normal or conventional scheme happens not to be colour-reversed. Perhaps it is just because a colour-reversed icon violates the standard procedure that it takes additional labour to process it.[3]

Now as a matter of fact I don't *believe* this story for a minute. It is important to emphasise, however, that there is an alternative to the explanation Wollheim intimates. Wollheim, rightly, thinks that the colour-reversed system just is, *au fond*, unnatural while the colour-normal system is natural, but given the availability of a different explanation, in terms of 'entrenchment', we have to probe deeper to find the source of Wollheim's intuition. Obviously, if you agree that the colour-reversed icon of a tree doesn't *depict* it in its true colour, you agree too. All that needs to be established is what precisely makes the colour-normal icon *iconic* in respect of colour while its inverted counterpart is non-iconic in respect of colour.

Wollheim's puzzle is just that. It doesn't tell us what the difference is between iconic systems and languages or even codes. Our intuitions about it, however, encourage us to think he is right to think the reversed system unnatural. The puzzle is a challenge to all theories of depiction. We may ask of them one simple question: Do they account for the asymmetry between the reversed system and the normal system? If not, consign them to the flames; if so, pay heed. The puzzle is more than a test of finished theories. It proposes a conundrum that will constantly inform the development of theory.

In this chapter I have asserted that convention alone doesn't make something iconic. Manifesting the intention that a symbol shall signify O makes it signify O (in your idiolect at least). By contrast, manifesting the intention that it shall depict O doesn't necessarily do the trick. This complements Wollheim's intuition. Manifesting an intention that the colour-reversed symbol shall iconify red with green will not do; you can make green signify red by manifesting the appropriate intention, but you cannot make it iconify red just by word magic.

So we have these intuitions: that convention maketh not the icon, that the colour-reversed icon is not iconic in respect of colour while the colour-normal icon is iconic in respect of colour, and that the difference between the colour-reversed icon and the colour-normal icon is not merely a matter of the entrenchment of the former and

---

[3] Compare Goodman's theory of predicate projectibility in terms of entrenchment in Goodman 1973.

the novelty of the latter. These propositions are interrelated. The first and second entail the third and the second and third entail the first.

So much for our intuitions. The job is now to explain them if we can.

3

A theory of depiction

I NATURAL GENERATIVITY

The innocent eye cannot always interpret an icon off the bat. Many a native son or mother-in-law has gone unrecognised and unheeded when presented pictorially to his or her nearest and dearest.[1] One might say that such pictorial innocents fail to see their relatives in the picture. And who can blame them? Surely it is a form of madness to see a robustly three-dimensional mother-in-law in a flat two-dimensional piece of glossy paper. But that is exactly what Western iconomanes apparently succeeded in doing, and not only with mothers-in-law, but with mountains, churches, cars, planes – in fact, if you can see it the chances are you can see it in pictures.

Although in some cases something like learning how to interpret icons occurs, once the coin has dropped and someone has succeeded in a first pictorial interpretation, they will then be able to go on to pictures of other things and, without further ado, say what the icon depicts, provided only that they are able to recognise the depicted object. In other words, once you have succeeded in an initial pictorial interpretation, perchance as the result of some tuition, you should then be able to interpret novel icons without being privy to additional stipulations given only that you can recognise the object or state of affairs depicted.

I call this property of iconic modes of representation 'natural generativity'. Natural generativity is what makes a symbol (system) iconic. The two dot systems which I contrived in the last chapter transparently lack this property. For example, suppose I tell you that this red coloured dot stands for Stalin and that the rectangle stands for a table. I now place the dot beside the rectangle. Naturally, given the purpose of the model, you will understand that I mean to indicate that Stalin occupies a certain position at the table in the scene I am envisaging with the model's help. Now I introduce

[1] For examples of difficulties encountered by non-Europeans trying to decode European pictorial representations see Deregowski 1980 (especially chapter 4).

43

another dot but I do not tell you what it stands for. I place it by the table. For all you know it could stand for anyone or anything.

Natural languages also seem to lack 'natural generativity'. If I teach you a few sentences of a new language you may grasp the grammar and some vocabulary, but sentences containing vocabulary for which I have not as yet stipulated a meaning will be Greek to you.

Let's take as a very crude first approximation to a theory of iconicity this claim:

> A system of representation is iconic just if once someone has interpreted any arbitrary member of it, they can proceed to interpret any other member of the system, provided only that they are able to recognise the object represented.

The point is roughly that when someone cannot recognise you they will not be able to interpret naturally an icon as being of you. But even so, it is an icon of you given the truth of the counterfactual claim that if they had been able to recognise you, then they would have known this was a picture of you. I need only to have got the hang of depiction by, say, interpreting a picture of a church and, lo and behold, I can interpret your picture too (provided I can recognise you).

To be sure this just scratches the surface. Two problems force themselves on us at once. First, it is obvious that not just any initial picture will do the trick (if a trick is needed) and second, not any mode of interpreting that picture will do. Both problems present difficulty, for they offer an unpleasant choice between admitting counter-examples to our theory and accepting that our analysis of iconicity is circular.

Suppose, first, that I take a picture of a white dot on a black background (perhaps it is a picture of a painting from the studio of Hans Hofmann). I show this to one of our imaginary natives and he says laconically 'It's a white dot on a black background' (he also claims that it's the moon, but we shall ignore this). Then I show him a picture of his mother-in-law and he draws a blank: it just looks like a welter of lines and colours – rather like those anamorphs that so pained Galileo. He makes nothing of the picture. I try the experiment with other natives and get the same result. This appears to be a resounding counter-example to the theory of natural generativity. The native has succeeded in interpreting an initial picture, but he can't get on with interpreting other pictures of recognisable objects.

Perhaps we should look to the clause in our definition which says that a system of representation is iconic just when someone who has interpreted 'any arbitrary member of it' can then proceed to any other member of it (given the relevant recognitional abilities). What is meant by 'arbitrary' here? If it means that any old picture will do for starters, the definition is defective; our native interprets his initial picture but then can't interpret novel pictures of recognisable people. Perhaps what we should say instead is that a system is iconic just if there are arbitrarily many symbols that will do for starters, although there are some symbols, perhaps arbitrarily many, which will not do for starters. We could then try to characterise the conditions which the initial picture must meet. Perhaps, for example, we should require the primal symbol to contain intimations of depth; but this condition promises to be neither necessary nor sufficient. It isn't necessary since it is easy to envisage iconic systems which do not iconically represent depth at all. Nor is the condition sufficient, since it is possible that our native, confronted with the picture of a white dot on a black background, claims to see the dot in front of the background. Even an ability to see the dot as being behind or in front of the black surface will not necessarily effect pictorial omnicompetence in our native.

But I think we are barking up the wrong tree by futzing about with 'arbitrarily' and by trying to place constraints on the Ur-icon. Take a picture of something as complex as you like, say a picture of the Palazzo del Tè. Now I show someone this picture and say 'This is the Palazzo del Tè.' They nod and register this pearl of wisdom. When shown this picture in the future they are apt to say 'This represents the Palazzo del Tè.' But it obviously doesn't follow that they will be able to interpret *novel* pictures. Perhaps every time we produce a new picture we have to tell them 'And now this is a picture of Dr Strabismus' and so on. So again we have a counter-example.

There are various ways of reacting to this problem. I think our intuition is that quite evidently our subject has understood the picture but they haven't understood it in that mysteriously right way which will give them iconic competence *überhaupt*. One wants to say that our subject simply doesn't *see* the Palazzo del Tè in the picture. Shall we then stipulate that our subject must come to see the depicted object in the Ur-icon?[2] But this condition would not solve the original problem about the native and the picture of the dot-on-black. Even if we assume that he *saw* the dot on the black background, this would hardly tend to ensure a generalised pictorial competence.

[2] On seeing-as and seeing-in see Wollheim 1974, Wollheim 1968 and Wollheim 1980.

Of course, if one threw caution to the wind one could say 'Look, the trouble is that there is pictorial interpretation and there is interpretation of pictures and they don't necessarily come to the same thing. Interpreting a picture – divining its content – one does not necessarily interpret it *pictorially*. The trouble with both the original native and the subject in the Palazzo experiment is that their interpretations were not pictorial. Both of them have to rely on verbal cues to elicit the meaning of novel icons since both lack pictorial competence.' Well, this rash voice has let the imp out of the bottle. If we have to specify that the interpretation of the Ur-icon is pictorial, our claim to have presented a non-circular analysis of depiction must perforce go up in smoke. It hardly seems like the dawn of enlightenment to be told 'Pictures are such that if you have pictorial competence then you can interpret them.' So what?

But in fact I believe our rash voice has focused on just the right point. We should begin by saying what pictorial competence is. Pictorial competence in a symbol system is the ability to generate naturally interpretations of arbitrarily many novel members of the system. When an initial interpretation of some symbol does in fact effect an ability in someone to interpret novel symbols without further ceremony, then that initial interpretation was iconic or pictorial, the symbol so interpreted was a picture, the system containing the symbols which he is then able to interpret without any prior baptismal song and dance is iconic and he may be said to have pictorial competence in the system. So the theory of natural generativity is, if I am right, a power to reckon with: it tells us what counts as a picture, what counts as a pictorial system and what counts as pictorial competence. Who could ask for more?

Of course, we must still phrase our claim carefully. It must be stressed that I am not claiming that given an ability to interpret pictorially one symbol, an ability to interpret any other picture follows. First, of course, there is the consideration that one may not recognise the depicted object and so may be unable to interpret a given picture. Let us take that as read. More importantly, we must recognise at least the *possibility* that (a) P has interpreted some symbol S iconically, (b) P has pictorial competence in a system to which S belongs (the S-system) and (c) there is a pictorial symbol S★ which P cannot interpret even though it represents some O he can recognise.

This presents no problem for our analysis. First, we can be assured of P's pictorial competence by the things he is in fact able to do. If he can generate interpretations of symbolic novelties without further semantic ceremony, we know that he is pictorially competent in at least some system. Furthermore, we know that S is pictorial because his interpretation of it leads him to greater things. And we can say of the novelties he is able to interpret without further tuition that they are members of some iconic system or other. (I shall come to the problem of system-individuation shortly.)

How then do we know that S* is pictorial? Doesn't P's disability with S*, given his other attainments, reflect rather badly on S*? It may, of course. But if there is someone or some population able to interpret S* in the right way, then S* is pictorial. If P*'s interpretation of S* is sweetened by similar success with novel symbols, then S* is iconic and so are those other symbols. And of course P* therein manifests his pictorial competence.

Our definition of an icon is not quite general yet because of course we have only explicitly defined the conditions which would make an Ur-icon an icon. But obviously we don't want to require that S is an icon only if S could be an Ur-icon. There may be many icons too complicated (or too simple) to be the arch-icon. However, granted that we have defined pictorial competence and a pictorial system, there is no difficulty in giving a perfectly general definition of a picture: it is something which someone with pictorial competence in some system could pictorially interpret. More briefly: it is a member of some pictorial system.

I will not make heavy weather of it now, but it should also be noted that this general form of theory should hold good for all other types of symbol which we consider iconic. I would expect to be able to extend the theory of natural generativity to other visual icons – gestures, sculpture and so on – as well as to other sense modalities (at least to hearing and perhaps to touch).

Latterly we have noted that pictorial competence is, in effect, system-relative. This is hardly cause for surprise since iconicity is defined in terms of pictorial competence; if there are distinct pictorial symbol systems, what could this mean other than that competence in any one of them does not entail competence in all of them? And if there is but one system, it is trivially true that pictorial competence is system-relative, since pictorial competence is competence in *that* system.

So systems are, for our purposes, to be individuated in terms of competence. Let's say that two symbols S and S* are members of the same (iconic) system if and only if *either* an understanding of S and an ability to recognise the object O or state of affairs p symbolised by S* are sufficient for some P to have the ability to interpret S* *or* there is some third symbol S★★ such that an ability to interpret it and an ability to recognise what S and S★ symbolise is sufficient for some P to interpret S and S★.

About this method of individuating pictorial systems I have a few comments to make. First, of course it must be confessed that for many purposes this method of individuation will be too crude. Art historians would want to bring in stylistic matters and historians generally would probably wish to bring in genetic considerations (that is, symbols in the same system should somehow be causally linked to one another perhaps in terms of a common origin). Since our concern is principally with the interpretation of pictorial systems my crude mode of individuation happens to suit our purpose best.

Second, the second disjunct is there for a reason. Suppose S is our famous picture of a white dot on a black background. I would want to say that S and S★ might still be members of the same system even though an ability to interpret S does not effect an ability to interpret S★. They still count as parts of the same system if an interpretation of both S and S★ would be available to someone who could interpret some third symbol S★★.

Third, given the way I have cast this definition, whether two symbols are co-systemic depends upon the population (P) in question. It is conceivable that for one population an ability to interpret S would generate an ability to interpret S★ naturally while for another population an ability to interpret S did not ensure an ability to interpret S★. For the first population S and S★ would be co-systemic, but not for the second.

Finally, it might be found necessary to refine this criterion of individuation by introducing some notion of directionality or hierarchy. For example it may be that anyone competent in an iconic system *S* could interpret members of *S★* (given the usual epistemic restrictions), but not vice versa. We would then have reason for saying that *S* and *S★* are not identical, contrary to the letter of our criterion. It would be natural to say that *S★* is part of *S* and that *S* is more powerful than *S★*.

Since the epistemic restrictions on iconic interpretation are central to the theory it is worth while to pause and bring out their logic somewhat further. Suppose someone interprets a symbol S; then he goes on to interpret other symbols without prior introduction to those symbols or to meaningful parts thereof. Does it follow that his initial and subsequent interpretations are iconic, that he has an iconic competence, and that the symbols he manages to interpret are iconic? I do not believe that it does. My reasons for this will emerge more fully in chapter 10. Suffice it to say now that it is essential to stress the role of recognitional ability. A truly iconic interpretation is one which *results* from (a) initiation if any into the system and (b) an ability to recognise the symbolised objects. The claim is that a truly pictorial interpretation is in some sense caused by or brought about by the relevant recognitional ability. If S depicts O that is because an ability to recognise O could be enough, given an initiation into the relevant symbol system, to explain differentially P's getting his interpretation of S right.

If this is right, then the logic of our theory resembles various causal theories of action, perception, knowledge and so on. We are characterising icons as those symbols whose interpretation can be causally explained by relevant recognitional abilities. An icon is iconic because its interpretation can be explained in a certain way; an interpretation that *is* explained in this way is iconic. Obviously it is possible for someone to have the relevant recognitional ability and not use it. Sergio may say 'That's a picture of Jim' because he has been told that S is a picture of Jim even though in fact his ability to recognise Jim would have been sufficient to allow him to interpret S. In this case S is indeed an icon of Jim, but Sergio's interpretation is not in fact an iconic one even though he had the relevant pictorial competence.

This by itself establishes, I think, that recognitional ability or something like it has a crucial role to play in the theory of iconicity. For if I am right, an interpretation is not pictorial unless it is brought about by the relevant recognitional ability. The mere coincidence between an interpretation that is based on recognitional ability and another interpretation is not sufficient to establish that the latter interpretation is iconic. The recognitional ability has actually to have been *engaged* in the interpretation in some way. But then, if recognitional ability is crucial to characterising the difference between real pictorial interpretations and 'sham' pictorial interpretations, it is crucial to the notion of pictorial competence (which is just the ability to deliver interpretations which are pictorial) and hence to the notion of a picture (since we are characterising pictures precisely in terms of the kind of competence required to understand them).

In what follows we shall repeatedly have recourse to the notion of recognitional ability, which we shall find very useful in clearing up several difficulties. I am concerned here simply to bring out the parallel between my account and a causal theory of action or perception. In the case of perception it is necessary to anticipate the possibility of two qualitatively similar perceptual experiences one of which is a veridical perception of O and one of which is simply a hallucinatory experience as of seeing O. We must also distinguish between two qualitatively similar veridical perceptions of different objects. The causal relation of a perception to its object is part of what it is for that perceptual experience to be veridical and it is also part of what it is for that perceptual experience to be of a particular object and not of any qualitatively similar object. We have already seen that two people may give the same interpretation of S, one interpretation being iconic and the other, non-iconic. I propose that the truly iconic one is the one which is in fact the result of the interpreter's ability to recognise the relevant object.

But at this point we must be careful to bring out an important epistemic restriction. If an interpretation is truly iconic it must satisfy two constraints: the relevant recognitional ability must play some causal role in producing the interpretation and it must be at least possible to purify the interpretation of all other influences except the recognitional one. If other items of knowledge play an essential, non-redundant role in explaining the interpretation it is not a purely iconic interpretation.

To illustrate the importance of this restriction let us compare two interpreters of S, Verbo and Icono. S is a picture of a peacock. When Verbo and Icono are asked what S symbolises they sing out in unison 'A peacock'. But when we ask Verbo why he says this he points to Icono and says 'He told me so.' We ask him whether he would have known this without asking Icono and he says 'Oh yes. But in fact I just took Icono's word for it.' As for Icono, we learn that he deciphered the picture on the basis of his recognitional ability alone. Now it could be replied that Verbo's recognitional ability played *some* role in his interpretation, because he could not have the concept of a peacock unless he were able to recognise one. I realise this is controversial for natural kinds, so substitute an example where you think it is not controversial (say 'table'). If in general you think that possessing concepts does not entail recognitional ability, that is grist to my mill. The problem does not arise. But let's go along with the idea that Verbo's recognitional ability does essentially enter into his possession of the peacock concept. Well, then it enters into his interpretation of the peacock picture too – for without this recognitional ability he would not have understood Icono's report about the peacock picture.

Obviously, we must distinguish the way in which Icono's recognitional ability generated his ability to interpret the picture and the way in which Verbo's ability to recognise peacocks affected his ability to interpret this particular picture. We might say that Icono's interpretation was purely iconic because his recognitional ability alone was efficacious in producing his interpretation. Verbo's recognitional ability only produced his interpretation thanks to the added prompting of Icono. Of course, verbal prompting may have helped Icono to acquire the ability to recognise a peacock in the first place. So we may allow that Icono draws on information that may be language dependent. The point is that this information pertains just to features of peacocks and not to this particular symbol. It is no part of my brief to deny that language informs recognitional ability. Essential to Verbo's interpretation was the verbal information that 'This picture is of —.' No such picture-specific verbal prompting was *essential* to Icono's interpretation. Of course, it may in fact be that his interpretation was overdetermined, because his girlfriend was whispering 'It's a peacock' in his ear just as he saw that indeed it was a picture of a peacock.

What are the asymmetries between pictorial understanding and linguistic understanding? Obviously there are some crucial respects in which languages and pictorial systems are similar – if there were not it would be of no interest to contrast them. Pictures, like sentences, are or can be treated as semantic vehicles, bearers of truth-value. Pictures, like sentences, can be used to communicate. And just as someone with mastery of a language can interpret novel sentences (without being told what they mean), so someone with pictorial competence can interpret novel icons. So where are the differences?

They are not hard to spot. Although someone can understand a sentence without having seen it before, the sentence must contain familiar words and it must be built up from these familiar words by familiar rules of grammar. Of course, even when these two conditions are met there is no guarantee that one will understand the resulting sentence ('Curious green ideas sleep furiously'). But it is a necessary condition of being able to understand systematically the novel sentences of a language that one should master its grammar and a largish chunk of its vocabulary. It seems to be a necessary condition of knowing the meaning of a sentence in a language that one should know the grammatical rules and the vocabulary which appears in that sentence. For our purposes we can abstract from the fact that word-understanding always involves knowing the grammatical role of the word (in the case of names, knowing that something *is* a name seems to be about all there is to mastering it on certain austere theories of what it is to master a name). We may also abstract from the question of a universal grammar. Even if there be some underlying deep structure – perhaps a logical syntax – such that the surface grammar of any language could be computationally derived from it given semantic and phonological input, the surface grammatical rules of languages are legion and are conventional or convention-dependent (even if they are also dependent on some 'deep structure').

Contrast this with understanding a novel picture. One can understand a novel picture without ever having encountered it or any of its meaningful parts before. If I am pictorially competent in the relevant system, I can tell you that S depicts O provided I can recognise O. That is all there is to it. I do not even have to remember the meaning of any picture of my prior acquaintance. I do not see the new picture as composed out of elements from previous pictures. No semantic memory at all is involved. I do not even have to recall the content of my Ur-picture (the first picture I interpreted pictorially). Of course, I don't remember my Ur-sentences either, but the chances are that I have never had to relearn the vocabulary in my Ur-sentences. But there is no pictorial vocabulary to learn, so there is none to remember.

A few caveats come to mind, but none of them alters the substance of the picture one iota. First, it goes without saying that a symbol may be iconic in some respects and not others. There may be more to an icon than its iconic content. The theory of natural generativity only aims to characterise the iconically available sense of an icon. Call it the icon-meaning or the iconic meaning of the icon. That an icon may be used to communicate more than its iconic content I have no doubt. For one thing the user's meaning may not coincide with the icon's meaning. Icons may insinuate more than they iconically contain: one has only to pick up a book by Saxl or Panofsky to see that. So the iconicity of a symbol is aspect-relative; it may be iconic *qua* one content and non-iconic *qua* another. Anonymous Botch's masterful 'Greengages' is iconic *qua* 'representation of greengages' but not *qua* 'homage to Orcutt'.

A painting may depict, inter alia, another painting. Painters would not be human if they did not take their own works and works of their own kind as suitable targets for depiction. One has only to think of Poussin's self-portrait, Courbet's *Interieur de mon atelier*, Zoffany's painting of the Tribuna in the Uffizi and Watteau's *L'Enseigne de Gersaint*: all cases in which a painting depicts another painting (fictive or otherwise) in such a way that (some of) the icon-

52

ically available content of the depicted painting is iconically available to anyone looking at the parasitic painting.

Now suppose that S depicts S★. Suppose that the iconically available sense of S★ is available to someone who looks at S. Suppose also (as seems plausible) that an ability to recognise S★ requires an ability to understand S★. (This could be made more precise, but precision must await further work on the notion of recognition. The reader is referred to chapter 5.) We now have the makings of a prima facie counter-example to the theory of natural generativity. I have claimed that if S is iconic, interpreting S should only require the ability to recognise what S depicts and that it should not require one to recall the content of icons other than S. But now we have a case where the ability to recognise what S depicts requires one to recollect the sense of another icon – viz S★. Otherwise one will not be able to look at S and say 'Oh, that's a picture of Botch's "Greengage".' Suppose we then say 'OK, working out what a depiction depicts doesn't require one to remember what other depictions depict unless the depiction in question depicts a picture'? This is fair enough, but it would be a rather circular way of trying to go about characterising depiction to use this in the analysans. I think it is best to dispense with the appearance of circularity by constructing a recursive definition. Thus: S is an icon of O provided that one can interpret S without remembering the content of previous icons *unless* O is an icon, O is an icon of O★ if one can interpret it without remembering previous icons unless O★ is an icon, O★ is an icon of . . . So it goes on. Eventually one will be able to get rid of any reference to 'icon' in the definiens. Incidentally, the occurrence of 'previous icons' in the definiens is inessential – it could be replaced by 'any other symbol' – unless of course S depicts a symbol. But there is no threat of circularity here.

In any case, the general point stands that the ability to recognise what S depicts is sufficient to generate an ability to interpret S, even if S depicts an icon or another symbol.

It is important to distinguish the question 'What makes S an icon?' from the question 'What makes an interpretation iconic?' It is generally true that an icon is something which it is possible for someone to understand without calling upon information garnered from past episodes of iconic interpretation. We have just dealt with the exception to this rule (icons which embed icons). However, it is by no means the case that *iconic interpretation* may not rely essentially on information gleaned from previous iconic encounters. The reason is obvious: once somebody is pictorially competent, they can learn to recognise people and so forth from their photographs (or what have you). It is a fact worth noting that when we told our pictorial incompetent 'This represents the Palazzo del Tè' we did not thereby instil in him an ability to recognise the Palazzo del Tè. Of course, if we had described the Palazzo in the picture we could have instilled the ability, but credit for this achievement would belong to our powers of description and not to the picture we held in our hands. The story is different if we show the picture to someone who is pictorially competent. Once we tell them 'This represents the Palazzo del Tè' they are able to recognise the Palazzo del Tè (under some of its poly-morphous aspects) provided that they do their bit by actually looking at the picture and interpreting it. Now when they see other pictures of the Palazzo del Tè they will say 'That's the Palazzo del Tè.' I want to say that their interpretation is iconic because it is based on a recognitional ability even though that ability and hence their interpretation is mediated by information they have picked up from an iconic source. Obviously it would be absurd to suppose otherwise. The essential points of the theory are untouched by this. It is still true that an icon of O is iconic in so far as one *could* interpret it on the basis of a recognitional ability that is unmediated by information drawn from other icons. And your interpretation of it, even if icon-dependent, remains iconic because it is based on a recognitional ability.

It is perhaps a good idea to sketch in a further caveat at this point. I think we will need some distinction between 'basic' icons and 'non-basic' icons, rather analogous in structure to the distinction between the embedded picture and the picture which embeds it. Consider the following dumbshow. Someone goes to the tap and make-believedly turns it on, places a make-believe glass under it and then make-believedly drinks from the imaginary glass. I want to say that he has iconically represented someone getting and drinking a glass of tapwater. This is a sequential icon. Some of the interpretations of later stages of the icon depend upon interpretations of earlier stages. When our mummer downs his imaginary draught of tapwater our ability to say that it is tapwater he is pretending to drink relies essentially on remembering his dumbshow at the tap. The basic icon is the icon earlier on in the chain which we can interpret on the basis of an ability to recognise someone's turning on the tap (plus perhaps some initiation, long since lost in the mists of time, into the *general idea* of gesticulatory icons). The non-basic icon is the icon later in the chain which we can interpret only on the basis of having recollected earlier segments of the show. The crucial point is that the show is iconic in so far as all we have to bring to it *ab initio* is our kit of recognitional skills and the general ability to spot gesticulatory representation. The recursive epicycles we thereby introduce into our theory are concentric to the ones already introduced to handle depictions of depictions. S is an icon of O (where O may now be a state of affairs such as 'someone's downing a glass of tapwater') if an ability to recognise O would suffice to give one the ability to interpret S, unless interpretation of S depends upon recognitional abilities plus recollection of some second icon S^*, of O^*; S^* is an icon of O^* if... and so on until you get to your basic, generative, bottom of the line, end of the road icon, an icon which *can* be understood in splendid isolation.

This modification in the definition of 'icon' requires a concomitant slackening in our rigorous notion of iconic interpretation. So far I have allowed that an interpretation may retain its iconic status despite its reliance on icons past provided that those icons mediate the interpretation by instilling a recognitional ability. Thus, when I walk up to a Titian in the Pitti and exclaim 'I've seen that man somewhere before – oh yes, I remember now, it's Pietro Aretino. I know why I recognise him – I saw another Titian portrait of him in the Frick' I allow that my interpretation is iconic because it relies on recognitional ability, albeit an ability mediated by another icon. By contrast, when I watch the mummer downing his imaginary tapwater the chances are that an ability to recognise 'someone's drinking water' would not suffice to give me the ability to interpret this mummery. I need to rely on recall of the previous mummery at the tap – and *not* because this mummery gave me the ability to recognise anything I couldn't have recognised before. So *is* the interpretation of the make-believe water-drinking iconic? I am inclined to call it only quasi-iconic because of its essential reliance on something outwith the relevant recognitional ability. But to keep terminology to a minimum I shall call it a non-basic iconic interpretation. It relies on a chain which terminates in a basically iconic interpretation – one dependent on recognitional ability alone.

2 NATURAL GENERATIVITY AND OTHER MODES OF RADICAL INTERPRETATION

In this chapter I have argued that pictorial understanding is 'naturally generated'. Of course, I do not mean by this that human beings are born with the ability to read off the content of any picture whatsoever immediately. On the contrary, it may well be some time before a native tribesman standing before a picture will see it as a picture of three-dimensional objects arranged in a three-space. He may, of course, already understand simple drawings of faces and animals that attempt no representation of depth, but it may take a while for his depth-recognitional abilities to become engaged by the picture. However, I do not suppose that anything but looking at the picture in the first instance will be necessary for his eventually coming to see it as a picture of three-dimensional objects in three-space. In particular, I do not think that any verbal cue from a third party could ever be indispensable. It may help him, of course, to be told that this picture stands to that ensemble of objects over there rather as a simple line drawing of a face stands to a face, but I do not think such help is ever strictly necessary. Verbal explanation may expedite pictorial understanding, but only by showing the interpreter what he would eventually have been able to see unaided.

Now observe that once the penny has dropped and our imaginary native interpreter has seen S as a picture in depth of animals, houses, and so on he will then be able to go on without prompting to interpret novel pictures which represent quite different objects from those depicted in S. Nor need he remember any of the *content* of S in order to interpret these new pictures. The importance of S is simply that in looking at it, our native's visual recognitional capacities become spontaneously engaged in producing a correct interpretation of its contents. And, in a normally intelligent and perceptive human being, this initial interpretative engagement of recognitional ability will lead to a general competence. Of course, it is no analytic truth that an initial engagement of visual recognitional ability by a given picture will lead, given the opportunity, to further interpretative success in future instances. However, it is a natural fact about us that such initial successes are fecund and generate a general ability to interpret novel pictorial symbols without further verbal badinage or remembrance of the contents of icons past, provided only that we possess the relevant visual recognitional abilities.

Bearing these points in mind, I want to look at an objection to my claim that natural generativity is a sufficient mark of the pictorial, an objection that is inspired by the work of Donald Davidson on radical interpretation.[3] Davidson has argued that the conventionality of language is not essential to it. For our purposes we may divide the conventions involved in language into two kinds. The first kind involves the convention in a given community to correlate

---

[3] Davidson 1984, Essay 18.

a lexicon with a given field of reference. Thus, it is natural to think of the fact that English speakers use 'tomato' to refer to tomatoes as a conventional fact. 'Tomato' might have referred to eggs and some other word might have been used to designate tomatoes. So it is natural to think that each English speaker co-ordinates his use of 'tomato' to bring it into line with the use he expects others would make of it. The second convention is independent of the first sort, though the first is dependent on the second. This sort of convention simply involves the thought that I continue to use a word with a given meaning because I know that this is the pattern of use you expect and your reason for expecting it is partly that you know that I know that it is what you expect me to do. Note that this convention does not preclude us from using quite different words – you may say 'tomato' when I say 'egg' – all that matters is that there is an implicit mutual understanding that each of us will be consistent in the use of our vocabulary.

Davidson is right to insist that neither sort of convention is necessary to language, although certainly the second sort of convention is a necessary condition of any very elaborate linguistic communication. It will be evident that if it is at least conceivable that a sufficiently intelligent Robinson Crusoe could evolve his own language, it is not necessary for him to worry about what others would expect him to do, still less to worry about whether others would fall in with his rules of usage. Suppose that Crusoe talks aloud and we come upon his island and observe him secretly. Obviously, it is possible that his island context will provide us with enough information so that, together with a basic understanding of Crusoe's natural wants, gestures and expressions, we shall be able to understand the language we overhear him speaking. All we need to do is uncover the self-imposed linguistic norms of Crusoe: what *he* considers correct and incorrect usage.

It is clear that in this case the observer is understanding Crusoe, though indeed there is no *communication* going on between them. Understanding Crusoe is a matter of uncovering the *intentions* governing his use of words, and these intentions need not make any reference to Crusoe's expectations about others. Now it may be that, unknown to the observer, another man, Friday, has appeared on the island who communicates with Crusoe in the language originally devised by Crusoe. In this case conventions of both types may govern Crusoe's use of language: he may use 'tomato' to mean tomato in part because he knows that this is what Friday will expect of him and in part because it is the word Friday uses for tomatoes.

The point is that the observer need not know about these conventions in order to understand Crusoe's words. He needs to understand the rules Crusoe uses – what Crusoe would consider correct and incorrect use of terms – but he need not know that these rules are accepted by Crusoe partly because they are also accepted and known by Friday.

Now we are in a position to make a couple of remarks about the parallels between the hidden radical interpreter on Crusoe's island and the pictorial interpreter. First, it is evidently the case that if the hidden interpreter is lucky enough, the context of Crusoe's utterances will almost always make it clear what Crusoe means by his words. Thus if the hidden interpreter finds Crusoe pointing to objects and uttering sounds, he may rightly guess that those sounds name or designate the indicated objects. Indeed, it may even be that the necessary objects are always on hand to illuminate Crusoe's remarks. In this case the hidden interpreter need not bother to memorise Crusoe's vocabulary, because the context will always make it clear. To be sure, we should have to imagine Crusoe operating at a linguistic level rather similar to the crude slab-language discussed in the opening sections of Wittgenstein's *Philosophical Investigations*. Nevertheless, this crude language would appear to be such that once our hidden interpreter grasps certain general features of Crusoe's style – what his pointing gestures mean, what expressions mean assent, and so on – then his having understood one Crusoe utterance might put him in a position to go on to interpret others correctly without remembering the content of Crusoe-utterance-parts past.

It is not difficult to see the asymmetry between this sort of radical interpretation and naturally generated interpretation. Either the radical interpreter has to acquire and retain a knowledge of Crusoe's stable linguistic intentions/rules or he must be able to pick up from scratch Crusoe's linguistic intention on each occasion of a Crusoe-utterance. Either way, he can know Crusoe's intentions only on the basis of various contextual cues – facts about the expressions and gestures that accompany Crusoe's utterances and facts about the immediate Crusoe-surroundings. Crusoe's intentions can be inferred only from the total context of behaviour and surrounding states of affairs in which Crusoe's utterance is embedded. But this is quite unlike pictorial interpretation. To understand a picture, I have been arguing, all you need do is look at it and your recognitional ability and basic nous will do the rest. Of course once you naturally conjecture a certain content ascription for a picture, this serves as a basis for inferring to the intention of the picture-maker.

A second remark is pertinent. From the fact that the content of a depiction can be retrieved without knowledge of conventions which govern the meaning of its parts it doesn't follow that there are no such conventions. We have seen a similar point in the case of Crusoe, where we noted that the radical interpreter can understand his utterances without knowing they conform to conventions. It would obviously be an error to infer from this that Crusoe's linguistic usage (of a term T) is not in fact governed by convention. So we must avoid two mistakes:

1 The inference that because the use of T is governed by conventions, T cannot be understood without knowing those conventions;
2 The inference that because T can be understood without adverting to any conventions, there are no conventions governing T.

A similar point applies to depiction. For example, it may well be that if one were to look at a painting by Piero done in accord with the strictest Albertian rules of perspective, one would be able to read off the spatial arrangement of the depicted objects without any tutelage in the Albertian system. One would just *look* at the Piero and immediately or eventually one's perspectival visual capacities would become engaged in interpreting the content of the picture. However, it doesn't follow from this that Piero's painting was not made in accord with a relevant *communicational* convention; the only conclusion we can draw from the natural interpretability of Piero's depiction of objects in perspective is that knowledge of such conventions, if there are any, is not required for *interpreting* his work (for retrieving its *pictorial* content). Nonetheless, it may well be that Piero intended to paint according to a stable system of perspectival projection because he believed that others expected him to do so and because he believed that his consistency in this matter would *expedite* general understanding of his work. Likewise, it may be that part of Piero's reason for adopting the Albertian rules was that, since other painters had adopted them, his doing so would facilitate understanding of his work among the cognoscenti.

So while communicative conventions are unnecessary in the case of depiction, they are also strictly dispensable for understanding linguistic utterances. However, as we have seen, there is still an important asymmetry between radical linguistic interpretation and radical pictorial interpretation, since the former requires, as the latter does not, a heavy input of information from the immediate context of the utterance. This asymmetry is grounded in the fact that the depiction by itself has the power naturally to engage the perceiver's visual recognitional abilities whereas an uttered or inscribed sentence does not. Although communicational conventions analogous to those in language may be found in depiction, they do not have as much importance for everyday pictorial understanding, since most actual pictorial understanding is in fact radical whereas most actual linguistic interpretation is not. This asymmetry is likewise explicable in terms of the theory of natural generativity, since in most cases of understanding pictures, our visual recognitional abilities are in fact spontaneously engaged in the business of making out a picture's content, whereas it is far from being the case that we usually have enough contextual information to comprehend radically an uttered or inscribed sentence.

Davidson's demarcation between issues of understanding and communication is very congenial to the approach to depiction I have adopted here. If it is possible for Crusoe to devise a language for himself, with no one else in earshot, it must be possible for him to amuse himself by making various drawings of the butterflies and birds on his island with no second person in view. Certainly, if Crusoe is painting pictures, and not randomly daubing marks on a surface, there is a standard of correctness implicit in his activities, a standard by which Crusoe could judge certain drawings as successful and others as failures. None of these judgements requires that Crusoe should think about others, but only that he should test his output to see whether he himself can naturally generate an interpretation of his own work. He will ask himself whether he is able spontaneously to interpret his work as being about just those objects as having just those features (whatever the objects and features may be: he need not be judging his pictures in accord with a standard of truth-to-the-actual-world of his island). So, of course depiction of necessity involves rule-following, since understanding a picture essentially involves having an idea of what its maker was trying to do, and hence of what counts, relative to his intention, as success or failure. It does not, however, strictly have to involve communicational conventions. These matters of course require further exploration, and they receive it in chapters 7 and 8.

Utterances and depictions are not the only things we can radically interpret. For example, I dare say that one could work out from scratch that thermometers are used for registering temperatures. After eliciting the temperature from one of these instruments, one might be able to go on reading off temperatures from new and quite novel sorts of thermometers. Of course, on occasion one might have to do a little further work to get the hang of a new sort of thermometer, but perhaps this is rather like what someone does when they look for the first time at perspectival painting after having seen only simply drawings of (for instance) faces in two-space.

I shall waive the question of whether a thermometer's registration should be taken to *mean* that the temperature in the room is such-and-such. The crucial point is that you can only radically understand thermometers – puzzle them out without any tutelage, instruction manuals, and so forth – if you can observe the correlation in certain contexts between changes in temperature and changes in the registration on the thermometer. After you have observed this correlation, it might strike you that the concomitance was no accident, that indeed this instrument was meant (intended) to perform the function of registering the temperature, and so on. So the question is: is this a case of naturally generated understanding?

There are three salient differences between understanding a thermometer and understanding a picture. The first is that one cannot understand a thermometer's registrations simply by looking at it. One must look at how its registrations change in harmony with fluctuations of temperature over time. I cannot conceive of any other non-miraculous way of coming radically to comprehend a thermometer's registrations. By contrast, understanding one's first picture need in principle involve no more than searching the surface of the pictorial symbol for cues which in fact unlock one's ability to recognise the represented objects; this unlocking or triggering of one's visual recognitional capacity in turn leads spontaneously to an ability to ascribe content correctly to the picture – i.e. to an understanding of just those conditions under which the symbol would be accurate.

The second disanalogy between depiction and thermometrical representation explains the first. It is obvious that a thermometer does not spontaneously engage our ability to recognise visually the phenomena it registers, for the evident reason that we have by and large no ability to recognise the temperature by sight. The final point of difference is that once you have got pictorial competence, you have the ability spontaneously to give radical interpretations of an indefinite range of symbols that can represent any visualisable state of affairs. That you have understood a thermometer may mean that you can now go on to interpret indefinitely many new thermometrical devices, but these will all represent the same sort of phenomenon: the temperature.

Maps are another sort of representation which we might come to understand radically. I might deduce what a map is and how to use one just by observing someone pantomime the use of a map. After watching what the map-reader does, and after looking at his map, I should be in a position to go on to use new maps to locate myself and navigate in new situations. I take it that we must, for the moment, prescind from the linguistic inscriptions which appear on most maps: for in so far as these are required, maps are clearly unlike depiction in the ways already explained. Moreover, of course, we are presumably concerned to contrast *non-pictorial* maps with pictorial representation. We must therefore delete from consideration maps that are in fact also topographical depictions, such as Saenredam's *Siege of Haarlem* or Micker's *View of Amsterdam*.[4] Once we do this, we are down to maps that are lines and dots, representing, let us say for the sake of simplicity, roads and places. Such a representation should exhibit a kind of isomorphism between the dots and lines on the page and the places and roads in the territory represented. It should be very easy to get the gist of this visualisable isomorphism after observing someone using a map; one will observe a certain correlation between their behaviour and their perception of the map. One will then be able to go on to make new and correct uses of the map. Of course, it is very doubtful that one will be able to make use of new maps of new territories without first having it indicated to you (possibly by making new observations of map-reading behaviour) that the new map is correlated with a certain territory. There will also be differences of scale to contend with (analogous to differences of calibration in thermometers). All of these variations will require the radical interpreter to have access to further contextual information when he interprets novel sorts of maps.

So, I conclude that some maps are clearly pictorial, since they are such that an ability to recognise visually the shape and layout of a terrain as the shape and arrangement of *that* terrain would result in their immediate recognition as maps of that terrain. The topographical maps mentioned above are good examples of this. Other maps will evidently be non-pictorial in that they will not engage the viewers' capacity to recognise the mapped terrain in such a way as to permit them to recognise spontaneously (without contextual input) which territories are mapped by which maps.

Similar considerations apply to ground plans of cathedrals,

---

[4] Alpers 1983.

palaces and colleges. That such a plan may be a picture of a building's layout is certain. Imagine a trip in which you fly over a certain island in the Aegean and see from above various ruined palaces and fortifications. Several years later and in quite a different place, you come upon some floor plans that are completely denuded of verbal or other explanation: they are pure floor plans. And you say (correctly) of each plan which palatial floor plan it represents. Here the only explanation is that these plans spontaneously engaged your visual recognitional abilities (perhaps you are an expert in spotting from the air the layouts of ruined buildings) and led you on to the correct assessment of the accuracy conditions of the given plans.

Of course, not all floor plans will have a similar power to engage our recognitional capacities. Moreover, there is an important difference between the most abstract pictorial representation of the volume of Notre-Dame Cathedral and a floor plan, however detailed, of that same building. A floor plan does not represent the overall volume and three-dimensional appearance of the building (though doubtless such information could be conjectured from it). A picture (usually so called) of a church outline or façade is a picture of that building from a more standard angle of view or recognition. Perhaps only the cognoscenti will be able to enjoy the esoteric delights of recognising churches in their ground plans. Indeed, perhaps of those who pore over ground plans, few will be able to interpret them naturally, radically or pictorially: nonetheless, the fact that they can be understood radically, on the basis of the relevant visual-recognitional abilities, makes them pictures. What distinguishes them from the pictures more usually so called is simply that they do not represent the appearance of the church from the usual angle of view – they represent it from an imaginary point of view in the air and as though the roof and the rest have been removed. Clearly such representations are abstract and abstruse (see chapter 8 for a discussion of abstraction versus realism in depiction): but abstraction alone certainly doesn't negative pictoricity, as the simple circle-dots-lines drawing of a face should show. The difference between the simple drawing of a face (recognisable as such by anyone able to recognise a face visually) and the floor plan of the church is simply that the iconic content of the face-drawing is more accessible. Human beings, thanks to various evolutionary causes, are keen to detect facial cues, but there is no similar natural human sensitivity to Gothic floor plans, though for those who have acquired the necessary sensitivity Gothic floor plans may become as pictorial as stained glass windows.

The example of floor plans illustrates the important point that a symbol may be pictorial even if it is not possible for many or most people to interpret it naturally. So the untrained will not experience X-ray diagrams of human anatomy as pictures, just as the untrained will not see floor plans as pictures of building lay-outs: but for all that, these symbols may very well become pictorial for those blessed with the relevant discriminatory powers vis-à-vis the objects they represent.

4

The absence of grammar

Evidently, if natural generativity is the hallmark of iconicity, there is no place for a grammar or syntax of pictures. Grammatical rules tell us how to compose whole sentences from items of the lexicon that have had their significance bestowed upon them by convention. It is by convention that the marks which express various logical operations, such as conjunction and disjunction, express those operations and not others. It is by convention that referring terms and predicates have been granted respectively their referents and their satisfaction conditions. Given the conventional interpretations of the lexical items in a sentence, and given rules of grammar, the interpretation of the whole sentence is fixed. No further conventional stipulation is required to determine the sense of the sentence.

This feature of natural languages we may call 'compositionality'. Compositionality is what allows us to generate and communicate with hordes of novel sentences; it is what allows us to interpret and cope with the flood of sentential novelty that daily washes over us. Compositionality is only necessary and not by itself sufficient for the fecundity and flexibility of natural language. For example, the Conference dot system introduced in chapter 2 is compositional, but its grammar and lexicon are severely restricted and parasitic on a linguistic environment. The dots represent participants (indexed by numbers on dots and lists of names) and the rectangle represents a table. The only well-formed statements of the system consist of putting dots around the rectangle. A dot standing for O placed next to the rectangle between dots standing for O$\star$ and O$\star\star$ means 'O seated at the table between O$\star$ and O$\star\star$'. The grammar of the system is 'quasi-natural' in that no special or prior stipulation seems to be required to explain the significance of compositions of dots with the rectangle. Placing a dot in a certain location is naturally taken to predicate a certain relative position of the dot's referent vis-à-vis the referents of the other dots and the rectangle.

Evidently, the grammar for predication in this system is too specific for it to have many uses; you can, potentially, extend the system infinitely but only by adding more dots. The system in effect has one predicate: '— is seated at t at position p relative to — and —'. Predication is quasi-natural and compositional but rather samely for all that.

Pictures, by contrast, have no grammatical rules, natural or conventional.[1] Yet pictorial systems, like natural languages and unlike the dot system, can be indefinitely fecund and flexible. There may be certain limits on what can be depicted by a system and there may be limits to what can be depicted *überhaupt,* but still a good pictorial system will be capable of generating arbitrarily high amounts of novelty. Anything one can visually recognise should be fair game for depiction if my surmise is right.

Now it is also my surmise that languages must be compositional in order to achieve their fecundity precisely because of the role of convention in establishing linguistic meaning. It is because linguistic meaning is meaning-by-convention that a truly flexible language must be compositional. By contrast, given that the total meaning of an icon can be generated on the basis of the ability to recognise the total scene depicted, no such rules are called for or admissible.

Of course icons have iconically significant parts; an iconically significant part *is* an icon. The truth of the whole icon depends upon the truth of its iconic parts (as I shall later argue, all iconic parts have a truth-value). Understanding the whole icon entails understanding its parts. But note that these parts do not get their meaning by stipulation, their meanings do not have to have been previously learnt and memorised, and going from part to whole does not require a grammar. Furthermore, it is not always possible, in the case of an icon, to understand a given part independently of its place in the whole icon. The mode of composition of icons into whole icons is itself iconic. An icon is built up iconically out of its parts just if

[1] There is no need for a grammar in Chomsky's sense (see Chomsky 1957 and Chomsky 1965) for iconic systems. For Chomsky, the grammar of a language tells you which sentences are to count as sentences of that language and which sentences do not count as sentences of that language. An ungrammatical string of symbols is thus something which isn't really part of the language in question. What would be the iconic analogue of a sentence that is ill-formed or ungrammatical in Chomsky's sense? The only thing I can think of is that a symbol is ill-formed, from the point of view of iconicity, if it isn't really an icon at all. So if S were intended to be iconic but failed, we should have something analogous to a Chomskian ungrammatical sentence. But then it is obvious why we don't need a Chomskian grammar for pictorial representations. The theory of natural generativity places constraints on iconicity just as a grammar of L places constraints on sentencehood in L. In so far as there is an iconic analogue of an ungrammatical sentence, the theory of natural generativity explains the failure of the symbol in question.

anyone able to recognise the objects or states of affairs represented by those parts can generate an interpretation of the whole based simply on these recognitional abilities.

In discussing 'compositionality' (or 'decomposability')[2] we may distinguish between weak compositional interpretability and strong compositional interpretability. A symbol is weakly compositional if an understanding of the whole symbol presupposes or entails an understanding of its parts. That is, if S is weakly compositional and x is some significant part of S, either you must understand x before you can be said fully to understand S, or, if you understand S, this implies that you understand x. A symbol is strongly compositional if understanding it requires prior knowledge of the conventionally prearranged significance of its parts and of the relevant grammatical rules governing their composition.

Pictures are weakly compositional; sentences are strongly so. The constraint of weak compositionality is a very weak one. If a symbol fails to meet it the symbol can in effect be treated as primitive and its parts can be treated as being without independent meaning. Many words in natural languages fail to be weakly compositional. The fact that their parts have no significance in themselves does not imply, of course, that those parts have no effect on the significance of the whole. The letters 'c' and 'm' have no semantic significance on their own, but they make a difference in 'cat' and 'mat' – interchange them and you change the identity of the resulting symbol.

Natural languages are weakly and strongly compositional at the level of sentences but neither weakly nor strongly compositional at the level of morphemes (units having an independent semantic status by convention but not composed of units having an independent semantic status). Pictures are weakly decomposable or compositional but not strongly so. But pictures decompose into iconic parts, not into words. These iconic parts can eventually be decomposed into parts which make a semantic difference to the picture but which on their own have no semantic status (a segment of a line, a dot, a point of colour). Let us call these parts 'sub-iconic'. The contribution such parts make to the significance of the whole is not determined conventionally. By itself a sub-iconic segment has no meaning, no independent and iconically recoverable meaning. (It may, but usually does not, have a non-iconic meaning, but it is logically true that the non-iconic meaning of a part cannot make an essential contribution to the iconically available meaning of the

---

[2] I borrow the concept of 'decomposability' exploited here from Simon 1969.

whole.) It is only in the context of the whole icon that a sub-iconic part makes a contribution to the iconic significance of the whole.

With pictures you simply have nothing which plays the role of a word. A word (or morpheme) is a unit of language which (a) is not weakly decomposable (and hence not decomposable at all) and (b) has an independent semantic status. To say that a segment has independent semantic status is to say that it makes a fixed contribution to the truth-conditions of any symbol in which it occurs. Thus 'and' is a word and 'c' happens not to be. Some marks are ambiguous; 'I' is sometimes a word, sometimes not. The letters 'ly' have independent semantic significance in 'stupidly' but not in 'lye'. (It is not the case that 'x has independent semantic status' entails that x is saturated in Frege's sense; for instance, predicates have independent semantic status. Token reflexives also have independent semantic status on my definition in that they make a fixed contribution to the truth-condition of an utterance.)

I am tempted to make the following claim about pictures: if x is a part of some pictorial symbol S, then if x has an independent iconically recoverable sense, x is weakly decomposable; if x is not weakly decomposable, x does not have an independent iconically recoverable sense. If x is non-decomposable it has no independent iconic sense, but it may affect what the icon depicts just as a letter of the alphabet which has no independent sense may affect the sense of word units in which it occurs. Thus whether we put 'c' or 'm' at the beginning of '— at' affects the sense of the resulting word even though 'c' and 'm' have no sense they can call their own. That is, the semantic relevance of a letter is contextual; there is no rule specifying what semantic difference 'c' will make to a word, sentence or utterance. The difference it makes depends upon the relevant alternatives and the given word. (The letters 'c' and 'k' may be interchangeable without impairing sense in some contexts and not others.) There is a rule that tells us what a word constructed by putting 'c' in front of 'a' and 't' means, but there are no rules taking the form '"c" added to the front of a word shall transform the word from — to —' (adjective to adverb or whatever).

But note that the semantic difference which 'c' makes when put in front of an 'a' which is in front of a 't' is conventional; that the resulting word, so spelt, should denote cats rather than mats is conventional; and so it is by convention that there is a rule that the word constructed by putting 'c' before 'a' and 't' shall denote cats and not mats. It is even by convention that certain letters are not interchangeable.

Now I am claiming that the sub-iconic parts of a picture have two things in common with letters of the alphabet: they have no independent semantic status (no independent iconic semantic status) and the difference they make to the iconic meaning of the whole is dependent on the context of other sub-iconic parts. The *difference* between sub-iconic parts and letters of the alphabet is that the difference the former make to the significance of the whole symbol is not fixed by convention. The difference 'c' makes to the various words in which it occurs is determined for each word by the conventions governing the spelling of the word and what the word so spelt shall mean. But we do not have to learn rules telling us that a certain configuration of dots and lines shall constitute a representation of a face.

All I claim is that a dot or a brush stroke can make a difference to what a symbol depicts even though that dot or brush stroke *by itself* would not depict anything. A painting by Paul Klee in the Stedelijk Museum in Amsterdam makes the point with the artist's typical wit. In the centre of the painting we see a primitive depiction of a face, like that a child might produce: two dots for the eyes, a line for a nose, a curve for the mouth, a circle for the head, and a few squiggles of hair. Surrounding this face are all the dots and circles, but strewn about randomly. The point is clear: it is the relative position of the marks which depicts a face; and it is only in the context of such a configuration that given marks iconify given features. And this points to a second very important difference between the sub-iconic marks in an icon and the letters of the alphabet. Whereas the 'letter-in-the-context-of-other-letters' makes a given semantic difference, it does not make this difference by itself playing a semantic role, such as denoting something. But the dots-in-the-context-of-certain-other-marks not only make a difference to what the whole iconifies – a face with eyes – they themselves play a semantic role: the dots represent eyes. I call them sub-iconic because the dots cannot iconify eyes except in the context of the whole. Just as they make a contribution to the whole, so the whole makes a contribution to them. Without them, these marks wouldn't add up to a pair of eyes. By contrast, if Rubens decides to depict the eyes of his mistress, he will go into plenty of detail, giving them a sparkle and identity they would retain even if they were seen on their own outwith the rest of the face. They are full-blooded icons. By contrast, the speck of white paint which in context iconifies a sparkle in Helen's eyes would, if that context were subtracted, iconify nothing. Furthermore, there are things which the eyes in context iconify that they wouldn't iconify outwith that context. For example, in the context of the whole picture these eyes belong to a smiling woman, a woman in furs, to Helen Fourment and so on.

Any given aspect of an icon that is itself an icon is weakly decomposable. If x is a part of an icon S and x cropped from S would iconify O, then x is weakly decomposable. That means that x has parts which are such that an understanding of x implies or presupposes an understanding of those parts. Call such parts 'iconically relevant'. The iconically relevant parts of x may either themselves be icons of things outwith the context of x or they may be iconic only in the context of x (and S). If the latter, these parts are sub-iconic. They have an iconic role in the context of the whole, but no iconic content outwith the whole. Given that x is iconic, it has some iconic content outwith the whole, but x may have an iconic relevance in the whole which it may lack outwith the whole. The difference, then, between an iconic and a sub-iconic part is that whereas the former has *some* iconic significance outwith the whole, the latter has none. Whereas some of the iconic significance of the former is context-dependent, *all* of the iconic significance of the latter is context-dependent.

Undoubtedly there is a small, nagging voice that proclaims 'How odd!' when told that one's understanding that a given ensemble of marks iconifies a face implies or presupposes that one knows that these dots represent eyes while understanding that these dots represent eyes itself implies or presupposes that one understands the significance of the other marks in the ensemble. Surely this is circular! How can an understanding of the other parts depend upon knowing what the dots represent while knowing what the dots represent depends upon knowing what the other marks severally or together represent?

The key seems to be that we comprehend these marks all at once and not seriatim. If we are given the marks in a temporal sequence, one bit at a time, obviously the sequence will not be an icon of a face. For *sub-iconic* parts, it is crucial that we see them together with the other relevant sub-iconic parts. Iconic parts of a painting can be processed sequentially and add up to something. Not so sub-iconic parts. We must hold all the marks in the child's drawing of a face in our 'awareness' – be it subliminal or not – if we are to understand it. Likewise, the sub-iconic parts of Rubens's depiction of one of his lady's eyes require to be seen together, all at once. A sequential peep at a series of those parts would not be an icon of an eye. If we are looking at a large work, like a Tiepolo wall decoration, a fresco by Piero or a vast ceiling by Pozzo, we can't take in the whole work at once. But the fact that we must look at it sequentially – albeit not in any particular or standard sequence – does not affect its iconicity. Sequentially interpreted icons can add up to a whole icon; it is sequentially interpreted sub-iconic parts that will not add up – for they must be seen together with other parts to have any iconic relevance at all.

We can reinforce this point by looking back at the sequential icon that diverted us in the last chapter, the mummery of turning on the tap and drinking tapwater. I said that the later gesture, in which the mummer make-believedly drinks tapwater, is an icon of 'drinking tapwater' only thanks to our recollecting an earlier stage of the mummery, when the actor make-believedly turned on the tap. Note that I called this later icon 'non-basic'. I should have been more precise: it is non-basic with respect to iconifying the content 'drinking tapwater'; it may be basic with respect to the content 'drinking something'. This gesture is thus not sub-iconic because it has some iconic significance outwith the total sequence and, in particular, independently of the mummery at the tap.

The drinking-gesture is basic *qua* the content 'drinking something', non-basic *qua* the content 'drinking the water from that tap'. This distinction applies not only to sequential icons, but also to pictures. A given area may be basic with respect to one icon and non-basic with respect to another. A spatial area A of a symbol S is basic with respect to an iconic part I of S with content p just if one can tell that A exemplifies I (and hence iconically represents p) independently of seeing other icon-exemplifying parts of S. An area A$\star$ is non-basic with respect to an icon $I\star$ which is part of S$\star$ when A$\star$ co-exemplifies $I\star$ with other spatial areas of S$\star$. In this case, seeing those areas without seeing A$\star$ is not seeing $I\star$; likewise, seeing A$\star$ without seeing those other areas is not seeing $I\star$. Strictly speaking, then, it is not icons which are basic or non-basic; rather, there are areas which basically exemplify icons and areas which non-basically or partially exemplify icons. An area which basically exemplifies one icon may be only part of the total area which exemplifies some other icon. I know that this way of putting things sounds as if it has more of the frightfully roundabout than the fruitful about it and I am distressed to see so much of what Collingwood called 'typographical jargon' in my definitions. As we shall soon see, however, it is quite important to distinguish between spatial parts of icons and iconic parts. The iconic parts of icons are not, I shall argue, reducible to spatial parts (therein will lie a bone of contention between my account and Goodman's mereological approach).

We may take a breather here to note that a sequential icon is one whose parts together iconify something more than the parts severally would iconify but whose parts do not all exist simultaneously. (I mean that the spatial and iconic parts of such an icon do not exist simultaneously; of course, the spatio-temporal parts or time-slices of icons both sequential and non-sequential do not – cannot logically – co-exist.) A non-sequential icon is one whose spatial and iconic parts exist simultaneously. A non-sequential icon may or may have to be experienced sequentially, as for example the splendid Room of Giants in the Palazzo del Tè or Michelangelo's gigantic *David*; however, because the parts of a non-sequential icon exist simultaneously, they do not impose upon the beholder a given order of experience, though there may be some orders of experience which are better than others.

Let me now stress one consequence of my claim that iconic parts of S are not basic or non-basic but rather that areas are basic or non-basic with respect to a particular iconic part (icon). The consequence is, of course, that one area may be basic with respect to *I* while another area, A*, may be non-basic with respect to *I*. For example, one area (perhaps the whole) may be basic with respect to 'icon of Helen' while another part is non-basic with respect to 'icon of Helen' in that it plays an essential role (it exemplifies some essential iconic parts) but it would not by itself exemplify an icon of Helen. Another example: the spatial part of the child's simple drawing of a face which has two dots on it would not by itself exemplify an eye-icon; it is thus non-basic with respect to the eye icon. It may be that nothing less than the whole spatial expanse of the drawing basically exemplifies icons of the various facial features. Nonetheless, the spatial area of the dots non-basically exemplifies the eyes in that it is essential for depicting them. It is also true – given that the whole minus the dots would not exemplify a face icon – that the area with dots non-basically exemplifies the face icon. The marks in an area which does not *basically* exemplify any icon are *sub-iconic*.

Now in the preceding paragraphs I have been discussing the distinction between areas which basically exemplify icons and areas which non-basically exemplify icons. This discussion has pertained to pictures and non-sequential icons and not to gestures and sequential icons. I mention this only to avoid terminological confusion. What makes an icon in a sequence of icons 'non-basic' is the fact that to interpret it requires *recollection* of the content of previous icons in the series. To be strict, again, it is the *gesture* which basically iconifies one icon and non-basically exemplifies another. It may basically exemplify an icon of drinking but non-basically exemplify an icon of drinking tapwater. Again, what this means is that this gesture does not, by itself, iconify 'drinking tapwater'. It is only this gesture plus other gestures which iconify drinking tapwater. It is, if you will, a certain sequence of gestures which iconifies 'drinking tapwater' basically. The gesture which basically exemplifies the drinking icon non-basically exemplifies the drinking-tapwater icon. But whereas 'memory' is involved in sequential icons (because one cannot see all the relevant icons at once) I want to say that memory is not always involved in non-sequential icons, though it may be when the icon must be experienced sequentially.

An iconic interpretation of a segment of a sequential icon is non-basic in so far as it relies on recollection of the contents of previous icons in the sequence. A gesture which exemplifies an icon which must be non-basically interpreted is non-basic with respect to that icon. Likewise, if a gesture is non-basic with respect to an icon, the interpretation of that gesture as exemplifying that icon will be non-basic.

An interpretation of an area of a nonsequential icon is non-basic with respect to I when awareness of that area alone would not suffice to generate the ability to interpret I in someone capable of recognising what I represents. In the case of non-sequential icons the temporally neutral notion of 'awareness' replaces the temporally charged notion of 'recollection'. But the important point is that just as there is non-basic iconic interpretation of sequential icons, so there is non-basic iconic interpretation of non-sequential icons.

I think in the case of the child's drawing we are inclined to say that he has depicted a face and he has depicted it as having eyes but he hasn't really depicted the eyes. On my view this comes down to the fact that he has basically depicted a face-with-eyes but there is no area which basically depicts the eyes *and nothing else*. The smallest area of the icon which counts as depicting the eyes might be the whole icon. If we are asked 'Does the child know how to draw eyes?' it will be misleading to say 'Yes' unless he can draw something which exemplifies an icon of the eyes and no other facial features. Yet, in slight tension with this, if we are asked to point to the eyes in the child's drawing, we would undoubtedly point to the dots. I am inclined to say that we take the dots as *representing* or *standing for* the eyes even though they do not basically iconify the eyes. If we used the drawing for voodoo, we should probably put out the victim's eyes by doing things to the dots in the drawing.

One final small point. It is not really possible to draw the eyes without also therein drawing features of the eyes. So it is not strictly possible for an area to exemplify an icon of the eyes without also exemplifying icons of various eye features. This area basically iconifies eyes in that, so to speak, it contains all the information the interpreter needs naturally to generate the 'eye' interpretation. It also basically iconifies other things – the colour of the eyes and so on. We might say the eye icon is in a sense constituted by these other icons which depict the various features of the eye. So the key thing is that someone who can draw eyes can draw something in A and make A alone iconify just the eyes and the eye features. Likewise, someone can draw a face or a building when they have the ability to make a face-icon or a building-icon in isolation. An artist may not be a master of, for example, leaf-depiction in this strict sense, because he can't draw something which is just an icon of a leaf and leaf-features, though he can certainly depict leaves as parts of trees, forests and landscapes.

This section has been rather long on nice distinctions and novel jargon, so it may help to have the ideas and terms summed up in a simple example, the child's drawing of a face which is a *simple* icon. An icon is simple when the configuration of its marks simply exemplifies it; a configuration of marks simply exemplifies an icon when the total configuration basically exemplifies an icon and when none of the marks, taken separately, basically exemplifies any icon.[3] In the case of the child's simple drawing, the totality of marks (the total *configuration*) basically exemplifies an icon of a face; it also basically exemplifies the various features of the face. A configuration of marks basically exemplifies an icon when awareness of that configuration alone would suffice to give someone with the requisite recognitional ability the ability to interpret the said icon. If we take the marks which comprise the child's drawing – the dots 'for the eyes', the line 'for the nose', and so forth – we find that these marks non-basically exemplify icons for eyes, noses, and the rest. In other words, the dots are sub-iconic because they basically exemplify no

[3] The definition of a simple icon must be modified to take account of the following point. There are spatial segments of the configuration of a child's drawing of a face which basically exemplify an icon of the face and of the face's features. Thus, if one took the child's drawing and covered a line segment one would thereby produce a configuration which was a proper part of the total configuration but which still managed to exemplify, basically, an icon of the face and its features. However, the crucial point is that any area that basically exemplifies an icon of any of the face's parts must exemplify an icon of the face. That is, an icon S of O simply iconifies O just when any spatial part of the configuration which basically exemplifies S will basically exemplify an icon of a proper part of O only if it basically exemplifies an icon of O and other parts of O.

icon though they do non-basically exemplify an icon. A mark non-basically exemplifies an icon when awareness of that mark is necessary but not by itself sufficient for the interpretation of the given icon. The various marks in the child's drawing non-basically exemplify icons for each facial feature; for example the 'line for the nose' non-basically exemplifies not only the nose icon but also the eye and mouth icon. The reason for this is obvious: since the whole configuration of marks is the only thing which basically exemplifies icons for the various features, and since each mark in the configuration is such that the configuration *would not iconify any facial features* without that mark, each mark has an essential effect upon what every other mark is able to do.

This shows, as I have said, that we cannot explain the representational properties of this particular face in terms of its iconic properties; we take the dots at their face value, as eyes, but from the point of view of the symbol as an icon the dots have no more right to be considered the eyes than any other part. We acknowledge this, as I have also said, when we say 'No, the child certainly can't depict eyes though he can depict a face with eyes.' The representational properties of many icons *can* be explained by their iconic properties, but not so with this particular example. The moral is clear: the 'iconification' or 'depiction' relation is not the same thing as the 'representation' relation.

One final point I would like to highlight from this section: it is imperative to realise that there are no basic or non-basic icons properly so called. There are only *configurations* of marks which either basically or non-basically exemplify a given icon. And note, a 'configuration' of marks is a given spatial arrangement of them – not just a set or an aggregate.

2 PICTORIAL QUOTATION

I would like to consolidate and extend the doctrines of the last section by giving further thought to pictorial quotation, a matter which I raised in the last chapter but which here promises to give us further instruction.[4]

It may happen that one picture S depicts another picture S★. From this it does not follow that S quotes S★. S quotes S★ only if the iconic contents of S★ are iconically available to the beholder of S. But if the contents of S★ are iconically available to the beholder of S, then S

---

[4] Compare Goodman 1978, pp. 44–50.

depicts not only S⋆ but the contents of S⋆. The relation of pictorial quotation seems to be in this respect analogous to the relation of 'same-saying' discussed by Davidson. We may say that pictorial quotation involves 'same-depiction'. But of course, 'same-depiction' is only a necessary and not by itself a sufficient condition of pictorial quotation. Two pictures which depict the same things do not therein quote each other. The relation must also be asymmetric (on pain of infinite regress): if S quotes S⋆, S⋆ cannot quote S. By 'quote' here I mean 'quote *in toto*'; S quotes S⋆ *in toto* only when S depicts everything which S⋆ depicts. It is obvious that S and S⋆ can both depict the same things, but not when one of them quotes the other *in toto*.

Thus when S pictorially quotes S⋆, S must *depict* S⋆ and depict the contents of S⋆. We might put it this way: when S pictorially quotes another picture S⋆, S not only depicts the content of S⋆ but depicts that content *as* belonging to S⋆.

To put this in terms of the theory of natural generativity, if S pictorially quotes S⋆, then someone who is able to recognise S⋆ must be able to generate the interpretation that S represents or signifies S⋆. Furthermore, anyone who is able to recognise the content of S⋆ must be able to generate the interpretation of S that it depicts a picture with that content. But then, if the ability to recognise something must be active in generating the (correct) iconic interpretation of S, I want to say that S must depict that thing. I ask you for the moment to accept this last point on faith. I shall argue for it in chapter 5.

Now it may be the case that when S pictorially quotes S⋆, there is an area of S, call it A⋆, which is such that anyone seeing A⋆ alone would take A⋆ to depict not S⋆ but the contents of S⋆. Thus, when we crop the rest of the painting and leave only the section which quotes the contents of S⋆ we no longer have a quotation of S⋆ but a depiction of S⋆'s contents! Cropping A⋆ from the rest of the picture seems to change the sense of A⋆. This is unlike verbal quotation, at least on Davidson's account. If I say 'Galileo said "Eppur si muove"', then on Davidson's account my utterance contains the contents of Galileo's.[5] Thus when I utter 'Eppur si muove', then on Davidson's account I am saying something with the same sense as the thing which Galileo said. Removing the quotation marks does not change the sense of 'Eppur si muove.' The quotation marks merely have the pragmatic force of flagging the fact that the speaker

[5] Davidson 1968–9.

doesn't necessarily believe or assent to the uttered remark. When, however, you block out the rest of S and leave only A⋆, you appear to change the sense of A⋆.

Given what I have said in the last section, I think we have a solution to this apparent problem that preserves the analogy between same-depiction and same-saying. The crucial point is that A⋆ – the spatial part of S which cropped from the rest of S depicts not S⋆ but the contents of S⋆ – does not basically exemplify an icon of S⋆. It basically exemplifies an icon of S⋆'s contents. The smallest area which iconifies S⋆ is larger than A⋆, though of course it must include A⋆. Call this area A. Then A⋆ basically exemplifies an icon of the contents of S⋆ but not an icon of S⋆; A basically exemplifies an icon of the content of S⋆ (in virtue of including A⋆) but it also exemplifies the icon of S⋆ in virtue of including further iconic information – about, for example, S⋆'s frame, the wall on which S⋆ hangs and so forth. So the area which basically exemplifies an icon of another icon S⋆ must basically iconify the content of S⋆, but it must also basically iconify more than the content of S⋆.

Now it should be obvious that the spatial areas of S cannot be identified with S's iconic parts. Take A. This area is, let us say, the smallest area that not only basically exemplifies an icon of S⋆'s contents but also basically exemplifies an icon of S⋆. This area must, if it is to be able to exemplify an icon of S⋆, exemplify icons of other things as well – S⋆'s frame, the wall on which S⋆ hangs and so forth. So a given area can play one iconic role only by playing others. There is no simple correspondence, therefore, of spatial parts and iconic parts of S. The iconic parts of S (the *icons* which constitute S) are not spatial parts of S but rather 'aspects' or property-exemplifications. 'Aspects' or 'states' of things intermingle and fuse (like colour, shape and texture).

I have asserted that an area of S could not basically exemplify an icon of S⋆ unless it also exemplified icons of things beside and around and other than S⋆. This is true of the example as I have envisaged it. It is possible, however, to envisage someone who depicts another painting in such great detail that this is not the case. He depicts the texture of S⋆, the light reflected from S⋆, the brush strokes, and so on. If we crop the area A⋆ that is the smallest area which basically exemplifies the contents of S⋆ we find that it also exemplifies S⋆! One can tell that this area exemplifies an icon of a painting – S⋆ – because it iconifies such features of S⋆ as texture, brush strokes, and the artist's signature. However, this has no tendency to detract from my point, since A⋆ in this painting again mul-

77

tiply exemplifies icons; it exemplifies not only an icon of S★'s content but also icons of S★'s surface properties.

3 THE ONTOLOGY OF DEPICTION

I should now like to pre-empt a terminological confusion to which my discussion may have unwittingly given some quarter. I have spoken of configurations of marks as exemplifying, basically or not, icons and iconic parts. But I have now said that icons are aspects or 'property-exemplifications'. A property-exemplification is an n-tuple of a place, a time and a property; it is the exemplification of a property ϕ at p at t. I borrow term and concept from Jaegwon Kim.[6] If an icon *is* a property-exemplification it is a particular; hence it cannot be a property. But if icons aren't properties it can only create confusion to speak of marks or spaces as 'exemplifying' icons. So an adjustment of terminology is called for. I would say that a configuration *constitutes* a given icon in virtue of exemplifying certain properties.[7] In virtue of exemplifying certain properties – of colour and shape – a given area exemplifies certain iconic properties. An area which exemplifies certain iconic properties 'constitutes' an icon. We might say that such an area 'is' an icon provided that we are clear that this 'is' is an 'is' of constitution rather than identity.

So strictly speaking we should speak neither of 'basic' and 'non-basic icons' nor of areas which exemplify, basically or non-basically, icons. Instead we should speak of areas which exemplify certain colour and shape properties and which therein exemplify certain iconic properties. Areas of marks which exemplify iconic properties constitute icons. Basic and non-basic constitution of an icon replace basic and non-basic exemplification of an icon.

If one does not distinguish the spatial parts of an icon from its iconic parts one will end up having to treat all icons and iconic parts as ambiguous. This is in fact where Goodman's nominalist and mereological project has landed him.[8] Because he refuses to acknowledge nonspatial parts of objects, he must necessarily treat iconic parts as spatial parts. But it is obvious that any given spatial part of an icon will have multiple iconic content. So icons and iconic parts are condemned to ambiguity. If, however, we adopt the more

---

[6] Kim 1969, Kim 1973 and Kim 1976.
[7] I borrow the notion of 'constitution' used here from David Wiggins, *Identity and Spatio-Temporal Continuity*, Oxford, 1967.
[8] See Goodman 1966 for the calculus of individuals.

fine-grained method of individuating icons which I suggest, the relation of icons and iconic content will be one–one.

In any case, either you postulate a one–one relation between spatial parts and icons, in which case the relation of icon to iconic content is one–many; or you postulate a one–one relation between iconic content and icon, in which case the relation between iconic part and spatial part is many–one. Either way the relation of iconic content and spatial part is not one–one. But how do we individuate icons if not in terms of iconic content? What is an icon if not an embodiment of iconic content? What is the point of taking iconic parts to be spatial parts and then declaring them all ambiguous?

I want to argue that what may seem like just a terminological dispute between Goodman and myself in fact reflects a crucial difference between his approach and that which I have adopted here. In particular, I want to argue that if we adopt a naturalistic attitude towards symbol systems, two things will happen. First, we will realise that the iconic properties of a picture are secondary properties. Secondly, we will realise that iconic meaning must be a matter of the functional role of the icon. Consequently, the individuation of icons must be functional. The fine-grained individuation of icons which I propose is generated by this naturalistic conception of iconic content. Once we realise that iconic properties are secondary, any pressure to reduce iconic parts to spatial parts is relieved. It is seen to be the result of a confusion between folk psychology and deeper levels of scientific explanation. Moreover, the naturalistic method for individuating content positively enjoins the fine-grained method for individuating icons (given certain principles of economy).

When is a property Q secondary? Let's say that Q is a secondary property or quality when an explanation of the form 'O's being Q caused x' can always be replaced by something of the form 'So and so's registering that O is Q caused x.' Furthermore, if Q is secondary it is not only causally redundant, it is causally inert. That is, 'O is Q' can never by itself play a causal role in bringing about an event x except via some agent's registering that O is Q. It is in this sense that red, for example, is a secondary property. The redness of a thing is causally inert; it never causes anything. What does cause things to happen is someone's registering that something is red. Primary qualities, by contrast, are things which have a causal role on their own, independently of being perceptually registered.

Other examples of secondary qualities are value-properties and semantic properties. 'Goodness' is causally inert; it is never something's being good which explains some event, but someone's registering that it is good. The semantic properties of a symbol, be it iconic or otherwise, can in themselves have no effect other than by people's taking the symbol as having a certain significance.

To say that Q is a secondary quality, on the naturalist view, is to make a meta-induction. It is never, for a naturalist, just *a priori* that a property is secondary. For him a property is secondary because that is the way it has been (or will be) treated by the framework which he regards as the most fundamental explanatory framework. Thus, for a naturalist, Q is absolutely secondary if F is the most fundamental explanatory framework and Q-exemplifications play no explanatory role in F-explanations at all. To say that Q is secondary is, therefore, doubly a matter of induction. First, it is a meta-induction that F will continue to be the most successful and powerful explanatory framework; but is also a meta-induction when one reasons from past F-theories to future ones, as one does when one says that because F-theories have not used Q in an explanatory office in the past, they are not likely to be required to do so in the future. So for the naturalist, as distinct from a transcendental idealist, the assertion that Q is secondary is always an *empirical assertion* which is empirically confirmable or refutable by the continued success and character of a given network of empirical explanatory theories.

To be sure, then, 'red' and 'good' and 'meaning' and so on may not be treated as secondary qualities at all levels of explanation. At the everyday level it is perfectly in order to say 'I saw the red pillar box because it was bright red' or 'I did it because it was the right thing to do.' But the naturalist *conjectures* that such modes of explanation will not be the fundamental ones. For example, he supposes that we will be able to eliminate all reference to red in the explanation of the perceptual experience which the agent describes as 'seeing a red pillar box'. Likewise, something's being a pillar box is a matter of how people see it and treat it. The meaning of a sentence is likewise a matter of how given marks are conventionally used in a society. The meaning of an utterance has efficacy only through being perceived or registered. Likewise, icons can only influence the course of world events by being registered upon someone's sensorium.

Of course, the things we call pictures have many primary properties. They can do many things which do not depend upon their being seen in certain ways by human or animate agents. One may prop up a wall with a picture or hit someone over the head with it. So the things we call pictures obviously have primary properties in abundance. I only claim that the iconic properties of pictures are secondary. The pictorial properties of pictures can have no causal effects upon the world except via agents who register those properties. 'S depicts O' can only explain events in the world through the fact that people (or other animals) register that S depicts O. Any explanation of an event in terms of the fact that S depicts O can be replaced, without explanatory loss, by an explanation in terms of the fact that someone or other registers that S depicts O. At the everyday level, of course, it is perfectly in order to treat pictorial properties as in themselves explanatory. The naturalist merely *conjectures* that they will not be treated as explanatory at the deepest level of explanation.

Given that icons are exemplifications by spatial and physical regions of secondary qualities (iconic properties), it is obviously foolish to try to reduce them to intrinsic physical parts of the icon. From the point of view of naturalism, there would simply be no point to such a reduction. There is simply no reason to seek a reduction or isomorphism between physical and iconic parts of an icon. This would be like trying to reduce the redness of an object to a spatial part of it.

So once we realise that icons are second-class ontological citizens, there can be no *a priori* naturalistic pressure to reduce them to spatial entities or spatial parts of entities. The only reason to seek a reduction of A-type things to B-type things is that you want to make A-type things part of your basic ontology but you think that all things in your basic ontology must be B-type. But for the naturalist there is no pressure to establish that icons are a part of the fundamental ontology of natural science! So there is no pressure to reduce them to spatial entities.

But this is to put the naturalistic argument against a reduction of icons to spatial entities at its weakest. The argument can be put more strongly. Given that the naturalistic approach to icons will be to treat them as secondary individuals (exemplifications of secondary qualities), obviously the iconicity of an object is not an intrinsic property of it. It is a functional or interactional property. Something is iconic only in virtue of the fact that perceiving agents interact with it in a certain way. So it is *logically impossible* to individuate icons in terms of the intrinsic spatial properties of an icon. We must individuate them in terms of their functional roles. But this is in accord with a general naturalistic tenet about meaning: that the meaning of a symbol is a matter of its use or role. The symbol is treated as something in the world, something coming into causal contact with world and agent alike, something which obtains its meaning in precisely that interaction.

Thus, if distinct recognitional abilities are required to interpret fully the iconic significance of a given expanse of depiction, then this expanse embodies distinct icons. The decomposition of an icon into its iconic parts is thus functional and not spatial. Recognitional abilities, in turn, are distinguished by the experimental method of variation. If someone can have one recognitional ability without another, the two abilities are distinct. I predict that iconic abilities co-vary with recognitional abilities. Given this, we can distinguish the iconic parts of an icon in terms of the distinct iconic abilities required to interpret those parts.

I have moved from the functional individuation of iconic content to the functional individuation of iconic parts or icons. This move seems justified. There is no other naturalistic or non-arbitrary way of individuating icons and iconic parts that I can think of. So, my method of individuating icons seems preferable to Goodman's from a naturalistic point of view (indeed Goodman really has no *method* of individuation at all).

Why do the distinct iconic parts of an icon thus spatially fuse and intermingle? What is the explanation for this fact? It is surely the fact that a given spatial area of an icon may be crowded with icons which 'explains' why awareness of that area can be awareness of so many icons at once. But what explains why this area crams in so many icons? I believe that the answer is that the iconic facts mirror the recognitional ones. Just as one can recognise several acts in one bodily movement, so one can recognise many representational or iconic parts in one theatrical gesture. An actress's gesture may constitute an indefinite number of icons: an icon of someone stabbing her husband (constituted non-basically), an icon of stabbing a king, an icon of stabbing a man, an icon of stabbing a man in purple and so on. This just seems to mirror the fact that if one were to witness a melancholy scene of this nature in real life, one would recognise in a single movement many different acts.

Likewise, just as one can visually recognise several property-exemplifications in a given spatial focus of awareness, so one can decipher many icons in a given area of a picture. If someone then asks how we can recognise so many things at once, I must reply that we just do. Any further explanation must be of a psychobiological kind. It is just a fact – at the everyday level – that we can visually take in many facts at once. The cognitive psychologist says that parallel processing must underlie this feat, and who is to gainsay him? For

82

my purposes the crucial point is that the facts about iconic interpretation mirror facts about recognitional ability. This reinforces the
position of recognitional ability as the central factor in iconic interpretation.

In this chapter I have discussed some peculiarities of what might
be called iconic ontology. Icons are not spatially decomposable in
the way that sentence inscriptions are; there is no way of mapping
the iconic parts of an icon on to its spatial parts. By contrast the
semantic units which one can decompose the inscription of a given
sentence can usually be assigned to spatially distinct detachable parts
of S's inscription. The following is roughly true of a sentence inscription: for each semantic unit represented by or expressed by S,
one can assign that unit a discrete spatial segment of the S inscription.[9] This breaks down only in the case of ambiguity, in which one
word or many may have two or more distinct semantic roles assigned to them. Such ambiguity is of necessity a deviant occurrence
in language. Redundancy, in which two distinct spatial segments of
a sentence's inscription play the same semantic role, does not violate
my rule, since each occurrence of something representing or
expressing that semantic role has a distinct spatial unit attached to it.

To explain this difference between sentences and icons I have ap-
pealed to the role of recognitional ability in pictorial interpretation.
The fact that a given spatial expanse of a picture may constitute
many distinct icons merely reflects the fact that many distinct recognitional abilities are engaged in decoding that area. Moreover, this
facet of iconic interpretation mirrors the fact that one is able to
recognise simultaneously many distinct property-exemplifications
in a given area of an object or scene.

If I were to try to explain why linguistic symbols are spatially
decomposable in a way which reflects their semantic composition I
would conjecture that their decomposability reflects an important
fact about how language is learnt. Language is learnt by piecemeal
acquisition of vocabulary. The piecemeal acquisition of vocabulary
is a necessary, though certainly not a sufficient, condition of
language mastery. This means that the language learner must be
able to pick up words one at a time. The inscriptions of words must,
therefore, be spatially articulate. (The same goes for utterances: the

---

[9] Compare de Saussure 1966, p. 104. Note also this statement by Diderot (quoted in
Aarsleff 1982, p. 157): '(o)ur mind is a moving picture from which we paint cease-
lessly . . . the mind does not go step by measured step like expression. The brush
executes only in the process of time what the painter's eye embraces in a flash. The
formation of languages demanded the decomposition.'

sound which embodies a word occupies a distinct time-slice of a given utterance.) The spatial (or temporal) distinctness of words allows us to attend to them separately. Given that the conventions governing each word must be learnt separately, it is an obvious hypothesis that their spatial (or temporal) segmentation facilitates our acquisition and exploitation of vocabulary.[10] By contrast, there is no need to acquire an iconic vocabulary, so there is no need for the iconic parts of an icon to be such that we can direct our attention to them separately and learn their meanings piecemeal.

4 ICONIC PARTS AND SEMANTIC PARTS

In this chapter I have used the notion of an 'iconic part'. But it is now important to be clearer about this notion. It is very important to see that iconic parts are nothing like spatial parts. In this chapter I have stated quite explicitly that every icon has iconic parts. But these iconic parts are themselves icons. So it might seem as though I am involved in an infinite regress. But I am going to claim that I am not. The reason is that the relation 'being an iconic part of' is not necessarily asymmetrical, unlike the relation 'being a spatial part of'. If x is a spatial part of y (a proper spatial part), then y is not a spatial part of x. This doesn't hold good for iconic parts. Once again, the calculus of individuals fails to hold for iconic parts.

Let's first note two different relations, the 'semantic parthood' relation and 'the iconic parthood' relation. It is essential to distinguish them. $S\star$ is a semantic part of S only if the truth of S presupposes the truth of $S\star$ but not vice versa (this is obviously 'proper' semantic parthood). But $S\star$ is an iconic part of S if the naturally generated

---

[10] Sampson 1980 has also stressed the importance of language's having evolved for our understanding of the structure of sentential units. Just as language is acquired by each individual in a piecemeal process of trial and error, so it evolves phylogenetically by trial and error. Sampson believes that he can account for the grammatical features which are universal in linguistic systems in terms of hierarchy theory (see Simon 1969). Sampson believes that only those linguistic systems whose units are decomposable according to certain hierarchical principles have any chance of evolving. It is worth noting that pictorial representation seems to constitute a counter-example to his general claim. Pictorial systems evolve in a piecemeal fashion (as Gombrich 1960 makes clear), but they exhibit none of the grammatical features of linguistic symbols. So the fact that a symbol system evolves in a piecemeal fashion doesn't entail its exhibiting any grammar at all, much less a grammar conforming to Sampson's constraints. The key factor seems to be whether interpretative competence in a system is acquired piecemeal or holistically. If I am right, interpretative competence in natural languages is acquired piecemeal (as stressed by Davidson 1968–9) but interpretative competence in pictorial systems is acquired in one go. Of course, the recognitional competences which underlie pictorial competence are themselves acquired piecemeal.

84

interpretation of S would be incomplete or impossible without the naturally generated interpretation of S*. It may also be the case that the naturally generated interpretation of S* would be impossible without the naturally generated interpretation of S.

To get the gist of this distinction we can consider once again the child's drawing of a face. Here the eye iconifying aspect of the face icon is a semantic part of the face icon, in that the whole icon is accurate or true only if the eye icon is true. The eye icon may be true even if the whole icon isn't, so obviously the whole icon is not a semantic part of the eye icon. The iconic interpretation of the eye icon is dependent (as we have seen) on the iconic interpretation of the whole icon, while the iconic interpretation of the whole icon is dependent on the iconic interpretation of this part. So, given our definition of 'iconic parthood', the eye icon is an iconic and semantic part of the face icon while the face icon is an iconic though not semantic part of the eye icon. The relation of 'iconic parthood' will be symmetrical whenever it is the case that one can naturally generate an interpretation of S only if one can naturally generate an interpretation of S* and vice versa (where S and S* are semantically distinct). The asymmetry between the eye icon and the face icon is at the level of semantics and not at the level of interpretation.

The fact that the iconic parthood relation may be symmetrical explains why it can be the case that each icon can have iconic parts *without* positing an infinite number of iconic parts for each icon. The whole of which S* is a part may itself be a part of S*. Obviously there would be a paradox if icons had to be interpreted sequentially, for then if S* were an iconic part of S and S were an iconic part of S, we would be saying something incoherent – namely, that S and S* were comprehensible but that S* had to be comprehended *before* S could be comprehended and that S had to be comprehended *before* S* could be comprehended. Obviously iconic interpretation of S and S* (when each bears the iconic parthood relation to the other) cannot be sequential. One of the great challenges facing empirical psychology is that of understanding so-called 'parallel processing'. I hope I have made it clear, at the conceptual level, why something like parallel processing must be postulated to explain iconic interpretation.

Given that the calculus of individuals fails so signally to apply to iconic wholes and iconic parts it may be wondered that I have retained the terminology of 'parts' at all. I sympathise with this objection. I would be happy to say that icons really don't have parts at all if parts are to be understood in terms of the calculus of individuals. It would be preferable to speak of iconic *functions* rather than of iconic parts. Let's say that S is an iconic function of S★ just if the generation of a complete natural interpretation of S presupposes or entails the generation of a natural interpretation of S★. Then, the point I am making is this: the 'iconic function' relation is not necessarily asymmetrical. S may be an iconic function of S★ which in turn is an iconic function of S.

Holism at the level of interpretation does not necessarily entail holism at the level of semantics. The truth of the eye icon does not depend upon the truth of the face icon – but its iconic interpretability is parasitic on the iconic interpretability of the whole. Once again we see the importance of the distinction to which I alluded in the first chapter between the question 'What is involved in interpreting S?' and the question 'What is the content of S?'

It should be stressed here that what is in question is an interdependency between the *naturally* generated interpretation of S and the *naturally* generated interpretation of S★. It is perfectly possible that some non-naturally generated interpretation of S★ may not depend upon the non-naturally (or naturally) generated interpretation of S even though the naturally generated interpretation of S★ depends upon the naturally generated interpretation of S. My point is that when S★ is an iconic part of S, one can't *naturally* generate a complete interpretation of S without also naturally generating an interpretation of S★. And this relation may be symmetrical.

Now it is important to note a distinction between the following four claims:

1. The complete interpretation of S could not be naturally generated without naturally generating a complete interpretation of S★.
2. Not even a partial interpretation of S could be naturally generated without naturally generating a complete interpretation of S★.
3. The complete interpretation of S could not be generated naturally without naturally generating at least a partial interpretation of S★.
4. Not even a partial interpretation of S could be naturally generated without at least naturally generating a partial interpretation of S★.

A complete interpretation is one stating the full content of S; a partial interpretation is one stating a part of the content of S. To see the importance of these distinctions, reflect on the case of the sparkle in the eye of Rubens' mistress. The icon of the sparkle in Helen's eye is dependent on the icon of the eye. There is no spatial part of the portrait that could iconify the sparkle without also iconifying the eye. So the sparkle-iconifying aspect is an iconic function of the eye icon (the eye icon is an iconic part of the sparkle icon). Clearly, we also want to say that the sparkle-depiction is part of the eye-depiction in the sense that a complete interpretation of Rubens's eye depiction must include the fact that he depicts the sparkle in his mistress's eye. However, a *partial* interpretation of the eye icon is possible without naturally generating any interpretation of the sparkle icon. The reverse is not true: *any* naturally generated interpretation of the sparkle icon requires the natural generation of an at least partial interpretation of the eye icon. So there is clearly an asymmetry here: the sparkle icon is more dependent on the eye-icon than the eye-icon is on the sparkle-icon. This will not always be the case, however. In the case of the child's drawing of a face, to generate naturally a partial interpretation of the face icon requires or presupposes that one naturally generates an interpretation of the eye icon and likewise even a partial interpretation of the eye icon requires a partial interpretation of the face icon.

Of course, the thesis may seem trivial if one isn't careful to understand it aright. The complete interpretation of a word in a sentence requires the partial interpretation of the sentence: namely, it requires the interpretation of that part which is constituted by the word itself. However, when I say that a partial interpretation of S is required for a complete interpretation of S* what I mean is that the interpretation of S* requires or presupposes the interpretation of parts of S which are semantically distinct from S*.

One final point. Someone might be alarmed that I have made a distinction between the 'semantic' parthood relation and the 'iconic' parthood relation. They might take this to imply that the relation between the iconic parts of a completely iconic symbol and the semantic parts of that symbol is not one–one. This is not so. What is in question is simply a distinction between two kinds of dependency that can subsist between icons. S can be truth-functionally dependent on S* even though S* is such that its iconic interpretation presupposes (is a function of) the iconic interpretation of S. But the S* which is a semantic part of S is not a different S* from the S* of which S is an iconic part.

If S* and S are icons and S* is a semantic part of S, then S* is an iconic part of S. S is an iconic function of S*. I have argued that S* may also be an iconic function of S. In the remainder of this essay I shall reserve the term 'iconic part' for S$\star$ when S$\star$ is a semantic part of S and S is an iconic function of S$\star$. 'Iconic part' used in this way *is* asymmetrical, and so the 'part' terminology is less misleading. The point of substance remains unaffected by this concession to ordinary usage: that there is a distinction between 'S is a semantic part of S$\star$' and 'S is an iconic function of S$\star$' and that the latter relation, unlike the former, may be symmetrical. All icons are iconic functions of other icons, but this doesn't lead to an infinite regress because even if S is an iconic function of S$\star$ it may also be that S$\star$ is an iconic function of S. So there are no atomic icons. All icons are complex in the sense of being iconic functions of other icons. Given our now official definition of iconic part, that S$\star$ is an iconic part of S just if S is a semantic and iconic function of S$\star$, there may be iconic parts which do not themselves have iconic parts since although they are iconic functions of other icons they are not semantic functions of other icons. For example, the sparkle icon in the painting of Rubens's mistress may be atomic in the sense that it has no iconic parts since it has no semantic parts (though it is an iconic function of other icons).

5

Recognition and iconic reference

I THE PUZZLES OF ICONIC REFERENCE

There is reference and there is iconic reference and it would be a dire mistake to confuse the two. It is in virtue of the reference of a name that we say the sentence 'Henry's pants are ablaze' is about Henry and no one else. Likewise, a picture of Henry with his pants ablaze is a picture of Henry and no one else. There is a third form of direct and rigid aboutness which we might call representational. If Henry's enemies set an effigy of him alight it is something which represents or stands for *Henry*, and no one else, that they have set alight.

All three relations – denotative, pictorial and representational – are instances of what we might call 'rigid aboutness'. In recent years, Saul Kripke has given us many insights about rigid designation ·(the denotative form of rigid aboutness).[1] He has argued, persuasively, that P can refer to O with 'N' if something like the following story is true: P recognises that 'N' is a name and that its semantic role is purely referential; he uses 'N' referentially. O was baptised with the name 'N' by some group of people. It may be that 'N' is P's nickname for O (perhaps O is the neighbour's cat and Henry has just nicknamed him Grimalkin). The people who baptise O with 'N' may or may not have been able to recognise O. It is quite possible that they, and every other user of 'N', lack the ability to recognise the thing which 'N' designates, at least under the description 'the thing which "N" designates'. Nonetheless, they have to have enjoyed some causal contact or rapport with O. It is the causal contact between the baptisers and O which establishes a real relation (as we might, after Hume, call it) between 'N' and O. These people have established a convention that 'N' shall designate O. It may be true that the original instigators of the use of 'N' must at least have some reference-fixing descriptions or modes of presentation which they associate with 'N', but users of 'N' further down the chain of transmission need not inherit these. They must, however, intend to

[1] Kripke 1980.

use 'N' to refer to whatever those who are earlier in the chain used 'N' to refer to.

Now we can, I think, directly apply this kind of story to the kind of representation involved in effigy. Henry's effigy is baptised as 'Henry'. R represents O for a social group when they baptise R with one of their names for O. Thus, the rigid aboutness of representation is parasitic on the rigid aboutness of names. The name for O is fictively applied to O's representation and the representation thereby becomes rigidly of the thing which its own fictive name rigidly designates. It is an important feature of rigid designation that when a term applies rigidly to O it applies to O in all possible situations. In particular, O does not have to have any particular properties, other than (tautologously) that of being called by the name which rigidly designates it, in order to merit the status of being rigidly designated by 'N'. Now representational aboutness is often of this kind: something can stand for or be something else regardless of what the represented object is like. This is most obvious when there is no 'natural' relation between the representational vehicle and the represented object. For example, I could take the pepper pot and the salt cellar and say 'Right, now let this pepper pot be Henry and let this salt cellar be a car: here's how the accident happened.' What I have done is to take two quite random objects and designate them fictively with terms I want to use rigidly, 'the car that struck Henry down' and 'Henry'. So not surprisingly, representational aboutness often reflects denotational aboutness.

Of course, anything can be used as a name or a representation if you establish the right conventions. I might take Mona's portrait and say 'Right, let this stand for Henry' or I might take a picture of a bird and say 'Right, let this be the name of the cat next door.' The picture, so used, will be rigidly about Henry or the cat next door. But there is a distinctive kind of pictorial aboutness which is exemplified by a portrait of Henry. Here again, of course, the portrait represents Henry, in that I may address words of abuse to the portrait and so on. But Henry's portrait is *iconically* and *rigidly* about Henry. We might say that it iconically refers to Henry. The icon ascribes many properties to someone, and it will be an accurate or true icon only if Henry is the person who has the properties ascribed. To say that Henry's portrait is accurate because someone else has the qualities ascribed in it to Henry would be as ludicrous as saying that 'Henry's pants are ablaze' is true because someone's pants are ablaze. No, Henry's portrait is a good 'likeness' only if Henry is the person who has the properties the portrait ascribes to him.

But there are really two rather distinct senses in which a picture can be, *qua* picture, about someone. Suppose we take a picture of Henry in travesty, through billows of smoke engendered by the malicious (or so it is said) ignition of his frock. *No one* who is able to recognise Henry would ever guess that this is a picture of him. Yet, in a rather left-handed way, it is certainly a picture of him. I mean it is a picture of someone whose frock is going up in smoke, and that someone happens to be Henry. And surely Henry, if perchance he witnessed the scene in a mirror, would be able to recognise it in a picture. So, there are at least some conditions in which it would be possible for someone who was able to recognise Henry, albeit under a rather bizarre aspect, to say 'Ah, this is Henry in the Dewsbury panto playing Cinderella. His frock was burnt to cinders. It seems someone had dipped his broom in the wassail bowl, and it was soaked in alcohol, and when poor Henry put it into the fire . . .'.

But it is possible for a child to make something which counts as pictorial, *qua* some of its content, even though it is not a picture of anyone in particular. One of the children at the performance may draw a blob of red flames surrounding someone vaguely recognisable as a person and say 'This is Cinderella on fire.' To be sure it is a picture of someone on fire, and given the child's expressed intentions it is of Cinderella-Henry, but it is clearly not a picture of Henry.

We have learnt two things from this little skit. First, recognitional ability is aspect-relative. Someone able to recognise Henry in his mid-morning aspect may be unable to identify him when he steals into the night wrapped up in scarf, top coat and wide-brimmed hat. Consequently, we can only claim that Sandy will recognise Henry in a picture S if Henry in the picture is depicted as having the features with which Sandy is used to recognising Henry. This needn't worry us overmuch. We can simply claim that S is pictorially or iconically of Henry just if someone able to recognise him under some of his aspects or in some of his guises would on the basis of that ability alone recognise him in the picture.

Of course this proposal begs a rather important question, for we need to ask: what makes this picture a picture *of* Henry and not someone else? Why isn't it a picture of anyone who happens to look like Henry? The answer will, of course, have to have something to do with the causal relation between Henry and the picture.

Now the second thing we have learnt is that something can be a picture and it can be of Henry without thereby counting as a picture of Henry (the child's drawing was an example). So for something to be both a *picture* of Henry and a picture *of* Henry we have to combine two things. Causation and intention explain the 'rigid of-ness' of the picture while the fact that the ability to recognise Henry causally engenders the ability to interpret the picture as being of Henry explains the iconicity of the picture's relation to Henry.

Now at once we spot an obvious asymmetry between pictorial aboutness and denotational aboutness. Recognitional ability is required for mastery of pictorial aboutness, but not for mastery of denotational aboutness. On the 'austere' theory of naming one knows the semantic role of a name when (a) the name refers (thanks to its causal credentials) and (b) one can recognise and use it as a name. That is it. When the name happens not to refer, then the name has no semantic role whatsoever, and therefore there is *nothing to know*. One cannot be master of it because there is *nothing to master*. (I shall return to vacuous and fictive names later.) Being *pictorially competent* in the reference of a picture is a matter of being able to specify the referent of the picture on the basis of an ability to recognise the referent of that picture. So to understand iconically the iconic reference of a picture one requires specific recognitional abilities.

But we meet the following question: if a picture iconically refers to Henry, surely it doesn't iconically refer to him in all possible worlds? That is, there are situations in which this very picture simply would not be a picture of him. This objector continues: rigid designation involves a name designating an object in all possible worlds. But surely this picture bears no analogously rigid relation to Henry.

This objection seems confused to me. Take a picture of Henry as a baby. Kill off everyone able to recognise him as a baby. Henry grows up. Is this picture still iconically of Henry? Of course it is! The fact remains that anyone able to recognise Henry as a baby would be able to say 'This is a picture of baby Henry.' The fact that there happen not to be any such people around is neither here nor there. The claim is counter-factual: if there *were* people able to recognise Henry as depicted, then they would know that this picture depicted him.

But the objector probably has a different case in mind. Imagine a picture of Henry in this world. It represents him as having certain recognition-triggering features. Anyone able to recognise Henry under the features in this cluster would be able to tell that Henry was indeed the man in the picture. The picture bears the right causal-cum-intentional relation to Henry. So let's grant that it is a picture of Henry. Now, transport this picture (in imagination, of course!)

to a different possible world. This is a world in which Henry lacks (indeed, has never had) the recognition-triggering features he has in the actual world. He is hideously disfigured as the result of an inferno which consumed his nursery in this counter-factual world. So no one able to recognise him in this counter-factual world would be able to say that this picture depicted him.

But it is easy to see that this picture we are imagining in the counter-factual world simply isn't the very same picture as the picture in the real world. Its causal relations to Henry just cannot be the same as they are in the real world, since the picture as described could not have been modelled on the Henry in the counter-factual world. All that we have succeeded in imagining is a situation in which a picture which is qualitatively similar to Henry's picture is not a picture of Henry. *That* is certainly possible. What is not possible is that a given picture of Henry, standing in the relation in which it actually does stand to Henry, is not a picture of Henry. Here it is perhaps once again necessary to stress that a picture is an essentially semantic entity and that it is not reducible to a physical object. The functional relations of a semantic entity are of its essence. If this picture has a certain causal origin, and in virtue of that origin has a certain semantic status, then it retains that causal origin in all possible situations. *It* cannot suddenly acquire new origins any more than I can acquire new biological parents.

So we must certainly agree that a picture which is qualitatively similar to Henry's is not necessarily a picture of Henry. It is not a picture of Henry if Henry played no role in causing it. To be sure, more needs to be said about the nature of the causal chains involved, but that is a tall order and would only side-track us here. Let's beg a host of questions now which I hope, thanks to the work of Peacocke and others, we can unbeg later and say that if there is a non-deviant causal chain between Henry and his picture, then this picture is of Henry and is a picture of Henry in all possible worlds. So I see no problem in allowing for the relation of 'rigid iconic aboutness'. We must of course acknowledge that the physical object which constitutes Henry's picture may come to be used for purposes other than Henry-depiction. Suppose that the picture lasts a few thousand years and, lo and behold, it is one day discovered by some people whose king happens to be a deadringer for Henry. Let us call him Henry II. They decide to use this newly unearthed portrait of Henry I as a portrait of Henry II. Have they not thereby altered the reference of Henry I's portrait? Not on your life! They have, of course, redeployed the physical object which constitutes Henry I's portrait.

It now *also* constitutes Henry II's portrait. If they start altering the physical substrate of Henry I's portrait, to make it a more suitable embodiment of Henry II's portrait, they may well alter the appearance of Henry I's portrait and may even destroy it. But they cannot make Henry I's portrait into a portrait of Henry II. Not even God could do that.

The story so far is perfectly parallel with a Kripkean story about proper names. A name is not a physical token, at least not in the sense in which it rigidly designates someone. Of course this very token of my name might be used to designate someone else, but it doesn't follow from that that my name, in the sense of that term which designates me in all possible worlds in which it designates at all, has changed its reference. If Kripke is right, and I think he is, the origin of a certain use is essential to it. The role Henry plays in the emergence of the 'Henry' naming practice is essential to that practice. It is the causal or functional role of a name which is of its essence. Obviously the physical token is in fact irrelevant, since my name can be realised in a variety of physical media. What is of the essence is the origin of any particular realisation of my name. Of course, I can have distinct names, but their distinctness consists in the fact that they originate in different baptismal rites and not in the fact that they have different physical realisations. Likewise, the essence of a picture is its functional role, as I have already argued in the last chapter. Its functional role is an abstract thing, not a concrete one. That is why Henry I's picture can *spatially* coincide with Henry II's picture, just as a given physical token might be used to realise physically two different names.

I claim that given that S depicts Henry, S depicts Henry in all possible worlds. This claim is ambiguous. I only intend to claim that given that S depicts Henry, then in any situation or world where there is something which S depicts, it is Henry that S depicts. This does not entail that S depicts Henry as he would look in any possible situation! Obviously nothing could do this.

The reluctance one may feel to accept that Henry's baby picture depicts Henry, now an adult, is likewise a product of scope confusion. If S is Henry's baby picture, and T is sometime in his adulthood, then my claim is that: there is someone at T, namely Henry, whom S depicts. Obviously I do not claim that S depicts Henry as he is in adulthood.

If S depicts Henry, then I require that someone able to recognise Henry should be able to interpret S as being of Henry on the basis of their ability to recognise Henry alone (given the obvious background conditions that they are pictorially competent and so on). If S meets this condition, and the further causal conditions (which involve Henry's role in the making of S), S is of Henry. However, it may well be that Sandy, who is able to recognise Henry only under his adult aspect, is unable to interpret Henry's baby picture. This shows that the picture doesn't depict Henry under the adult aspects which enable Sandy to recognise Henry. It hardly shows that it doesn't depict Henry at all.

Another confusion may involve the existence of S. If W is a world or situation in which S does not exist, this does not affect the fact that Henry may be the person in W whom S depicts. If 'N' is a childhood nickname of Henry's that has long been forgotten by everyone, Henry included, it is still true that Henry is the person designated by 'N'. Likewise, 'Henry' designates Henry even in worlds where he is not called 'Henry'.

So, given that S depicts Henry in the real world, Henry is the person it depicts in a counter-factual world W even though W is a world or situation in which Henry looks nothing like he does in the real world. Pictures of Henry as he looks in W obviously won't look like Henry's pictures in the actual world. That is why S cannot exist in such a world; something qualitatively similar to S may exist in W, but it wouldn't be a picture of Henry, so it wouldn't be S.

2 DEPICTION AND DOUBLES

I have admitted that two qualitatively identical pictures may represent different objects. Phenomenal similarity does not guarantee sameness of content. This may appear to put the theory of natural generativity in a pickle. I shall argue that it does not. To show the fly the way out of the pickling bottle I am going to discuss Ralph and Sam and their respective pictures. Ralph and Sam are homozygotic twin brothers. They are deadringers. Suppose I know what they both look like: they both look the same. I can't tell them apart. Obviously knowing everything about what O looks like need not generate an ability to recognise O. Not surprisingly, my recognitional disability carries over to pictures of Ralph and Sam. This is just what we should predict, given that iconic competence varies with recognitional competence. Just as Ralph and Sam look alike, so their pictures look alike (they make no attempt to distinguish themselves). Just as I can't discriminate them, I can't discriminate their pictures.

Now if I had said that 'Knowing what O looks like is sufficient to generate an ability to interpret S if S depicts O' this example would have been sufficient to scupper the theory of natural generativity. But that is not my claim. My claim is that the ability to recognise O, if S depicts O, is sufficient for a person to be able to interpret S. The twin case, as so far presented, presents no problems for this analysis. Recognitional ability and iconic competence are both defeated by the *Doppelgänger*. I only predict that the two abilities will co–vary. What would refute my proposal would be an instance of a depiction that could not be interpreted by at least someone with the ability to recognise the depicted object. I should be more precise: if P can recognise O under F and if P is pictorially competent in the system of which S is a member, and if S depicts O as F, then if P has a chance visually to inspect S under optimum conditions, and he has all his wits about him, and so forth, he should be able to tell us that S is of O. If he can't, this will refute my theory.

In any case, it is obvious that the Ralph and Sam case does not refute my theory. But that is not the end of it. I am now proposing two distinct theories. One is a theory of iconic reference and the other is a theory of iconicity. The Ralph and Sam case may pose problems for neither theory separately, but it may bring out a contradiction between them. What makes the icon of Sam an icon of Sam rather than Ralph? The fact that someone able to recognise Sam would be able to say that S is of Sam plus the fact that Sam bears the right relation to S. But what about this causal relation? Knowing whether S depicts Sam depends upon knowing whether S can be traced causally, somehow, to Sam. Perhaps it even depends on the intention of the artist. Imagine that Sam is the mayor and Ralph, his twin brother, is unemployed. The mayor is too busy to sit for his portrait so he asks Ralph to sit for it. Ralph gladly does so. Now given the intentions of the artist and the whole point of portraiture, it is obvious that the resulting artifact is both a picture and a portrait of Sam. We might say that it bears the right relation to Sam through the intention of the artist. (The result may also be that the artifact re-alises a picture of Ralph. It is not, however, a *portrait* of Ralph, since it is not meant to commemorate Ralph.) In any case, this just adds fuel to the fire. If to know that S depicts O we must know a causal story and perhaps even a story about the intentions of some artificer or user of S, it surely follows that the ability to recognise O is *not* sufficient to know that S depicts O. So the theory of natural generativity goes up in a puff of smoke.

My primary claim is that if S depicts O, the ability to recognise O will, ceteris paribus, give one the ability to generate the interpretation that S is of O. Furthermore, if I interpret S as being of O on the basis of a recognitional ability, I probably would not have made this interpretation unless it were the right one. In general, knowing that an interpretation which I generate is the correct one may require me to know something about the causal origin of S. But I would claim that this knowledge can be a consequence of my interpretation rather than a cause of it. It may be *because* I naturally generate the interpretation that S depicts O that I surmise that S was produced or used with the intention of representing O. The interpretation comes first. Then, on the basis of a naturally generated interpretation, I explain the interpretation in terms of a plausible hypothesis: I naturally generate the interpretation that S is of O *because* someone intended that I should generate this interpretation. Further down the line, if I am a speculative philosopher, I might give some thought to the fact that O must play a causal role in the origin of S.

Someone who has iconic competence in a system of icons is able to track their content; that is, he would not believe that S has the content *p* unless S has the content *p*. My claim is that what distinguishes iconic systems from other systems is that we can track an icon's content with or because of our ability to recognise the object it depicts. That is, our ability to recognise the depicted object is what explains our ability to interpret S. Furthermore, there is in fact, whether we know it or not, a mechanism, call it M, which ensures that our recognitionally generated interpretations are likely to be right. This mechanism is the practice of depiction. The artist A would not have made S in the way he did if he did not think someone with the ability to recognise O could interpret S. So, given the intentions of the artist (or the mechanism of the camera), there is bound to be a reliable connection between our naturally generated interpretations and the correct ones. But knowledge of such a mechanism – though it may be readily available – is not actually required for the mechanism to do its job. Since, unlike the brain mechanism designed by evolution, the pictorial mechanism M is an artifact, it is of course the case that someone, somewhere along the line, must have an inkling of M if the mechanism is to work. The artist, producer and user, for example, must be aware of M. But my point is that the interpreter need not be. M can do its work, of co-ordinating producer's intention with interpreter's interpretation, without the interpreter being aware of it at all.

Of course, much the same goes for the conventions which govern language. We don't have to be aware of them. But they have to be there. What distinguishes pictorial interpretation from linguistic interpretation is that what results in the co-ordination of producer's intention and interpreter's interpretation in the pictorial case is not a convention at all. It is the fact that producer and interpreter alike share a set of recognitional abilities and that they can apply these abilities to pictorial symbols that explains the correspondence of producer's intention and interpreter's interpretation. It is because the artist can himself *naturally generate* the interpretation of S that he expects others will be able to do so. In the case of a word, it is because I expect you to use it in a given way that I use it in that way; or perhaps I use it in that way because I expect that you will expect me to use it in that way. It is a web of reciprocal and interlocking expectations based on entrenched habits of use that governs the use of words. Not so with pictures. The artist experiments until he gets something which he can naturally understand on the basis of the relevant recognitional abilities. He then puts it before the public in the belief that their recognitional abilities, being similar to his, will result in an ability to interpret it.

We might say that it is part of the functional essence of an icon that it should be interpretable on the basis of recognitional abilities alone. An icon is the way it is *because* its being that way allows it to be interpreted on the basis of the recognitional abilities. Just as we conjecture that something is a chair because we can sit comfortably in it, so we conjecture that an object constitutes an icon because we can interpret it naturally. In either case we may be mistaken, but it is the fact that *x* performs a certain function F which leads us to conjecture that its performing that function *explains* its existence. And since chairs and icons are artifacts and not products of natural selection, they imply a designing agent. But whether something serves as a chair or an icon does not depend solely on convention or the artificer's intentions. It depends upon *performance*. You can make any set of marks you like into a word or symbol provided you manifest your intention that it should be used in a certain way. Your success in coining a term will depend entirely upon whether people accept the word as a designator for a given object (or whatever). But something doesn't become a chair just because people accept it as one. It has actually to perform a certain function. It has to be successful, to a degree, in performing that function. Likewise with an icon: something doesn't become a picture of Henry just because people treat it as one or just because the artist manifests his intention that it should be so regarded by the beholder. It becomes an icon of Henry only if it serves the purpose of being such that Henry's friends, those able to recognise Henry, will, on the basis of their recognitional ability, interpret it as being of Henry. And just as a carpenter might test the success of a chair by sitting on it, so the artist can only test his iconic success by asking himself 'Would I see Henry in this just on the basis of recognising Henry and being pictorially competent?' He may even perform a thought experiment in which he puts himself in the place of someone coming to the painting cold.

A difference between the chair and an icon (or any other symbol) is that a chair could serve its chair function even if the fact that it is serving that function did not register on the user. An icon can serve its function only if it is recognised as serving that function. It can serve its function only if its purpose is understood. As we shall see, this necessarily implies an awareness of the artist's intention or an awareness of some convention. But the difference between an icon and a word is important. The word fulfils its purpose once its intended function is understood. We might say that a word's being understood as intended to perform a certain function *is* its performing that function. If S is a linguistic symbol, S performs its function by virtue of the mere fact that its function is understood. This is not the case, as we have seen, with icons. But we must come back to this in chapter 7.

So we have the following contrasts and similarities. An icon is like a chair in that the fact that an icon performs its function is not to be explained simply by the fact that it is taken to perform a given function. Unlike a chair, and like a word, an icon cannot perform its function unless its function is understood. But an icon does not perform its function merely by making its function manifest, whereas a word does perform its function in so far as its purpose is manifest.

3 THE TWO OFFICES OF RECOGNITION

We have distinguished, in a rather rough and ready way, two kinds of recognitional failure. One kind of recognitional failure is based upon not knowing what someone looks like in a given context. So when Henry goes black tie for an evening out I don't recognise him under his elegant aspect. Recognitional ability is always aspect-relative. This applies to recognising individuals as instances of types as well as to recognising them as individuals. So when Henry dresses up to play the bear in *The Winter's Tale*, the local drunk takes him for a bear. He doesn't recognise that he is just a human actor in a bear outfit.

But there is a second sort of recognitional failure which we have encountered with our twins Ralph and Sam. We may know everything about what Ralph and Sam look like but not be able to discriminate them. Here our ability to recognise, say, Sam, may *misfire*. We may walk up to Ralph and say 'Hello Sam'. When I fail to recognise Henry in his evening gear I do not necessarily confuse him with anyone else. My ability to recognise Henry simply isn't engaged by the right object. We might say that my recognitional ability is simply disengaged or that it fails to translate into the new context. This is not the problem with Ralph and Sam. My ability to recognise Sam is engaged all right – it is simply engaged by the wrong object. We might say that it is misengaged.

When my ability to fire off a Henry-identification is confined by my limited acquaintance with Henry's guises my ability is not *robust* enough. On the other hand when my ability to recognise Sam misfires and tends to get triggered by the wrong object, we can say that my ability is not discriminating enough. Now, a given recognitional mishap can involve both sorts of disabilities at once, as the case of the drunk who mistakes Henry for a bear shows. Each of these two types of recognitional mishap corresponds to a distinct office of recognitional ability. One office of recognitional ability is to identify someone over time, to slot the time-slices of someone or something into the right spatio-temporal worm. The second office of recognitional ability is to discriminate one individual from other individuals. The first office involves tracking someone through time, and the second involves tracking someone through populations. The first office is especially vulnerable to change in the individual over time, while the second is especially vulnerable to population changes. To illustrate the latter sort of change, if you clone Henries all of a sudden, this population shift can affect your recognitional ability. Likewise, if you take Henry's chair, which normally stands in splendid isolation, and put it in amongst a sea of samely chairs, you can wash away Henry's ability to recognise his chair.

Of course, these are unseasoned generalisations, and I intend them to be taken with a grain of salt. It is obvious that the two 'offices' of recognition and the corresponding pathologies of recognition are intimately related. With enough ingenuity and pedantry you might even be able to reduce one pathology to the other. I have only been concerned to bring out these two dimensions of recognitional mischance because they correspond so neatly with two different dimensions in which iconic competence can fail. I can fail to see that S depicts Henry because it depicts Henry in a guise under which I am unable to identify him; here I fail because I don't know what Henry looks like in this guise: I cannot put the appearance and Henry together. I can also fail to see that S depicts O because O has a *Doppelgänger* O★. I know what both O and O★ look like: I just can't tell them apart.

Two further kinds of recognitional mishap may befall iconic interpretation, but these involve not so much an inability with respect to the depicted objects as an inability with respect to the picture itself. We have already seen that two qualitatively similar pictures may nonetheless be different pictures. Henry I's picture resembles Henry II's picture, and they may even be parasitic on the same physical object. Now, it may be that in fact I am able to distinguish Henry I and Henry II. They are both neighbours of mine, each living with his seventh wife. But they don't look as similar as their pictures do. Their pictures have been done by yet a third friend of mine, Anonymous Botch. Call these pictures S and S★. The point is that it is easy to confuse S and S★ and think that S depicts O★ and that S★ depicts O (whereas it's the other way round). Now S depicts O because there are conditions in which just the ability to recognise O would result in the correct interpretation of S as being of O and O does stand in the right relationship (causally speaking) to S. The same story goes for S★ and O★. However, it is easy for people who know O and O★, Henry I and Henry II in our story, to confuse S and S★ even though they have no recognitional disability *qua* Henry I and Henry II. The explanation is simple: Botch isn't a very good artist and he realised he could get away with duplicating his efforts. He forgot to put in certain distinguishing features of Henry I and Henry II, however. He left out the huge mole on Henry I's cheek, and he omitted the wart on Henry II's nose. So the result is that their pictures, S and S★, look rather similar though the two Henries do not look as similar as they are in their pictures. Now this in fact presents no problem for my claim that iconic competence mirrors recognitional ability. Why? Because if Henry I and Henry II were in fact *as depicted* we would be unable to tell them apart. That is, if we imagine a recognitional situation in which Henry I and Henry II both look as they are depicted in Botch's portraits, and in which the visual information is all that I have to go on, I would probably be unable to tell them apart.

There is another kind of recognitional mishap which can befall iconic interpretation. Something which is an icon may look just like something which isn't one at all. Here I may identify the non-iconic symbol as an icon when it is not. My interpretation may fail as a result. I shall discuss this problem in chapter 7.

Now, given what I have said about iconic interpretation, it should be clear that failure to identify different time-slices of S should not in itself constitute an interference with my iconic ability to interpret S. To interpret S I do not have to recall having seen it before. To interpret a word I have to recognise an inscription as realising that word. I have to recognise a word as one I know. But I do not have to be able to recognise icons over time in order to be able to interpret them. I do have to be able to track icons through populations, in order to distinguish non-iconic symbols from iconic ones, and to distinguish iconic symbols from things which are not symbols at all. The population-tracking office of recognition is required. But I do not need to be able to track S over time. If I am able to recognise what S depicts, and I am able to distinguish S as being iconic, I can work out what S depicts. Again I should stress that my belief that S is an icon is probably based on my ability to interpret it naturally, to make sense of it on the basis of a recognitional ability alone.

4 AN ANALYSIS OF PICTORIAL REFERENCE

We started this chapter by noting that some pictures are 'rigidly' of what they depict. A portrait of Churchill as bulldog-faced is accurate just in case *Churchill* is bulldog-faced, just as the sentence 'Churchill is angry' is true just if *Churchill* is angry.

We immediately noted, however, that S can be a depiction and it can be rigidly of O without being a depiction of O. We distinguished:

(1)   S is a depiction and S is of O.
(2)   S is a depiction of O.

Sentence (1) is a necessary but not sufficient condition of (2). A child who draws a stick figure and says it is of Henry has created something which satisfies (1) but does not satisfy (2). It is an icon *qua* the content 'a person' but not *qua* the content 'Henry'. What do we have to add to (1) to get to (2)? It may help to compare (1) and (2) with the following:

(3)   S depicts something which is F.
(4)   S depicts something as F.

Here, of course, (3) is neither necessary nor sufficient for (4). It is not necessary because S could depict Henry as sporting a green carnation even if he never wears one; it is not sufficient because the fact that S depicts a dog with a tail does not entail that S depicts the dog *as* having a tail. In the next chapter I shall define both 'S depicts something as F' and 'S depicts O as F.' In this chapter I have made essential use of the former locution. Obviously an analysis of iconic reference cannot, without begging the question, make use of the latter locution.

What then is the relation of (1) and (2) to (4)? First it should be clear that something can be a *picture* and it can be *of* Henry and it can be of Henry *as* F without its being a *picture of Henry as F*. Someone shows us a picture of a blob running out of a burning building and says 'There's Henry!' This is a picture, and it is of Henry as running out of a burning building, but it is not necessarily a picture of Henry as running out of a burning building (though why it is not is admittedly a delicate matter). It is not 'iconically of' Henry, to use a locution I have employed repeatedly in this chapter. So what do we need to add to

(5a)   S is a depiction and S is of O as F

to get

(6)   S is a depiction of O as F?

I have claimed that what we need is something like

(5b)   S depicts something as F and F is a cluster of properties such that there is someone who believes that if something is F it is O and who on the basis of that belief is able to recognise O.

So I claim that we can derive (6) from *something like* (5a) and (5b). The causal part of the 'iconically of' relation is presupposed by (5a). The fact that S causally originates from O (in that mysteriously right non-deviant way) and that S has a content which is iconically available gets us to (5a). If something satisfies (5a) but not (6), it follows that not all of its content is iconically available; in particular, the fact that the accuracy of S depends upon how it is with O is not iconically recoverable. So we need to add something like (5b). Sentence (5a) tells us (partially at least) what it is for S to be of O. Sentence (5b) tells us what it is for that 'ofness' to be iconically recoverable.

It is apparent that (5b) as it stands is not quite adequate. It is both too permissive and too strict; it needs to be both tightened and relaxed in certain ways. For example, it does not seem to exclude the picture of the blob running out of the burning building from being a picture of Henry. Imagine that Henry is the only person who lives in the building in question; he has no family, no friends and no visitors. P. knows this. So when P. sees a blob emerging from the building he knows it is Henry. P. lives at some distance from Henry's house but his sitting-room window affords an admirable view of Henry's comings and goings. ('P.' is a first initial, not a variable.) P. goes on holiday. One day he glances at the *Daily Mirror* and he sees a picture of a blob emerging from Henry's burning house. He immediately (and correctly) identifies it as Henry. Obviously he has relied on his ability to identify the building, and has inferred that the dot must represent Henry. His interpretation seems to meet (5b). But the photograph is surely not iconically of Henry. Or is it? Incidentally, P. is a business associate of Henry, so he knows perfectly well what Henry looks like. P.'s ability to recognise Henry is both robust and discriminating. Let's call the picture in supposition *Inferno*. If we want to prevent *Inferno* from masquerading as a picture of Henry, what shall we do?

I suggest that we should require that an icon of O should depict something as having properties which are *robustly* recognition-triggering. What do I mean by that? F is a robustly recognition-triggering cluster of properties (with respect to O) just if the following is true: if P believes that something which is F is O this gives P the ability to recognise O in a large variety of contexts. The information about Henry contained in *Inferno* is not a basis for a suitably robust capacity for Henry-recognition. So we may tighten (5b) by adding that

(5c) F is a recognition-triggering cluster such that someone who knows that something which is F is O has (in virtue of that knowledge alone) a reasonably robust and discriminating ability to recognise O.

One can test for the qualities desiderated in (5c) by taking someone of known pictorial competence and asking whether showing them S would impart a robust and discriminating ability to recognise O. It must be frankly admitted that (5c) imports an element of vagueness into the notion of 'iconic reference', since the notion of a 'reasonably robust and discriminating' recognitional capacity is itself a vague one. Obviously some depictions are going to be 'more iconically' of what they depict than others. This seems to me to match the facts.[2] One might say that if S meets (5a) and (5b) but not (5c) it *loosely* iconifies O whereas if it meets (5c) as well as (5a) and (5b) it strictly iconifies O.

---

[2] The 'ofness' of an icon is not a matter of degree, but the iconicity of the 'ofness' relation is.

In fact it may occur to the reader that there is an analogy between the way in which the *Inferno* picture depicts Henry (loosely) and the way in which the child's very abstract drawing of a face which we discussed in the last chapter depicts various facial features (loosely). Just as the dots alone do not even loosely depict eyes, so the blob in the *Inferno* picture does not even loosely depict Henry. The blob-area of the picture non-basically iconifies Henry. This area is essential to the Henry-depicting pretensions of the *Inferno* picture, but by itself it does not depict Henry (constitute a Henry-depiction). There is no area of the *Inferno* picture which both basically constitutes a depiction of Henry and does not constitute basically a depiction of things other than Henry and Henry's parts. So this might provide an alternative account of loose depiction:

(5d) S *loosely* depicts O if it meets (5a) and (5b) and is such that there is *no* spatial part (area) A of S which is such that A basically constitutes a depiction of O and O's parts and A does not constitute basically a depiction of anything other than O and O's parts.

This definition will not quite do, however, and it fails not just because the notion of O's parts is somewhat vague, but because it seems possible that A might basically constitute a depiction of O as seen through a haze. There might be no area which constitutes an O-depiction which does not also constitute a depiction of haze (maybe the picture was taken in Chicago on a particularly sultry day in the summer). So I do not believe we can define loose and strict depiction in terms of basic and non-basic constitution of O-depictions. We can say that an artist is not really able to depict O unless he *can* create an icon which satisfies (5d). What we cannot claim is that S loosely depicts O just if it satisfies (5d).

So for the moment, at least, we are stuck with (5c) as a necessary tightener of our definition of strictly depicting O. However it is evident that (5b) also needs to be made a bit more permissive. For example, we want to grant that S is a picture of Sam and S★ is a picture of Ralph even though Ralph and Sam, as depicted and in real life, are deadringers. Ralph and Sam are both depicted as F. But then it would appear that S depicts Sam as F even though someone who is F is not necessarily recognisable as Sam – because of course he might be Ralph.

I would be tempted to say that if Ralph and Sam are doubles then their pictures are not really their pictures – pictures of them – at all, if it were not that the consequences of saying this would be so bizarre. Suppose Ralph is a thief. We apprehend him thanks to some excellent photographs showing him in the act of robbing a bank. At the trial he produces a learned treatise on depiction and argues that it is logically impossible for these pictures to depict *him*. When asked why, he produces his *Doppelgänger* Sam. If the existence of a *Doppelgänger* means that you cannot be depicted, Ralph can't be depicted, so these pictures can't depict him and his case should be thrown out of court. But it is absurd to claim that the mere existence of a *Doppelgänger* of O entails that O cannot be depicted (even if we imagine a bizarre world in which Ralph and Sam act, look and dress alike). So before the Kray brothers cotton on to this defence we had better abandon the idea that S and S★ are not pictures of Sam and Ralph respectively just because Sam and Ralph are deadringers.

So to handle this case I have introduced a 'counter-factual' test. The Ralph and Sam pictures are deadringers and so are Ralph and Sam. S depicts Sam as F and S★ depicts Ralph as F. The problem with F is that in the real world there are two alternative interpretations of an F-array; either it's Sam or it's Ralph. So we have to imagine a situation in which only one of the alternative interpretations is relevant. So let's imagine Ralph away. Suppose he never existed, suppose he is dead, suppose he was separated at birth from Sam and lives on another continent or another planet. Suppose what you like, but suppose a world in which the Ralph-interpretation of the F-array is simply not a relevant alternative to the Sam-interpretation. Now I claim that anyone able to recognise Sam on the basis of the F-array in this new situation would be able to say that S depicted Sam on the basis of that ability alone (plus pictorial competence, visual ability, sanity, etc. etc.). So S in the real world depicts Sam if this story is true.

To this fairytale someone might object: 'Surely you've weakened the notion of iconic ofness too much. For example, suppose I draw something which is taken to depict a table by those who are able to recognise tables. It is not, *ex hypothesi*, a picture of a particular table, though in fact while drawing it I studied my table. My table was the model for this drawing. But the ability to recognise my table would trigger no shock of recognition in the beholder of my drawing. It is far too abstract. But now, imagine a world in which my table is the only table! Surely this drawing would naturally be taken to refer to this table. So since my drawing, call it S, passes the same counter-factual test which Sam's picture passed, it should get accorded the same honours: it must count as a picture of my table.'

However, this objection involves a crucial misuse of the counter-factual test. In the case of the twins, Ralph and Sam, we allowed a test in which we imagined a world in which just Sam's double or look-alike had been eliminated. If people in that world could interpret S as being of Sam solely on the basis of their ability to recognise Sam, then we should allow that S depicted Sam even though in the actual world people cannot naturally generate an interpretation of S because of Sam's having an identical twin brother. Now it is utterly impermissible to extend this counter-factual test to allow the imaginary elimination of all tables. The counter-factual test allows only the elimination of those tables that look exactly like the table in question. So the results of the test proposed by my objector are simply irrelevant since the test is not the one which I applied in the Ralph and Sam case.

The counter-factual elimination of look-alikes test applies not only to Ralph and Sam but a variety of things in the world which have duplicates (look-alikes): leaves, chairs, knives, forks and so on. If S depicts a knife (if it is as it were a portrait of a knife), then S must pass the relevant counter-factual test in which we imagine away all of the knife's look-alikes (*and no more*). In this world, would S be naturally interpretable as being of this knife? If the answer is 'Yes' and this knife stands in the right relation to S, then S depicts this knife.

Again, I don't expect this test to deliver crystal-clear results. There will be intermediate cases in which the way of the world and the way of the artist are equally to blame for a lapse in pictorial recognition. Recall Botch's portraits of Henry I and Henry II. Henry I and Henry II look rather alike, but they are by and large distinguishable from each other by certain features at once prominent and immutable. Their portraits by Botch are a different story. They are qualitatively indistinguishable. Maybe Henry I, unbeknownst to himself or anyone else, has a picture of his hated enemy Henry II hanging in his drawing-room! Now, each picture passes the counter-factual test. S is of Henry I because anyone would take S to be of Henry I in a world in which we imagine away Henry II. Yet here the fault does not entirely or primarily rest with the world for having produced near look-alikes; it rests rather with Botch for having produced *pictorial* look-alikes. So it may be unclear here that we are entitled to use the counter-factual test. I am inclined to say that we are, since the fact that Henry I and Henry II look so nearly alike is an essential part of the reason why we get their portraits mixed up. But if you want to be strict and demand that if the artist's failure plays any part in the failure to recognise which picture is which then we are not entitled to use the counter-factual test, I shall not object too strongly.

It needs to be stressed that the causal relation of S to Sam is of the utmost importance. If we imagine S in a world in which we had Ralph and no Sam, people would, no doubt, take S to be of Ralph. They would be wrong. S cannot be of Ralph because it isn't connected to him in the right way. If Ralph and Sam are impecunious skinflints they may have commissioned Botch to do one portrait of both of them. They may sit in alternation for it, or perhaps one of them does all the modelling. The result would be a single object which, thanks to its rather baroque origins, constituted two icons, one of Sam and one of Ralph. To be sure the origin of the artifact is not always the only important thing. After Sam dies Ralph might take over Sam's portrait and use it as his own. Again, he has not really turned Sam's picture into a picture of himself (that I have argued is logically impossible). Instead, he has taken an object which had previously just constituted a Sam-depiction and turned it into something which now also constitutes a Ralph-depiction.

It is obvious that S may be causally related to Sam and S may be such that those able to recognise Sam would take S to be a Sam-depiction even though S is not a Sam-depiction. What then is the *right sort* of causal relation? The key is to focus on the fact that an icon of Sam is constituted by many iconic parts; these iconic parts are icons of Sam's features (they are *not* spatial parts). Each iconic part of Sam's portrait must be causally related to the features of Sam which that part depicts. I suppose if the relation of S to Sam might be causally deviant, it is also true that the relation of any iconic part of S to a feature of Sam might also be deviant. Of course, it would be fantastically improbable for the whole set of S's iconic parts to be deviantly caused by the appropriate feature of Sam. I suppose, however, that it is logically and conceptually possible. I suggest that a further constraint needs to be placed on the kind of explanation linking a given feature of Sam to the iconic part which depicts that feature. We might require that the explanation should be *functional*. In other words, an iconic part S* of S depicts a particular feature F of Sam just if its function is to be such that someone able to recognise someone as F would interpret S as depicting, inter alia, someone as F. Let this be our account of what it is for S* to be non-deviantly related to F; then S is non-deviantly related to Sam in virtue of the fact that S's iconic parts are non-deviantly related to Sam's features.[3]

What does it mean to say that doing or being φ is the function of X? It means that the fact that X exists is a causal function of the fact that X does φ. It is X's doing φ that explains X's existence. So what I am claiming is that where S* non-deviantly depicts O as F, this is because it is S*'s function to make S naturally interpretable as representing O as F. Now admittedly, this will appear to beg many questions since the functional explanation of an icon will involve human agents, directly or indirectly. And one is bound to want a further account of the intentionality of the agents' purposes themselves. I conjecture, however, that the notion of functional explanation will also be required for this task, but this time in an evolutionary form which does not presuppose a purposive agent. But since my purpose here is not to give an account of intentionality in general but only of iconic ofness I must beg off from these grander issues.

5 FICTIVE PICTORIAL REFERENCE

How can S depict O when O doesn't exist? The answer is quite simple: it cannot. Yet, a unicorn-picture is quite distinctly a unicorn-picture and not a griffin-picture or a manticore-picture. All these pictures are pictures of nothing. Yet, somehow, they seem to be pictures of different nothings!

You might think the answer is simple. Although there are no unicorns, one would know it if one met one. So one has the ability to recognise unicorns. So since this picture is interpreted as being of a unicorn by those with the unicorn-recognising abilities on the basis of those abilities, it is a picture of a unicorn.

Unfortunately, given that unicorns do not exist and have never existed, there can be no such thing as an ability to recognise unicorns. A unicorn, clearly, is not just anything having certain qualities. It is regarded as a kind of animal, as a natural kind of animal. There are, of course, stereotyped unicornish properties. One cannot have an ability to recognise K-type things unless that recognitional ability has causally originated from contact with K-type things, where K-type things are natural kinds. The reason is clear: many distinct kinds of natural kinds may exemplify unicornish properties. Which of these kinds would be unicorns is just logically unde-

---

[3] This analysis is a modification of the one presented in Christopher Peacocke's *Holistic Explanation*, Oxford, 1978.

cidable unless one of these natural kinds is causally responsible for our unicorn-recognising abilities. So recognitional ability with respect to a natural kind K presupposes that that ability has originated via some causal route leading back to K-type things. An ability to recognise K-type things is distinct from an ability to recognise K*-type things, even if K-type things and K*-type things are phenomenally indistinguishable.[4]

This can be illustrated by Hilary Putnam's famous story about Twin Earth. Twin Earth is qualitatively just like Earth. However, there are certain underlying physical facts about Twin that distinguish it from Earth. One of these is that what Twin English speakers call 'water' is in fact not H_2O, though it looks, tastes and functions just like what we call water. So Twin water* isn't Earth water; and Twin 'water*' isn't semantically or functionally equivalent to 'water'. The ability to recognise water* is simply not the ability to recognise water and vice versa. As long as Twin and Earth are far away, 'water*' is not a relevant alternative to the 'water' interpretation of water, so the recognitional abilities on the respective planets are not impaired. It would be wrong to say that someone who is transported from Twin to Earth can recognise water. He no doubt thinks he can, as so do all his Earthling friends. But in fact he is systematically wrong. Because when he says that Earth water is 'water*' he is of course identifying it, wrongly, with the stuff which he drinks at home. He may discover that although Earthlings can drink the stuff, he can't. So his mistake may cost him dear.

It seems clear, then, that the causal origin of a recognitional ability is of its essence. And, from an evolutionary perspective, this is just what one would expect. The function of the Twin Earthling's ability to recognise water* is precisely to help him to identify something which is essential for his survival. When he is transported to a new environment, the recognitional ability which evolved in the old environment may play him false in the new one: such is the way of natural selection. It tends to make one fit in fitnesses which can so easily become unfit in a new situation. The contextual nature of recognition is of its essence.

Now the long and short of it is that there can be no such thing as an ability to recognise unicorns, given that there are and never have been such things. If something with unicornish properties evolved, it would not be a unicorn. No doubt we would dub it a 'unicorn',

---

[4] Recognitional ability is no more solely dependent upon factors within the head than knowledge or meaning. One cannot have the ability to recognise O if O doesn't exist.

but this would be a new entry in the lexicon. So obviously, unicorn pictures are not unicorn pictures in virtue of the fact that people able to recognise unicorns say that they are unicorn pictures. There are no such people: no one can recognise unicorns.

'Unicorn' as a natural kind term is vacuous; one other possibility is that it is fictive. There is a world of difference between fictive names and vacuous names. Whether a given name is fictive or vacuous depends upon its origin. Some names, such as 'Sherlock Holmes', are fictive rather than vacuous. That is, they are not really part of English at all. They are imaginary extensions of English. A name gets into English only through a rite of dubbing in accordance with a certain convention. If we dub a natural kind which happens not to exist, we have introduced a name into the language which does not refer. Thus, some historians believe that the notion of a centaur originated from the peasant's first glimpse of men on horseback. If we imagine that 'centaur' was introduced to designate the kind of animal monster the peasant supposed himself to be seeing, this term is vacuous rather than fictive. Of course, given that it is no longer used in accord with the naming convention, 'centaur' is really no longer a name in the language. It is instead a fictive or imaginary name, like 'Sherlock Holmes' or 'Frodo Baggins'.

What is clear, however, is that something having the grammatical standard form of a name can function, logically and semantically, like a predicate. Thus we can attach a kind of meaning to 'Sherlock Holmes', but not *qua* name. *Qua* name, 'Sherlock Holmes' does not exist in the language at all. It was not introduced as something which functions as a name. Though grammatically name-like, it is logically and semantically something else. It is a kind of term for a lot of properties. The term doesn't, of course, *designate* someone with these properties, because it doesn't designate anyone at all. Nonetheless, it is a kind of index of certain properties. One could describe a friend who works as a private detective as 'a Sherlock Holmes' and one would know what was meant.

For such quasi-names, there is a text in which they are associated with certain properties. It is imagined that there is someone called 'Sherlock Holmes' and that he has certain properties. In other words, it is imagined that there is a slight extension of English in which 'Sherlock Holmes' is added. The man who, it is imagined, has this name also has certain properties. Thus, certain properties get associated with the name. But no one has even ostensibly been given the name 'Sherlock Holmes'. Even the name is imaginary. Fictive names present no problem for a theory of reference because there are no such names. Of course, typographical equivalents of these imaginary names get into the language and they may be grammatically name-like. But in so far as they have any function at all, they are not names. Of course, some private dick may change his name by deed poll to 'Sherlock Holmes', but then a *new* name enters the language.

To say that 'There is someone called "S.H." in Doyle's stories' is to say

'There is someone called "S.H.". Doyle imagined that.'

All occurrences of 'S.H.' occur within the scope of the 'imagined that' operator. 'Sherlock Holmes is clever' is fictively true just if:

'Someone called "Sherlock Holmes" is clever. Doyle imagined that.'

Statements of this form are obviously susceptible of truth-valuation. Statements of this form fix the properties we associate with the term 'Sherlock Holmes'. In so far as a similar-sounding term is introduced into English, it is obviously not a name (because no one believes it refers; no one believes that Doyle dubbed some real person with that name – obviously the names in a roman-à-clef may not be fictive in as much as they may be just the author's nicknames for real persons. 'London' is obviously meant to have its usual referent in the Doyle stories).

What does Doyle mean when he writes 'Sherlock Holmes lives at 221B Baker Street'? He means 'Someone called "S.H." lives at 221B Baker Street. I imagine that.' There is no more need for Doyle to use 'S.H.' as a name than there is for his readers to use it as a name.

Now it might be asked: 'How can we understand this fictive English?' Most of it isn't fictive. Most of it is standard English. How then do we understand the fictive parts of it, such as the fictive term 'S.H.'? The answer is: obviously we do not understand this term We understand *Doyle*. We understand that he has imagined an extension of English in which there is someone who is called 'S.H.'. If you want to put it in Davidsonian terms, we imagine a version of English in which '"S.H." refers to S.H.'. These are things we imagine. We do not actually add 'S.H.' to English! (It is not in accordance with naming conventions and hence not used as a name.)

In this sense, many terms which were once vacuous names in some language are no longer names in ours. 'Centaur' might be an example of this. Maybe it was once used by Greek speakers as a name. It fails to refer. So wherever it was used as a name, the resulting sentence was strictly meaningless (the *sentence* would have been devoid of *semantic content*). However, 'centaur' is simply no longer used as a name. We no longer believe that once upon a time centaurs were dubbed 'centaurs' and that the name has been handed down to us from this time. We can imagine people who use 'centaur' as a name, we can remember them, we might even watch them – but *we* don't use it that way.

Now what about pictures of – as we say – centaurs and unicorns and other fictive creatures? What makes S a unicorn picture and S* a centaur picture? There are properties stereotypically associated with the fictive name 'unicorn' which we might call unicornish properties. The ability to recognise these properties suffices to give one the ability to interpret this picture as being of something with unicornish properties. But furthermore, there is an element of fiction: one pretends that this is a picture of a unicorn. That is, one pretends that there is a creature such that 'unicorn' applies to that creature and such that this picture depicts that creature. But this is all make-believe. There are no such creatures, there is no such name (any longer) and there can be no such pictures.[5]

Let me round off this section on 'fictive' iconic reference by distinguishing two ways in which iconic reference may be fictive. It may be fictively or make-believedly true that S depicts O either because O does not really exist or because no one, including the person responsible for making S, knows what O looks like. Thus, a picture of Pickwick is make-believedly a picture of Pickwick because although there is no such person, we may well pretend or make-believe that a particular picture is *of* Pickwick. This amounts to pretending that 'Pickwick' refers and the picture S refers and to pretending that they refer to the same thing.

However, it is important to see that S may make-believedly depict O even though O existed and stands in some appropriate causal relation to S. Take a picture (as we say) of Christ. Here is what Ernst Kitzinger and Elizabeth Senior said: 'We all have a very distinct idea of Christ's physical appearance ... [but] when we enquire whether there is any representation or description that dates from the time of Christ and can therefore claim to be authentic we find that there is none, and that even the most venerable of His portraits were produced by later generations' (*Portraits of Christ*, London, 1940). Now, it stares one in the face that such portraits of Christ cannot literally depict him in my sense, since it is likely that

---

[5] I have borrowed the idea of make-believe reference from Kendall Walton's 'Fearing Fictions', *Journal of Philosophy*, 74, 1978, 5–27.

people who could have recognised Christ would not have been able to interpret the symbols that pass for portraits of him on the basis of having a robust and discriminating ability to recognise him. Consequently, although these pictures may be of Christ, they are not iconically of him. But nonetheless, we may make-believe that they are pictures of him, that they are *iconically* of him. In doing so, we pretend that Christ in the pictures of him would have been recognisable to his friends.

Of course, that there should be these two distinctive kinds of fictive pictorial reference is just what one would expect on my view, since I have been careful to distinguish the question of whether S is *of* O tout court from the question of whether S is *iconically* of O. Of course, if S is not of O, *a fortiori* it is not iconically of O; but S may be of O even if it is only make-believe that S is iconically of O.[6]

[6] The problem of depicting unrecognisable historical personages was put to me by Richard Wollheim and Antonia Phillips.

6

Saying it with pictures: what's in an icon?

I ICONIC 'PREDICATION'

A picture not only depicts its subject, but has something to say about it. Indeed, as I have argued in the last chapter, no picture can depict something without having something to say about what it depicts. A picture that doesn't say anything is not a picture.

Yet of course pictures do not literally speak – they are 'mute poetry'. Nor do *pictures* literally ascribe properties to objects; the artist ascribes properties to objects *with* his pictures. In the picture objects are depicted as having certain properties. Obviously there are no names or predicates in pictures, and although pictures admit of decomposition they do not decompose into names, unsaturated expressions, operators of various sorts, etc. How then does iconic 'predication' work? (Of course we observe the usual Fregean distinction between predication and assertion.)

A picture depicts Brando because there is that about the picture which invites those who recognise Brando to see him in the picture. And what is it in the picture that explains their ability to see Brando in it if not the fact that it depicts Brando as having certain properties? Of course, to depict a man who is surly is not necessarily to depict him *as* surly. What is it to depict not only a surly man but to depict him as surly? Perhaps we can say that a picture of Brando iconically represents him as surly just when anyone who is able to recognise Brando and anyone who is able to recognise an individual as surly could generate, on the basis of his ability, the interpretation that the picture is true or accurate only if Brando is surly. So let's say

> S depicts O as F just if anyone who is able to recognise O and anyone who is able to recognise something as F-type would generate the interpretation that S is true or accurate only if O is F.

I take it that the interpretation could be generated under the epistemic restrictions which mark an interpretation as natural in my sense.

We must attend to the 'only if' in this definition. Why not 'just if'? The reason is obvious: the picture, S, as a whole will be true only if each depicted individual is as depicted. Thus if S is a picture which ascribes many properties to many things or many properties to one thing the substitution of 'just if' for 'only if' in the above definition would result in absurdity, for the fact that O is F need not make S as a whole true.

However, we cannot repose our theory of iconic property ascription on this analysis, for as it stands it implies that all pictures depict tautologies, since for any picture, this picture will be accurate or true only if Reagan's real hair colour is either green or not green. Surely we don't want pictures to depict all necessary truths. However, we may note that there will be a proper iconic part of S – an aspect, not a spatial part – that will be true if and only if O is F, but there is no part of the picture that is true if and only if Reagan's hair colour is either green or not green. Our analysis of iconic ascription becomes:

> S depicts O as F just if there is a proper part of S, S★, such that anyone who is able to recognise O and anyone who is able to recognise something as F-type would generate naturally the interpretation that S★ is accurate or true just if O is F.

And of course, S is true only if S★ is true, since S★ is an iconic part of S.

We see once again how important it is for our project that we reject the mereological approach to symbol systems advocated by Nelson Goodman. Obviously, if by 'a part of S' we meant a spatial part, then the above analysis would be inapplicable, since a given spatial area of S will constitute many icons and hence have numerous truth-conditions.

It may be asked on what basis we postulate these separate iconic parts of S. Do we do so just as an ad hoc way of defining iconic predication? As I have already argued, we individuate the iconic parts of pictures functionally. That is, to the extent that you can distinguish the recognitional competences required to understand a given picture or a given spatial area thereof, you can discriminate the semantically important aspects of the picture or spatial part. You may be able to do this even if the iconic aspects fuse and interpenetrate. That is why we have to treat them, ontologically, as aspects or states of the material object rather than as spatial entities. In short, to individuate iconic parts of S as I have recommended one simply employs a perfectly respectable empirical methodology. Although the nominalist may treat us as being in a state of sin, our empiricist credentials are untarnished. But of course, Goodman is not really a naturalist. He doesn't treat symbol systems as part of the world; he regards them as world-makers. I approach them as parts of the world that must be understood by the naturalist, just as he must come to terms with other secondary qualities (colour, linguistic meaning and so on). The naturalist doesn't come equipped with an *a priori* ontology that tells him what the world must be like. No doubt Goodman wouldn't put it this way, but the basis of his approach is that of a dogmatic nominalist who wants to restrict the range of tolerable worlds to those comprised of concrete individuals and parts thereof. The naturalist is by contrast prepared to countenance the objects which turn up in his best theory of the world. Our best understanding of pictures requires us to treat them as made up of iconic parts which simply cannot be treated as decomposing into spatial segments of the picture (though indeed, they are constituted by the material object which constitutes the whole picture and are, in a rather left-handed sense, individuals of a kind).

Let's take a picture of Brando in his leather cap. This picture depicts a leather cap and it depicts it as Brando's. Are these distinct semantically or spatially or both? The answer appears to be that they are distinct both semantically and spatially. You can isolate an area which depicts the hat but doesn't depict it as Brando's. Another area, which includes this one, constitutes a depiction of the hat as Brando's (as the one he is wearing). So these two parts are spatially distinct. What about a picture of Brando's surly expression? Here we can't separate spatially the picture of Brando's face from the picture of it as surly; but we can separate these aspects functionally. Someone might be able to recognise either one of these aspects of the depiction without recognising the other. Someone might be able to recognise the surliness but not Brando, while someone else might be able to recognise Brando but not surliness. Of course, there are subtle questions here. Take Brando's nose. Now, if you isolate the nose, you have got a picture of a nose, but have you got a picture of Brando's nose? I don't mean have you got a picture of that nose as Brando's, but have you got a picture of *that* nose? That obviously depends upon whether the nose is so depicted as to be recognisable as that nose even in Gogolian detachment. We may permit the use of the counter-factual test to eliminate *Doppelgängen* of this nose. Imagine that you've got a connoisseur of noses, a man with a nose for noses, who has devoted his life to the discrimination of nose-types (he has a kind of nosological interest in noses as symptoms of character). Now if he were able to interpret this picture as being of this particular nose on the basis of being able to recognise it, this spatial part would indeed constitute a picture of Brando's particular nose.

The iconic parts of an icon are themselves icons. Sentences may be broken down into significant units which are not sentences. Not so with icons. We may break a sentence down into name and un-saturated expression (a predicate like '— is surly'). Obviously we cannot break down a depiction of Brando as surly into a part which barely denotes Brando (like 'Brando') and an expression which takes objects into truth-values (like '— is surly', which is a function taking objects as arguments and yielding the value true or false depending upon whether the object is surly or not. According to Frege this is an incomplete or unsaturated expression because it denotes no object, whereas 'Brando' denotes Brando and 'Brando is surly' denotes a truth-value). By contrast, we break icons down into other icons. Thus the aspect of the Brando icon which depicts his surliness is the one which is true just if Brando is surly (there is another aspect which depicts a man's surliness, and another which depicts someone's surliness and so on). In other words, this aspect expresses a whole proposition. It is, in Frege's terms, saturated. Consequently, although icons are decomposable into iconic parts, each of which contributes to the content of the whole, you do not reach a level of decomposition which is both iconically significant and which consists of parts of the icon which are not icons. Of course, you do get sub-iconic marks, but these are, as I have argued, more like letters than words in that they have no independent semantic status.

But perhaps we should take care over the assertion that all iconic aspects of icons depict states of affairs. We have already repeatedly faced the fact that a given spatial part of a picture may embody many icons. For example, there is a part of Brando's picture which expresses propositions such as that Brando is surly, a man is surly, someone is surly, or Brando's face looks so-and-so. Furthermore, and this is the crucial point, we cannot distinguish these aspects spatially. We cannot point to an area and associate with it one of these aspects but not the other.

Now, can't we distinguish the aspect of the icon that represents a hair and the aspect which represents it as brown? To be sure, these may not be spatially distinct. But isn't that like separating a name and a predicate? But there cannot be an area which represents iconi-cally the hair and which does not represent it as having certain properties. The aspect which represents the hair iconically is necessarily composed out of or constituted by aspects which represent the hair as having this or that property. To represent iconically someone's hair just is to represent something as having certain properties which are recognisably those of hair. I conclude that all the iconic parts of a depiction are icons having a propositional content of their own.

This may seem to pose a problem: how can an icon be a vehicle of truth if its truth-conditions are so complicated? Some people have, I think, shied away from the idea that icons could have a semantic content precisely because they are so unlike what they take to be the paradigm of semantic content, a sentence. I shall address these worries in chapter 8, where I shall discuss the fact that icons are selectively committal. For example, black-and-white photographs aren't committal about the colour of what they depict. But this discussion will build on the discussion of conventionality and depiction which I undertake in the next two chapters.

Not all icons are definite icons; that is, not all icons purport to refer to individuals. Even an icon which depicts an individual will have iconic aspects which do not purport to be about particular individuals – though these indefinite iconic parts may be spatially coincident with the definite icons. Try to separate spatially the part of a Piero which depicts a man as having a broken nose from the part which depicts Montefeltro as having a broken nose. They are not the same, though we may speak of one including the other, since anything which depicts Montefeltro as having a broken nose must depict a man as having a broken nose. In any case we need an account of indefinite iconic predication. Let's say

> S indefinitely depicts an O as F just if there is a proper iconic part of S, S★, such that anyone who is able to recognise individuals as F-type would be able to generate naturally the interpretation that S★ is true or accurate just if some object is F.

There is an interesting distinction between two kinds of indefinite icon. Imagine an icon of a duck which incorporates just enough information to detect that a duck is at issue, perhaps ascribing some particular properties to make it as a particular kind of duck. This is something which is true just if there is a duck having certain properties. No particular duck has to have these properties for this icon to be accurate. However, one may also imagine a different depiction in which an imaginary duck is represented; it doesn't purport merely to be a general depiction of a kind of duck, but purports to be a depiction of a particular duck. It ascribes various properties to the duck and turns it into a regular individual. We may even follow *it* from picture to picture – even though there is no *it* which we are following. It isn't enough to say that each of these pictures is true just if there is some duck having properties of a particular kind. The duck in each of these pictures must be the *same* duck. The duck who has a meal in S is the same as the one who has a swim in S★. Here we meet the problem of 'intentional identity' in roughly the form in which Peter Geach introduced it.

I want to suggest that his is not a semantic problem but, if you will, an aesthetic one. We pretend or make-believe that S and S★ refer to a particular duck and that they refer to the same duck, though in reality neither of these pictures is about a particular duck and so in reality they cannot be about the same duck. But for the purposes of make-believe we pretend that they are about the same duck. Likewise, when we weave a fantasy around fictional characters, we simply pretend that we are thinking about given individuals and that we can refer to them with their fictive names. Our thoughts 'about' Othello are not really about Othello, so they are not really about the same thing. But we pretend that they are: this is just part of the convention of fiction and make-believe. I believe this dissolves Geach's problem of intentional identity. Gog and Magog each believe that Grimalkin has soured their cow's milk. But Grimalkin doesn't exist. When we present the beliefs of Gog and Magog phenomenologically we pretend to go along with their assumption that there is such a witch and that she has soured the local milk. Of course, semantically we must say that given the failure of reference, Gog and Magog's beliefs aren't co-referential. But when we imaginatively identify with them we pretend or make-believe that there is co-reference where there is no reference at all.

2 WHAT CAN BE SAID PICTORIALLY?

There are numerous questions we may raise about the semantics of depiction. Can pictures express 'universally quantified' propositions? I don't see why not. Cézanne can depict the fact that all the oranges on the table are spherical. Perhaps one cannot depict the fact that all oranges in the world are spheroid, so there may be universally quantified propositions expressible in sentences but not in pictures.

It appears that depiction abhors a vacuum. One cannot depict a negative state of affairs directly or 'barely', though one can depict a state of affairs which excludes others and so indirectly depict the negation of other states of affairs. One cannot barely depict the fact that Reagan's hair isn't green – one can only depict it as having some colour which excludes the possibility of its being green. Can one depict a negative existential? Obviously, one cannot depict the fact that there are no thinking oranges, but one could depict the fact that no oranges on the table are non-spheroid. But one only depicts this by depicting the fact that all the oranges on the table are spheroid. By and large one cannot depict a disjunction without depicting one of its disjuncts. And if we are to let semantic mania carry us away and allow the possibility of depicted tautologies, let us at least mention that they cannot be directly depicted; the only way to depict a tautology is to depict one of the infinity of states of affairs from which it follows.

But of course, the question which must be considered before all others is whether depicting p entails depicting all that follows from p. Intuitively, this seems preposterous. Am I committed to it? It would appear that we sponsor this absurdity as long as we embrace the conceit that to understand a picture is to know in what situation it would be true. For if depicting O as F means depicting the conditions in which 'O is F' is true, doesn't that entail depicting all tautologies? And if you depict O as F, don't you depict it as F or G? To avoid the problem that all true pictures have the same content (since 'p just if q' is true just when p and q have the same truth-value) we have to go model theoretic and say that the content of the picture is that state of affairs which *must* obtain for it to be true. Thus, if a picture could be accurate in a world where q is false, the picture doesn't depict q. This should allow us to individuate the content of distinct pictures quite easily. However, it still leaves us with the problem that a picture depicts all necessary truths. But this is absurd.

I believe we can solve this problem by saying that a picture only depicts the recognitionally relevant features in a situation. Let us say that F is a recognitionally relevant feature just if there is some object O and some situation or condition C and some person P such that P's knowing that O is F would help him to identify or recognise O in C.

Obviously, O's being such that p or not-p could never be relevant to recognising O. O's spatial position could be recognitionally relevant and so could various features of O's shape and colour. What about existence and self-identity? Can S depict O as existing? It is true that P could not recognise O unless O existed (as we have seen, there could be no such thing as an ability to recognise O unless O exists). However, O's existing and O's being self-identical (which is obviously a condition of being able to identify O) do not distinguish O from other objects. Let's say that F can be recognitionally relevant only if O's having F could distinguish O from some other object in some possible situation. Existence and self-identity are not recognitionally relevant; I suppose that being in space isn't either (except in a left-handed way), though being in a certain spatial position relative to other objects is recognitionally relevant. Of course, the picture's undepicted content contains the fact that O exists as a non-trivial part. (The non-trivial part of the undepicted content of a picture is the contingent part. O might not have existed, so the fact that O exists is a non-trivial part of the non-pictorial content of a depiction of O.)

If F is a necessary property of O does it follow that it is recognitionally irrelevant? Obviously not. Churchill's portrait depicts him as a human being and this is no contingent fact about him but a necessary one. It is obviously recognitionally relevant. There are situations in which knowing that Churchill was a man could aid recognition. Although every object has the property of being such that Churchill is a man not every object has the property of being a man. The latter and not the former is recognitionally relevant. There can be no depicting O as being such that Churchill is a human, but obviously one can depict Churchill as a man.

It is self-evident that 'X's being such that p or not-p' is hardly equivalent to 'p or not-p' since the latter is true in all worlds, the former only in those worlds where X exists. But obviously both facts are recognitionally irrelevant; the only fact which the former adds to the latter is the recognitionally irrelevant fact that X exists.

So 'Churchill is a man' is recognitionally relevant. It is a necessary truth. It is both recognitionally relevant and necessary: so why is it not part of the depicted content of every picture? The reason: Churchill is not part of the content of a picture unless recognising Churchill is the basis for generating an interpretation of that picture or an iconic part thereof. Knowing that Churchill is a man could be recognitionally relevant to the task of recognising any given person P. Who is P? P is the woman standing next to Churchill. Who is Churchill? That man. But knowing that Churchill is a man could then also affect the ability to interpret a picture of P. Just after being told that P is the person next to Churchill, that man, I turn to look at S and say 'Ah, a depiction of the woman next to Churchill'. Why then is Churchill not part of the content of this picture? Recognising him has, albeit indirectly, played a crucial role in interpreting this picture. The answer is surely obvious: first, recognising Churchill is not essential to being able to interpret S and second, someone able to recognise Churchill but not P would not be able to generate naturally an interpretation of S (given that S depicts P). Moreover, of course, Churchill does not stand in the right sort of causal relation to S (he may have painted it, but he doesn't stand in the sort of causal relation to S which I defined at the end of the last chapter, a relation R in virtue of which O's bearing R to S guarantees that S is of O and not anything else).

So, O* is not part of the content of a depiction S unless there is an iconic part of S such that the ability to recognise O* alone would, given the other standing conditions we have specified, give someone the ability to interpret that iconic part of S. Facts of the form 'O* is F' are not a part of S unless S refers, in part at least, to O*. So that's why the fact that 'Churchill is a man' is not part of the depicted content of every picture. The same argument applies, as far as I can see, to any necessary truth which could be potentially recognitionally relevant, since it must involve an individual (or a natural kind) in the referential position of '— is F'.

What emerges from this is that we have two distinct reasons for excluding necessary truths from the pictorial content of a given picture and two distinct kinds of necessary truth to exclude. There are some necessary truths – logical, mathematical, metaphysical, or conceptual – which are never recognitionally relevant. They are thus part of the pictorial content of no picture. There are other necessary truths which are sometimes depicted. They may be recognitionally relevant. However, these truths always involve individuals or natural kinds. We have already dealt with what makes S depict an individual O in the last chapter; and we have dealt with what makes S depict O as F (where F may be a natural kind) in the first section of this chapter. So we need add nothing to our account of iconic reference and predication to explain when a given necessary truth of the form 'O is F' forms a part of the iconic content of a given picture S: it forms part of that picture only when S depicts O as F according to the criteria already laid down. Of course, what makes F depictable, in general terms, is the fact that it is recognitionally relevant.

Though necessary truths are sometimes depictable, they are never depictable as necessary. Why not? The necessity of a property is not recognitionally relevant. It may be recognitionally relevant that O is F, but that O is necessarily F adds no recognitionally useful content. So truths cannot be depicted as necessary. Likewise, if S includes $S^\star$ as an iconic part, and we call p the content of S and q the content of $S^\star$, p entails q. But $S^\star$ cannot depict the fact that p entails q; this is a logically necessary truth and hence recognitionally irrelevant and hence undepictable.

Where e is merely evidence for O, depicting e is not depicting O. Depicting my cat's footprint is not depicting my cat. Sometimes, the evidence for something bears an internal or *a priori* relation to that thing; the reason is that sometimes knowing that e is evidence for O is part of what it is to have the concept of O. Evidence of this sort is called criterial and is usually distinguished from symptomatic or *a posteriori* evidence. Although e is *a priori* ground for positing an O-type thing (event, state, process) it is still defeasible. For example, certain behavioural patterns are criterial for anger; call these C. It is possible for someone to display C and not be angry. But there is an *a priori* weighting in favour of P's being angry if P displays C; the burden of proof lies with anyone who wants to challenge the anger-hypothesis given C. Recognising anger is a matter of recognising the states which are criterial for it; likewise, depicting anger (or any other state of mind) is a matter of depicting the states which are criterial for that state of mind. S depicts O as angry just if S depicts O as C.

What about disjunctions and negations? Of course these can be recognitionally relevant, so they can be part of the depicted content of the picture. Two facts are worth noting. Negations and disjunctions are never directly depicted. A negative state of affairs (O's not being F) can be depicted only by depicting a state of affairs which precludes it. I can be portrayed as not angry by being depicted as complacent. In this case I am only indirectly depicted as not angry. Likewise a disjunction is only depictable by something which depicts one of its disjuncts. Let us therefore divide the depicted content of S into the directly and the indirectly depicted content. A content q is indirectly depicted by S just when S depicts p, p entails q and one would not suppose q to be part of the content of S unless one had supposed p to be. That is, S's depicting p is the only ground for saying that S depicts q and the fact that it depicts p entails that it depicts q, but p and q are not logically equivalent.

The fact that S (as it stands) depicts Brando in a leather cap entails that it depicts him as having a hat or having an alligator. But this latter fact is only indirectly depicted because this picture (as it stands) depicts it only because it depicts Brando as having a hat. There is an iconic part of S of which it is necessarily true that it depicts Brando as having a hat; and it is true of S that it is because of

S's having that part (S*) that it depicts Brando as having a hat or an alligator. Contrast this with the relation between the fact that a picture depicts Brando and the fact that it depicts a man. It is true that the fact that it is of Brando entails that it depicts a man. Nonetheless, one could tell that it was a picture of a man without knowing that it was a picture of Brando, so it also directly depicts a man. But one could not have told that S depicted the disjunction in question without knowing that it depicted Brando as having a hat.

The gist of my suggestion is that we first divide the contents (truth-conditions) of a picture into the depicted and the undepicted contents on the basis of the tests proposed: recognitional relevance, plus our account of iconic reference and iconic predication. Then we make a further division of the depicted content into the directly depicted and the indirectly depicted. Let us call the directly depicted content of a picture what it strictly depicts. We often speak as though the picture depicted only what it strictly depicts.

One upshot of this chapter is that what can be depicted, strictly or loosely, corresponds roughly to what the Tractarian Wittgenstein thought could be said. The undepictable contents of pictures correspond roughly to that which can only be shown. He may have been wrong about what we can say with language, but he seems to have been close to the mark regarding what we can say with pictures. *Given* his picture theory of language and given the nature of depiction, his views about the sayable would follow.

7

Convention and content

It is possible that S is an icon of O, S* is a symbol perceptually indiscriminable from S and that S is not an icon of O or indeed of anything else. I might stumble upon a strange symbol that looks to me
for all the world like the portrait of a pear but which turns out to be,
upon anthropological investigation, an abstract symbol of the local
native godhead. What distinguishes this symbol from an icon of a
pear? Obviously not just natural generativity, for in both cases one
might naturally generate the interpretation 'It's a pear.' Of course in
one case, the iconic case, this naturally generated interpretation is
the correct one while in the other, the totemic case, it is not. So what
makes the naturally generated interpretation the correct one when it
is the correct one?

As it happens, this problem is formally identical with the problem of the colour-reversed icon. A colour-reversed icon is one in
which some or all of the colours have exchanged places with other
colours so that, for example, red pigment on the canvas would represent an object as green while green pigment on the canvas would
represent it as red. Wollheim posed the crucial question: 'What
makes a colour-reversed icon less natural than the normal icon?' He
rightly points out that many accounts of depiction cannot answer it.
Goodman too notices this possibility in *Languages of Art*:[1] 'colors
may stand for their complementaries or for sizes, perspective may
be reversed or otherwise transformed, and so on.' But he implies
that the difference between a colour-reversed symbol and a colour-
normal one is merely a matter of entrenchment; just as we project
'green' and not 'grue' out of habit and so find 'green' natural and
'grue' unnatural, so it is because we are in the habit of dealing with
colour-normal icons (following the green-for-green rule) rather
than colour-reversed (green-for-red) icons that we find the former
natural and the latter unnatural. Just as the grue-user would find our
colour vocabulary bizarre and unnatural, so the colour invert would

[1] Goodman 1968, p. 231.

find the colour-normal system unnatural. The upshot, for Goodman, is clear: 'The often stressed distinction between iconic and other signs becomes transient and trivial; thus does heresy breed iconoclasm.'[2] Pictures are no less conventional than words. Wollheim, correctly, believes that there must be more to the distinction between colour-normal and colour-inverted icons than the entrenchment of the former and the novelty of the latter. I believe he is right. I shall discuss his own account of this distinction in chapter 10 on 'seeing-as'. In this chapter, meanwhile, I wish to indicate how the theory of natural generativity can explain why the colour-reversed icon is not iconic in respect of its colour-representing features.

Of course, we have moved a long way from our original position in chapter 2 where the colour-reversal problem was first broached. We now have to hand a theory of iconicity that appears to do just the sort of work, including the sorting of the iconic from the non-iconic, that we want it to do. Yet we have not yet discussed the colour-reversal problem. Perhaps it will be easy to conjure away with our brand new theory. Yet, as we shall see, there is a residue of the problem that sticks and will not go away and in solving the problem we shall see that convention must be accorded a central role in the theory of iconicity. This residual problem is formally identical with the problem we kicked off with, of what distinguishes S and S* when they are perceptually identical, S being an icon and S* not being an icon.

Suppose someone paints a picture of a tree, a green-leaved tree, but uses red pigment to designate greenness. This icon is, evidently, not iconic with respect to tree colour, for one is not able to tell that it represents the tree as green-leaved just on the basis of being able to recognise trees and being able to recognise green things. In addition to such recognitional abilities, one needs to know the artist's special code: red pigment stands for green. So it is clear that the colour-reversed icon is not iconic with respect to those colours that have been reversed. So far, so good. Colour-reversed icons do not pass the natural generativity test and Wollheim's intuition has been essentially vindicated: even if the colour-reversed icon were entrenched and the colour-normal icon were a novelty, the normal icon would be iconic in respect of colour whereas the inverted icon would be non-iconic in respect of colour. The theory of natural generativity vindicates our intuition that one system is more natural than the other.

2 *Ibid.*

127

However, consider that a colour-reversed icon may be the *Doppelgänger* of an icon that is normal in point of colour. This time the problem is not that the depicted objects are perceptually indiscriminable, for they are precisely discriminable in respect of their colour, but that the icons which depict them are perceptually indiscriminable but semantically distinct. An icon of a tree with red leaves, one which depicts the tree as having red leaves, may be perceptually identical with a colour-reversed icon which represents a tree as having green leaves by using the inverted convention that red pigment means 'green'. So what is the difference? What makes the naturally generated interpretation of the normal icon correct whereas the same naturally generated interpretation of the deviant icon would be wrong? The former interpretation is true and the latter would be false, true enough! But in virtue of what? This goes to the heart of the problem, for the question is of what gives an icon the content or sense that it has. Let it not be supposed that these iconic *Doppelgängen* threaten the core of the theory of natural generativity. They do not. For we are still able to distinguish the iconic depiction of tree colour from the non-iconic representation of it: in the former case, the naturally generated interpretation is correct, while in the latter case it is not. However, as with our original *doppelgänger* problem, there is an indirect threat to the theory; we have to show that the account of how an icon gets its sense is compatible with our account of how that sense is grasped.

We have already given an account of what makes the non-naturally generated interpretation the correct one in the colour-reversed case and in the native totem case. In each case what one needs to know is a convention. Thus, an artist will succeed in communicating to me that the tree is green-leaved with his use of red pigment if it is common knowledge that red pigment means 'green'. That is, he intends red pigment to mean green, he thinks I know this, I do know this and I know that he knows that I know and so on. I give 'red pigment means "green"' a truth-theoretic gloss. The red pigment on his canvas represents O as green just because this aspect of the canvas will be true just if O is green. Of course, all that matters for communicative success is that there is an established custom regarding his works which is common knowledge between himself and his audience.

What makes the naturally generated interpretation of an icon the correct one? It might seem as if our account of iconicity precludes an account of the content of an icon that is symmetric with the conventionalist account of the content of a non-iconic symbol.

If the content of an icon is convention-dependent, like the content of the colour-reversed icon, then what is the difference between them?

It might be suggested that icons can get their content in some natural, convention-independent way. Perhaps the difference between the colour-reversed icon and the colour-normal icon is just that the colour-reversed icon gets its content conventionally whereas the colour-normal icon gets its content 'naturally', without the help of any convention. This is, of course, unilluminating because it does not tell us anything about the natural process whereby an icon acquires content. Is the 'natural' process merely a matter of the object's causing the icon? This obviously isn't enough. Suppose a given mark is the result of an impress of a scarab in the sand; suppose also that it looks quite like something which is an icon of a scarab, a sand painting of a scarab. Someone who sees the mark left by the scarab might take it to depict a scarab on the basis of an ability to recognise scarabs. Obviously, this doesn't entail that it is a depiction of a scarab. So even though this mark 'specifically reflects' a scarab, each feature of the mark having been brought about by a feature of the scarab, and even though this object might be taken to be a sand painting which depicts a scarab, this mark is not an icon or depiction of a scarab. Intuitively, the reason it is not a picture of a scarab is that it is not functioning as a depiction. But the question before us is: if S functions as a depiction does that entail that S's contents are convention-dependent in some way? In other words, if S is such that its being naturally interpretable as being of O functionally explains the features of S in virtue of which it is so interpretable, does this involve a convention?

Let us now spread out before the mind's eye a range of cases which one might suppose to be problematic. 'Problem' cases are those in which X looks as though it might be an icon but isn't.

First, there are naturally formed objects. These are of two kinds, those which causally depend upon the objects which they might mistakenly be thought to represent and those which do not. A rock formation may, quite by accident, look as though it were a sculpted face. Here X (the rock formation) does not causally depend upon the human face. X might have existed had no human face existed. This suffices to rule out X as an icon of a face. In our example of the scarab's imprint in the sand there is a causal dependency between X and the object it might be thought to represent. But still X is no icon. Causal dependency, even of the most intimate kind, does not make an X an icon of O even if X would be naturally taken to represent O by some of those able to recognise O. Let us suppose that the rock face and the scarab imprint fail to be icons because they are not artifacts. Icons have to be artifacts. But why? What kind of artifact?

If X is an artifact which might naturally be taken to represent O, it does not follow that X depicts O. Someone might make something which looks vaguely pear-like with the intention of deceiving someone into thinking it is a pear. He fails, and instead of being taken for a pear X is taken to be a Claes Oldenburg sculptural representation of a pear. The object which is made with the intention that it will deceive people into thinking it is O when it is not O is not an icon of O. Being a pear decoy is just not the same sort of thing as being a representation of a pear. The deceptive function and the representational function are quite distinct. Indeed, they vary inversely; the nearer X comes to being a successful pear decoy, the less likely it becomes that we would naturally generate the interpretation that X represents or depicts a pear. From this it does not follow that illusion has no role at all to play in understanding iconic representation, as we shall see in chapter 9. The crucial point here is that the function of the artifact seems paramount; if X is such that those able to recognise O would take it that X represents O, it does not follow that X represents O – even if X causally depends upon O – unless its function is to be taken to represent O. But since pictures unlike pears don't grow on trees, the purpose of an icon is a function of a human agent's purpose.

It might be thought that the problem with the pear decoy is that it was not meant to *symbolise* a pear. So perhaps we should say that if X causally depends upon O, is naturally interpretable as being of O and is intended to be a symbol of O, X depicts O. Yet this will not do. Let's suppose that we have a tribe called, totemistically, the Scarabs (they speak a version of Scarabic). They idolise the scarab. Unfortunately, they have no idea what one looks like – *no idea whatsoever*. They wouldn't be able to recognise one if it crept into bed with them. They use a certain device, a sand-painting, as a symbol of the scarab which they idolise. This symbol is made by taking an object and impressing it into the sand. They happen to like the resulting design, so they have adopted it as the insignia of the scarab – even though they do not know what one looks like. Now, unknown to them, the object which they use to make this mark in the sand *is* a scarab. I am quite sure that you will agree with me that in this example the resulting symbol is not an icon of a scarab even though there is a tribe across the river from the Scarab tribe who do recognise scarabs and who would naturally take the Scarabic sand-painting to be a representation of a scarab. So the upshot is that (a) S causally depends upon, indeed specifically reflects, O; (b) S is intended to symbolise O; (c) S is such that anyone able to recognise O would take S to represent O. Yet S is not an icon of O! And the reason seems to be that the Scarabs can't be taking S to function as an icon because they lack the relevant recognitional ability.

The final type of problem case we have already alluded to in our discussion of colour-reversal. S* might be iconic *qua* some content but non-iconic with respect to some other content and yet resemble S, which is iconic with respect to all its content.

Now in each of these cases, the difficulty is that the function of the object, if it has a function, is not of the right kind; the natural formations are ruled out because they have no functional explanation whatsoever; the pear decoy is ruled out because it isn't intended to function as a symbol. S can be a symbol, can function as a symbol, only if S is known to function as a symbol – it is part of S's functioning as a symbol of O that it is known to be a symbol of O. A pear decoy can serve its function only by hiding the fact that it is serving that function. The scarab symbol is indeed serving a symbolic function. The trouble is that it is not functioning as an icon. It is not functioning as an icon because its function is not to be naturally interpretable as being of a scarab. So, clearly for S to be an icon it must be intended to be such that someone able to recognise what the artificer wants to represent would be able to tell that S represents O. But someone can tell this only if he knows or guesses the function of S. So clearly, the artificer must want the function of S to be manifest and the beholder must be aware of its function. However, making the function of the icon manifest is clearly not enough. It must actually fulfil the function. The function of a word is fulfilled just when its intended function is understood. Not so, obviously, with an icon. Its function is to be such that one can naturally generate an interpretation of it; it does not fulfil its function by making its function manifest – it fulfils its function only by *making its function manifest by performing its function*.

The upshot of all of this appears to be that common knowledge of the function of S is a necessary (though not sufficient) condition of S's being an icon. So we are back to the question 'What is the form of the relevant common knowledge? What kind of convention is involved in depiction?'

131

Because a given S which is an icon (is indeed necessarily an icon if 'S' refers to the icon and not to its substrate) might be a deadringer for an X which is not an icon, interpreting S presents a problem to which there is more than one solution. It is possible to take S for an icon, but it is possible to take it in other ways. Since there are diverse ways of taking it, which way one ought to take it must be determined by the intention of the artist. But must we know the intentions of the artist in each separate case before we can interpret an icon? No indeed: as I have stressed, we can generate the interpretation of S – assign it truth-conditions – based on our ability to recognise what S depicts. Conventions do not explain the interpretations we generate; the iconic convention merely determines whether the naturally generated interpretation is the right one. So the convention governing iconic systems is simplicity itself:

C: If S admits a naturally generated interpretation p,
     S means that p.

In other words, if S is an icon, Convention C governs S; the naturally generated interpretation is the correct one.

We immediately see that there is an important difference between the role of Convention C in iconic interpretation and the role of conventions in linguistic systems. In the case of a language, or in the case of the dot systems discussed in chapter 2, there is a separate convention governing each meaningful constituent of the language and one's mastery of the language requires remembering a host of distinct conventions. These separate conventions, given the rules of syntax, yield an interpretation of the sentences (truth-bearing constituents) of the system.

The colour-reversed system is parasitic on an iconic system; it is just a bit of conventional vocabulary added to an otherwise iconic system. The point remains that to interpret a colour-reversed icon one must remember, as it were, an item of vocabulary – that red pigments mean 'green' and so on. Convention C, by contrast, does not assign any particular meanings to anything; it doesn't operate on particular iconic signs to tell us that they mean this or that. Knowing that Convention C governed an icon would not, in itself, tell you what it meant; knowing the convention governing the meaning of a word *is* knowing what the word means.

If we review our list of problem cases we find that none of them are icons despite their perceptual similarity to icons. In the case of natural objects, the rock face and the imprint left by a scarab, there is no communicative intention whatsoever, and *a fortiori* Convention C does not apply. In the case of the pear decoy again there is no communicative intent, so Convention C does not apply. In the case of the rather elaborate story about the Scarabs and their symbol, there is a sort of communicative intent involved in their god symbol, but again they do not intend the symbol to be read under the auspices of Convention C. Finally, in the case of the colour-reversed icon Convention C applies only differentially; in particular, while it applies with respect to some of the content of the icon it does not apply with respect to the colour of the represented objects. Understanding the colour-reversed icon involves negativing a certain naturally generated interpretation in favour of one dictated by a certain convention, such as that red paint shall stand for green in the depicted object.

I must stress once again that the colour-reversal conventions are parasites. They operate in the context of a symbol which is by and large such that Convention C applies. If this were not so, the full extent of the unnaturalness involved in them would become immediately apparent. But the colour-reversal convention says: the interpretation of S as depicting O as red which you would naturally generate is wrong; wherever you would naturally generate the red interpretation, substitute the green interpretation. If the colour-reversed icons did not to this extent rely on the naturally generated interpretation, if only to negate it, the conventions for interpreting them would be unmanageably complex. Thus, Goodman is quite wrong to suppose that a reversed system is just as 'natural' as the normal one once you have got the hang of it. It demonstrably involves more labour, in that one has to decode it; moreover, in so far as the example works at all, the colour-reversal conventions are parasitic on the normal ones. The theory of natural generativity fully vindicates Wollheim's intuition that the colour-normal system is natural whereas the colour-reversed system is not. The colour-reversed system by definition involves simply reversing the naturally generated interpretations and substituting others.

Moreover, it should be noted that the rule for 'predication' in the colour-reversed system would have to be directly parasitic on the iconic rule for predication. For the question naturally arises, for the colour-reversed symbol, to what does it ascribe colour? The answer must be something like this: if S is such that you would naturally take it as, say, depicting a tree as green-leaved on the basis of your ability to recognise trees, leaves and the colour green, take it instead to predicate *red* of the tree leaves. So the fact that S, by the use of the colour green, represents the tree as having red leaves is essentially parasitic on the fact that the colour-reversed system leaves the iconic rule of predication (discussed in the previous chapter) intact. Even understanding how the colour-reversed system could operate requires us to see that it depends on the naturally generated interpretations of the reversed symbol.

An object can signal the fact that it is to be understood under the auspices of Convention C in a variety of ways. By and large there will be no difficulty in spotting objects made under the sign of Convention C. Of course, there will be a degree of cultural relativity here, in that some ways of embodying icons may seem quite strange; for example, a Western European might not immediately cotton on to the possibility of painting in sand, while it appears that many native Africans have great difficulty with the idea of two-dimensional icons of three-dimensional reality (though the same natives have no difficulty with sculptural representation).

Obviously we cannot require that visual inspection of the object will yield some mark that guarantees or makes certain that S adheres to Convention C; we will find plenty of criterial indicators – the most important indicator of all being that we are able to make sense of the symbol, explain it, on the hypothesis that its function is to be understood as representing what we have naturally interpreted it to represent. Our being able to 'make sense' of S by generating naturally an interpretation of it is prima facie reason to suppose (a) that Convention C applies to S and hence that (b) our interpretation is correct.

Special circumstances may, of course, negative the presumption in favour of Convention C; but let's say that being able to generate naturally an interpretation of S and on that basis to make sense of or to explain S constitutes an *a priori* (though defeasible) ground for taking Convention C to be in force. There will then have to be special reasons for negativing the naturally generated interpretation. For example, one would not give the colour-reversed reading of an icon unless *explicitly* told that the icon was colour-reversed. I shall discuss further reasons for selectively applying Convention C in the next chapter on convention, commitment and realism.

So the sequence which I posit – as an ideal type – is something like this. I confront S. I am able to generate naturally an interpretation *I* of S. I conjecture, on this basis, that S's function is to be naturally interpretatable. That is, that Convention C applies. So, I conclude that *I* is the correct interpretation unless there are grounds, either internal to S or external to S, for supposing otherwise.

To say that S depicts O in virtue (partly) of the fact that S is made or used in accord with Convention C does not imply that S represents O only if someone intends S to represent O. This is a merit in the criterion, since it is obvious that S can be an icon of O *even if no one intended it to be*. A painter may canvas a tree he takes to be an elm. What he has really depicted is a beech. He has made his painting in accord with Convention C and anyone who can recognise beeches and tell elms and beeches apart will say that it is a picture of a beech, and they are right: it is a picture of a beech. Of course, in this case it is important that the painter intended to paint *that* tree (a tree which is in fact a beech).

With photographs we may have an even more radical divorce between intended content and actual content. A photograph can have content of which no one is aware. I am told that in certain observatories hundreds of pictures of the night sky are taken every minute and – of course – the bulk of these have never been seen by human eyes. They are taken automatically. But even in normal circumstances, a photographer will discover content in his photograph that he did not intend or expect to be there (the same goes for a painter). Yet the mechanism which produces these photographs is designed with the intention that it should produce depictions which are interpretable by those able to recognise the depicted objects. Thus, even when a camera clicks away automatically the pictures it produces are manufactured in accord with Convention C, albeit indirectly.

This means that S can depict O (where S is a photograph) even if no person has ever come into causal contact with O. It is impossible to conceive of a word which refers to O even though no person has come into contact with O. It is easy for us to explain the asymmetry here using the theory of natural generativity. Words latch on to things only via people who come into contact with those things, either directly or indirectly. Then what the word refers to is a function of what the originator of the word, the godfather of the object in question, intended it to refer to. This is very imprecise, but it will do for our purposes. The originator of the word intended it to refer to something and he picked it out with a demonstrative. However, S can depict O even though no one has come into any kind of contact with O. Given that there is a mechanism M which can produce symbols of things on contact with those things, and given that M was designed with the intention that if S is a symbol produced by M, Convention C applies to S, and given that a particular symbol S has been produced by contact with O, and given that if someone were able to recognise O he would naturally generate an O-interpretation of S, then – given this story – S depicts O. Obviously O needs somehow to impinge upon M for this to be possible, but M need not be a person. It might be a camera.

Is Convention C enough? Do we not have to add further constraints to it? Obviously the fact that someone able to recognise Sam would naturally take Ralph's picture to be a picture of Sam doesn't entail that it is a picture of Sam. It is a picture of Ralph. Ralph is the person who stands in the right causal relation to S. Furthermore, if the artist knew of Ralph's *Doppelgänger*, he could hardly have made S under the auspices of Convention C! For he would expect people who recognise Sam to give the Sam interpretation to S – and he would claim that they were wrong. So, he has depicted Ralph but he has not depicted him under the auspices of Convention C.

I believe that this points to an important fact. There are in fact two levels to the question 'How does S get its iconic content?' At one level, the answer is: 'It is in virtue of facts about the artist's intention and the causation of S that S gets its content. It is because S is intended to be of O that S is of O.' However, the question is: 'What makes S *iconically* of O?' And here the answer is: 'The artist intends that the fact that S is of O should be recoverable by those able to recognise O.' So once again, it is important to distinguish the question 'Does S refer to O?' from the question 'Does S iconically refer to O?' My claim is that facts about S's causation and the intentions of S's maker fix the answer to the first question; the answer to the second question is that S iconically refers to O if the artist intends that those able to recognise O shall, on that basis, be able to recover from S the fact that S is of or about O.

This still leaves us with the question about the *Doppelgänger*. Because of Ralph's *Doppelgänger*, the painter of Ralph's portrait can't have intended that any naturally generated interpretation should be correct. But that's not the point. What the artist intends when S depicts O is that *those able to recognise O* should be able to interpret S.

The problem with the *Doppelgänger* brothers is that one *can't* recognise them. So obviously the artist's intention has to be put in counter-factual form: he intends that if someone were able to recognise the object of his depiction, he would then be able to generate naturally the correct interpretation.

So what fixes the correctness of the interpretation is indeed the artist's intention (or in the case of a photograph the photograph's causation). However, what fixes the given content as *iconic* is the fact that the artist has followed Convention C: given that S is of O, the artist intends that those able to recognise O should be able to interpret S as being of O.

This becomes crystal clear if we look at the case of the Scarabs once again. They represent a scarab by creating something which could be naturally interpreted to be of a scarab. They do indeed intend their symbols to be of scarabs; but they do not intend the scarab interpretation to be naturally generated. So their symbols are not icons. The reference of their symbols – or rather, the representational 'ofness' of their symbols – is fixed by their intentions. It is the fact that they do not intend the reference of the symbol to be iconically recoverable that explains why their symbols are not in fact icons.

What then is the difference between a photograph of a scarab produced by a camera which clicks away automatically and the fossilised imprint of a scarab? In virtue of what is the photograph an icon of a scarab, while the fossil is no kind of icon of a scarab at all? In each case the object has been caused by a scarab, but obviously the photographs have both a symbolic and an iconic function. We might put it this way. The camera is a mechanism designed with the following intentions: first that the photographs produced by it should be of whatever causes them in a non-deviant way (of whatever they 'specifically reflect'), and secondly that the photographs should be naturally interpretable by anyone who can recognise the objects which cause them. The second of these intentions is, of course, just the intention that the resulting symbols should be interpreted in accord with Convention C. The first intention fixes what the content of the photograph is of – and it is in virtue of this intention that the photograph has content at all. It is in virtue of the *second* intention – Convention C – that the photograph has iconic content.

The upshot is that our original statement of Convention C was a bit too loose. Convention C should read

C: Given that S is of O, it is intended that those who are able to recognise O should be able, on that basis, to interpret S.[3]

It is obvious, now, that Convention C does not and should not pretend to explain the fact that S refers to O. That is explained by the artist's intention plus some causal story. What does C explain? It explains what it is for S's content to be iconic. If S is of O (by causation and artist's intention) and if S is intended to be iconically of O

---

[3] NB: The original version of Convention C is valid if we prescind from doubles. In the rest of this book I shall use the pristine version of Convention C unless I say otherwise.

(by Convention C), and if it is naturally interpretable as being of O (in virtue of the ability to recognise O), then S is an icon of O. That is the full definition of what it is to be an icon.

Convention C is the only convention involved in iconic interpretation. It is the only convention which the interpreter must know to be in force. Hence it is the only essential pictorial communicative convention. What does the interpreter know in virtue of knowing that Convention C applies to S? He knows that whatever S refers to, it is intended that someone who is able to recognise that thing, whatever it is, should be able to interpret S. Thus, knowing that C applies to S is merely knowing that S is intended by its maker to be an icon of something or other. So obviously, knowing that C applies to S doesn't entail one's knowing what S means.

So we can now say more precisely in what the difference between language and depiction consists. In linguistic communication and iconic communication alike, the speaker/maker wants to communicate something to a hearer/beholder. This requires that speaker/maker and hearer/beholder should agree upon the content of a symbol. In the case of linguistic communication agreement on the specific content of a symbol is entailed by agreement on the conventions governing that symbol. What co-ordinates the content ascription of the hearer with the content ascription intended by the speaker is simply that, thanks to conventions regarding the meaning of the constituents in the speaker's utterance (plus rules of grammar), there is a prearranged significance for the whole which both speaker and hearer know. They know that each other knows it and so on. In the case of an icon, however, what co-ordinates maker and beholder as far as the specific content of S is concerned is not a convention at all. It is the fact that they both naturally generate a certain interpretation p and they believe that the other believes he will generate the p-interpretation and so on. But no convention is required to start the process; the level at which one generates the interpretation is not convention-governed at all. However, it is when one asks oneself 'Did the maker intend me to generate this interpretation and to take his icon as signifying the naturally generated content p in virtue of my believing that this is the content he expected me to generate naturally for S?' that Convention C comes in. Where Convention C is in force, the answer to this question is 'Yes'.

So the role of Convention C is quite unlike the role of convention in language. Convention C merely explains what it is for a given content to be iconic; it explains neither how S comes by the content it has (causation and intention do that) nor does it explain how the interpreter comes to know the content of S (recognitional ability is responsible for that). Knowing that Convention C applies to S tells you nothing about the content of S except that whatever it is, it's iconic. Knowing the communicative convention governing a word *is* knowing its content.

I have suggested that we distinguish, for analytic purposes, the following questions:

1. What is the content of S?
2. Is it intended that S's content should be iconic?
3. Is the content of S in fact iconic?

The answer to the first depends upon the artist's intention and the causal relation of S to O. The answer to the second depends upon whether S is manufactured with the intention that Convention C should apply to it. The answer to the third question depends upon the answer to the first and second plus a further fact. Given that S is of O, and given that it is supposed to be an icon of O, is it the case that someone able to recognise O can on that basis alone (given all the obvious background conditions) interpret S as being of O? If the answer is 'Yes', then S iconifies O.

Now the division between these questions is good only for analytic purposes. We must acknowledge the importance of the interdependencies among them. For example, it may be precisely because the artist can naturally generate an interpretation of S as being of O that he takes S to be of O. The fact that he takes S to be of O, that he intends it to be, is not a fact which is independent of his being able to generate naturally an O-interpretation of S. Likewise, for the beholder of S, his reason for thinking that S is intended to be iconically of O is precisely that he, the viewer, can naturally generate an O-interpretation of S. So the fact that S is of O is not something that the artist decides prior to making S iconify O. Equally, deciding that S refers to O is not something that the beholder decides prior to deciding what S iconifies; if it were, his interpretation of S would not be iconic, since an iconic interpretation of S is precisely one in which the fact that one can recognise O explains one's taking S to be of O.

Thus I want to dispel the idea that the artist first makes S designate O by a private ritual of willing or intending that S should designate O and then goes on to make this intention public and to give S's content an iconic embodiment rather than some other kind. Such a picture I utterly reject. It is obvious that just as the beholder takes S to be about O because his ability to recognise O suffices to give him the ability to interpret S as being of O, so the artist intends that S is to be of O because he finds himself able to generate naturally the O-interpretation of S. And just as the beholder reasons that since he can naturally generate the O-interpretation of S, the artist must also have generated that interpretation, so the artist reasons that since he can generate naturally the O-interpretation of S, any beholder will likewise be able to generate the O-interpretation of S. And then of course the artist reasons: 'and since the beholder will generate the O-interpretation of S, he will see that I too generated the O-interpretation of S'; likewise the beholder will reason: 'since the artist no doubt generated the O-interpretation of S, he expected that I too would generate the O-interpretation of S'. And so the artist reasons: 'since the beholder realises that I too generate the O-interpretation of S, he will reason that I intended *him* to generate the O-interpretation of S and, on that basis, to conclude that S is about O'. And the beholder reasons: 'since the artist expected me to generate the O-interpretation, he must have intended me to see that that is the interpretation he expected me to generate and so, on that basis, he must have expected me to see that S is about O'.

I have thus far been rather non-committal on the question of whether S can be a picture even if it is not made with the intention that it should be a picture. I have spoken non-committally of S's being made or used in accord with Convention C. Obviously this is a point common to all artifacts. There is a distinction between being a vase and being used as a vase. Something is a vase if it was made with the intention that it should hold flowers; something is used as a vase when it is put to the use normally assigned to a vase. Likewise, perhaps we should distinguish between being a picture and being used as a picture. S is strictly a picture only if the purpose of S is to convey its contents iconically and this purpose explains S's existence and explains some of S's features (namely, its iconic features). X is used as a picture when, although it was not made with the intention of being a picture of O, it can nonetheless be used as a picture of O.[4]

[4] This chapter relies heavily on Grice 1957 and Lewis 1969.

8

Convention and realism

I GOMBRICH AND THE LANGUAGE MODEL OF DEPICTION

Two heresies have dominated the most interesting work to date on pictorial perception. According to the first heresy, a pictorial system is really an arbitrary sign-system or language for describing reality; the users of the system, both the senders and the receivers of pictorial messages, must learn the conventions for the pictorial sign before they can interpret it. Different cultures, different traditions, different artists and styles, even different media and techniques of representation, all carry with them distinct conventions which the intelligent decoder must learn before he is able to decipher the content of the pictorial symbol. I shall call this first heresy the semiological heresy.

A second heresy pervades art historical writing. It is the doctrine that the depiction of an object gives you an illusion of seeing that object. The pictorial artist strives to dazzle the beholder with a mirage of reality. According to this view, the progress of pictorial representation since the Renaissance rupture with medieval art has been a story of ever-increasing illusionistic effects. A claim which is a typical expression of this heresy is that Giotto's paintings achieve an illusion of space which is quite absent from the work of Cimabue. I shall call this heresy the illusionist heresy.

I regard the first as infinitely the more dangerous and misleading of these two orthodoxies – for indeed both heresies have now the status of pervasive dogma. The semiological heresy is the more pernicious view not just because, of the two heresies, it is the one which is more obviously incompatible with my own view, though indeed this is naturally a factor in my disinclination to accept it. The semiological heresy is especially dangerous because it has a habit of consorting with another heresy, what we might call the relativist heresy. According to this view, all pictorial systems are equally good at representing the world. The pictorial system available to the medieval artist is really not an inferior mode of depicting the world, it is not a less successful system of depiction than that available to the world of classical antiquity or the world of the Renaissance and modern times. Such 'value' judgements are really just subjective and 'ethnocentric'. In fact, the system of medieval depiction is simply a *different* way of depicting the world, and is just as good, on its own terms, as the Renaissance system. Of course we flatter ourselves that the Renaissance mode of depiction is better than the Gothic style, but that is only because our minds have been conditioned to accept and approve the post-Renaissance style. In reality, to claim that one system of depiction is better than another at iconifying reality is just as silly as claiming that one language is better than another for describing reality. One language may be better than another for certain specific purposes – such as remarking the infinite gradations in the colour and texture of snow – but no language is better than another tout court, and even in the case of a language which is inferior to another in some specialised descriptive task, the vocabulary of the inferior language could always be enriched to handle the task. Languages are simply different conventional and arbitrary solutions to rather similar co-ordination problems, and each language represents a reasonably adequate solution to the problem. Likewise, each pictorial system is simply a conventional solution to a given problem, and there is no sense in making the absolute judgement that one system more adequately reflects reality than another.[1] Of course, historians and philosophers of science will recognise the argument, for the relativist heresy is widespread there too, as a look at the works of Kuhn, Feyerabend and Foucault will show. The relativist heresy does not really have the status of a dogma in the philosophy of science – thanks to the opposition of a remarkable variety of philosophers who have perceived that modern science is a distinct improvement on old belief-systems – but such relativism is rampant in the social sciences, especially anthropology. Though such relativism is far too big a target for a

---

[1] Goodman 1968 and Goodman 1972 (chapter 3, section 6). For the common view that there is no fact of the matter about which if either of two depictions S and S★ of the same thing is the more realistic see Honour and Fleming, *A World History of Art*, London, 1982. On p. 8 they speak of the 'illusion of progress' and make it clear that by this they mean the belief that painters advance 'ever closer to the goal of visual truth'. It is evident that they think the very idea of such progress – even local progress – makes little sense. I believe they have conflated the claim that one can objectively assess whether S is more realistic than S★ with the claim that realistic depiction is the paramount goal of art. The latter claim is obviously false. Moreover, it is evident that one should distinguish between these empirical claims and the judgemental claim that visual truth is itself a good thing to strive for. I do not see why we should be reluctant to envisage both objective aesthetic and objective technical progress. Perhaps it makes no sense to speak of all art history as a grand progress towards greater visual realism, but surely it can be true of some periods that there is progress towards realism within those periods.

work directed primarily at an understanding of pictorial representation, it is well to note the parallel. In this chapter I hope to strike a blow for the anti-relativist cause. I intend to show that pictorial systems are not like arbitrary sign-systems and that it is quite wrong to think of them as 'languages'. Different sign-systems are not just different languages for describing reality, any more than different belief-systems or theories simply represent different (and perhaps incommensurable) vocabularies for representing the world. It is possible – at least in principle – to assess the varying degrees to which different pictorial systems *iconically* represent reality. Just as the non-relativist philosopher of science believes it is possible to measure and compare the verisimilitude of competing theories, so I believe that it is possible to compare and measure the different degrees of success in iconic representation that attach to different pictorial styles and traditions.

It is necessary right away to clear up one source of confusion. If someone says that one painting is more 'realistic' than another painting (of, let us say, the same subject), he is not thereby committed to *preferring* the more realistic picture to the less. The question of what value if any should attach to realistic depiction should be kept quite distinct from the question of whether it is possible meaningfully to assert that one mode of depiction is more realistic than another. I believe that the view that realistic depiction is essentially boring and (thanks to the camera) redundant has attained a degree of popular acceptance quite out of proportion to its merit. Realistic representation is by no means the banausic enterprise its detractors have made it out to be. But we must pick off the foe one at a time and so I start with the relativist heresy; in particular I want to attack the semiological heresy which forms the linchpin of the bandwagon in which the relativist is riding to his pyrrhic victory (for as commentators too numerous to requisition here have pointed out, relativism is ultimately self-defeating).

I must now face an embarrassing fact, and that is that the most powerful proponent of the view I wish to attack is Sir Ernst Gombrich. Indeed, with respect to the semiological heresy, Gombrich has some claim to the status of a heresiarch. His book *Art and Illusion* is, perhaps together with Goodman's *Languages of Art*, the most persuasive and elegant available vessel of this heresy. Yet Gombrich is certainly no relativist and, when it comes to defending the value of realistic depiction, no one has been more eloquent. Gombrich's view is a subtle amalgam of the heresy of illusion and the heresy of semiology. Each heresy tempers the other and the illusionist heresy in particular allows Gombrich to get away with claiming that one system of representation can do a better job of depicting the world than another. Yet there is a tension between these two heresies and it is not clear that Gombrich's view is ultimately coherent. How, one might ask, is it possible to decode a canvas, to extract the meaning from its semiotic vessel, while at the same time one is subject to the illusion that one is seeing what is depicted? Gombrich's solution is that we switch rapidly back and forth between seeing the sign and seeing the signifier. But it is not obvious that this is in fact what we do, nor indeed is it obvious that we can make sense of Gombrich's story. If indeed the pictorial sign is the vessel of its meaning, then it is a mystery to me how we can ask it to disclose its meaning to us without our being *aware* of it. The comparison Gombrich makes with the duck-rabbit figure only enforces my scepticism about his solution of the paradox. The duck-rabbit figure, as every school-child knows, is a figure which it is possible to see either as a duck or as a rabbit. It is not possible to see it, simultaneously, as both. Now if we imagine that the duck and rabbit figures each encode some message, it is hard to make sense of the suggestion that one could be visually decoding the message which has been encoded in the rabbit while one is only aware of seeing the duck. Consequently, I have a strong suspicion that Gombrich is able to dodge the relativistic con-sequences of the semiological heresy only by combining it with an incompatible heresy, the heresy of illusion. In this chapter I shall lavish my critical attentions on the semiological heresy and save my scrutiny of the illusionist heresy for the next chapter.

In drawing up my brief against Gombrich, I must follow the juri-dical custom of distinguishing the *quid juris* (question of right) from the *quid facti* (question of fact). But of course, I want to do more than establish that Gombrich has embraced a dubious doctrine. I want also to understand the overall project which Gombrich's great work proposes, so that we can have a standard whereby to measure other pretenders to the truth.

As I see it, Gombrich has proposed two facts for our consider-ation. The first datum is the enormous diversity of pictorial modes. Why are there so many different ways of depicting the world? But the second phenomenon he wants to understand is the evolution of realistic depiction. Why is it that a truly powerful system of realistic depiction has evolved only twice? What are the factors influencing its evolution? The two heresies I detect in Gombrich tend to swim into focus on different occasions. When he is trying to explain the diversity of pictorial modes, he stresses that they are conventional or arbitrary solutions to the problem of depiction. When he is trying to say just what it is that realistic modes of depiction have got that less realistic modes of depiction lack, he stresses the illusionistic virtues of realistic pictures.

But the interplay between the two views is subtler than this suggests. Gombrich believes that the development of pictorial realism is the result of a long history of trial, error and correction. In fact, we can envisage the evolution of pictorial realism as somewhat analogous to evolution by natural selection. We can think of the different pictorial repertoires as constituting a kind of population. The selective pressure is the desire to maximise illusionistic effect. The repertoires which can contribute to illusionistic effect survive in the realistic tradition. Repertoires which do not enhance the illusionistic effect are not taken up into the realistic tradition. Of course, for the evolution to take place, novel repertoires must be generated and tested for their illusionistic possibilities. Now, the new techniques will be randomly generated and hence, in a sense, they are 'arbitrary'. They get taken up into the traditions simply because they had the luck to have been the first to be thought of.[2] Pictorial sign systems, even realistic ones, are arbitrary in that they begin with random or arbitrary 'guesses'. These arbitrary initial ideas constitute the raw material on which the selective pressure of illusionism operates.

Here too, however, it is possible to detect an instability in Gombrich's theory. Although the starting-point of pictorial evolution may be random or arbitrary, the system should become progressively less 'arbitrary' over time. No representational technique is secure from modification. If someone can think of a way of making the technique yield more realistic results, or of a completely different technique which has more realistic results, the original technique may be modified or abandoned. Thus, the fact that a system has an arbitrary starting-point is no reason for regarding the later stages of the system as equally arbitrary. Evolution is the result of a rhythmic interplay of chance and necessity, but the factor of necessity obviously plays an increasingly important role in later stages as the results of 'selection' accumulate.[3]

---

[2] Gombrich frequently acknowledges his debt to Popper. See Gombrich 1960.

[3] Popper is guilty of mistakes that are similar to those I am laying at Gombrich's door. As many of his critics have pointed out, Popper's famous anti-inductivism (see *The Logic of Discovery*) overlooks two important forms of induction other than the simple Millian sort (the necessity for which cannot in any case be reasonably doubted): meta-induction and cross-induction (terms coined by Putnam and Reichenbach respectively). Meta-induction involves inferring from the success (or failure) of a past theory to its continued success (or failure); cross-induction involves inferring from the success of one theory T to the likely success of another theory $T^\star$ which is similar to T in certain relevant respects.

Indeed, if one is trying to characterise the difference between post-Renaissance or 'modern' representation and representational systems which are traditional or pre-modern, one could do worse than suggest that the modern system achieves a degree of naturalness in representation thanks to a ruthless willingness to experiment and to discard solutions which fail and retain only solutions which work. Traditional systems are conventional and stable inasmuch as they do not subject themselves to intense selective pressure. Indeed, as studies of primitive art such as that by Robin Horton in *Kalabari Sculpture*[4] make abundantly clear, the traditional artist is much more interested in sticking to traditional models than he is in trying to achieve a match with reality. This is for the very good reason that their pictorial representations are meant to serve as vehicles for communication between men and gods and it would be a foolish man indeed who attempted to experiment with the prescribed method for effecting such interactions. The primitive artist is not trying to maximise the realism of his representation; he is trying to be careful that his work duplicates the ritually prescribed formulae for representing the gods who control nature and man's fate.[5]

The modern system is thus to be distinguished by the avidity with which the artist freed from Byzantine ritual constraint is able to pursue the perhaps quixotic goal of maximising the realism of his depiction. Perhaps the correct way to put this is: modern post-Renaissance art was, from one point of view at least, the endeavour to enhance as far as possible the artist's arsenal for realistic iconification. The ambition of making any given painting as realistic as possible in all respects is perhaps incoherent. As Gombrich emphasises, it is often impossible to paint a picture with equal fidelity to local colour and to those tonal gradations which suggest distance and space. He instances Claude as an artist who sacrificed local colour to

---

[4] Robin Horton, *Kalabari Sculpture*, Lagos, 1965.

[5] Panofsky 1964 makes the striking suggestion that whereas Egyptian sculpture was intended to aid the deceased in the afterlife, classical Greek funerary sculpture sought to recollect the dead person to the world of the living. The magical use of sculpture does not require realism. Realistic depiction becomes important when the goal is commemoration of the dead person. To put the contrast in terms drawn from J. L. Austin, we might say that the Egyptian is depicted and *thereby* is helped to survive while the Greek is depicted and *therein* survives. Panofsky's discussion provokes the hypothesis that the realistic and magical uses of depiction vary inversely; Kris and Kurz 1979 confirm this guess, while Gombrich and Kris in *Caricature*, London, 1940 make the suggestion that portrait caricature supplants some of the functions of the magical image.

the project of depicting tonal gradation. Such a preference for tonal gradation and what it is able to propose to the eye no doubt explains the widespread preference for black-and-white photographs.

Be that as it may, the important point is that it is possible to view the evolution of realistic depiction as a collective enterprise in which the goal was to enhance the realism on tap. The project was to add to the artist's bag of tricks as many techniques for realistic depiction as possible. With such a goal in mind, it is natural that artists should specialise. A similar point applies to the vocation of the modern scientist. Obviously, no scientist is trying to come up with a single theory that explains everything, any more than any painter would entertain the Borgesian ambition of painting an infinitely realistic painting of the whole universe. Instead, each painter tries to develop a certain line of inquiry – this one studies light, this one shape, another colour and yet another the effect of light on the colour of water – just as each scientist is trying to add an essential component to the overall network of explanatory scientific theory.

Now the fact that artists specialise in their endeavour to enhance the total bag of illusionistic tricks available to the brotherhood entails that there will be a plurality of styles, techniques, media and subject matter. Each given style, technique or medium can only claim to reflect a corner of reality. Consider, for example, this list: stick-drawings, red-figure vases, black-and-white photography, woodcuts, Flemish painting, fauviste and expressionist art, pencil drawings, marble statues, and limewood sculpture.

Now, Gombrich is inclined to treat the different styles and techniques within the realistic post-Renaissance tradition as though they constituted distinct sign-systems or codes, each having distinctive conventions which it is necessary to learn before one can enter into their meaning. Thus, if one were to misunderstand the conventions of black-and-white photography one might foolishly think Cecil Beaton meant to portray his friends as black-and-white two-dimensional ensembles of tonal gradation (though this might be exactly what someone like Whistler tries to do!). To avoid such misunderstanding, one needs to be privy to the special conventions of black-and-white photography. At one point Gombrich says 'When we step in front of a bust we understand what we are expected to look for. We do not as a rule take it to be a representation of a cut off head . . .' (p. 60).[6] On Gombrich's view, we don't make this stupid

---

[6] All page references to Gombrich in this chapter are to Gombrich 1960.

mistake because we are on familiar terms with the conventional idiom of the bust.

Curiously, although Gombrich holds that pictorial systems constitute 'codes' (p. 39), 'languages' with a grammar and semantics (p. 9), or 'cryptograms' (pp. 44 and 58), he does not believe that pictures are ever literally true or false (pp. 67–8). People who believe that a picture can have a truth-value of its own are muddled. They have confused the picture with the use that is made of it. It is only when a picture is used to tell a lie that it is false (p. 68).

I am afraid that Gombrich himself is somewhat snarled up here. If pictorial systems constitute a language with a semantics and a grammar, it is hard to see how pictorial symbols can lack truth-value. As it is, I think Gombrich has got the truth the wrong way round. Pictures are indeed semantic vehicles, bearers of truth-value, but pictorial systems are in all other respects quite unlike natural languages and in particular pictorial systems are not codes with a grammar for constructing sentential bearers of truth-value out of a vocabulary.

Moreover, Gombrich is himself guilty of a confusion when he supposes that whether a picture is true or false depends upon what it is used to say. There are two quite distinct senses in which meaning might be a matter of 'use'. At one level, the words of a language receive their meaning thanks to conventions governing what they are used to designate. But although the significance of the words is fixed by convention, *given* the meaning of the words and the grammar of the language, *no further* convention or intention is required to fix the truth-condition of the sentence (though I dogmatically assert this, it seems to be precisely what Wittgenstein wants to deny in the *Foundations*).[7] Hence a sentence can quite by itself have a truth-value, regardless of the particular use to which it is put (*given* that it is constructed from a certain stock of vocabulary to which meaning has already been assigned and provided it is constructed via accredited rules of grammatical composition).

If I am right about pictorial systems, we cannot apply such a story to them. However, if Gombrich were right, we would be able to treat pictures as built up out of vocabulary of prearranged significance via the accredited rules of grammar or 'pictorial syntax' (the phrase is William Ivins's).[8] Hence, on Gombrich's *own* account, a picture should be like a sentence and hence should be capable of bearing a truth-value quite independently of what any language user

[7] See Craig 1975.
[8] W. Ivins, *Prints and Visual Communication*, Cambridge, Mass., 1969.

does with it. Meaning may be used at the level of vocabulary, but not at the level of the sentence.

However, an *ad hominem* argument here would be quite hollow since I do not agree with my antagonist's premise that there is a pictorial syntax. If I am right pictures *do* indeed have a truth-value which is independent of any particular use we put them to even though there is no pictorial grammar. They have to satisfy only two conditions: if Convention C applies to S and we naturally generate the interpretation that S is true just if *p*, then S will have a truth-value, thanks to C, that is quite independent of any particular thing we do with or say about S. Just as the meaning of a sentence is fixed by the meaning of its parts plus syntax, so the meaning of the picture is fixed by Convention C plus whatever interpretation we naturally give to it. Just as there is no need for a further convention to determine the truth-condition of the sentence once the conventions governing the meaning of its parts have been fixed, so there is no need for a further convention governing the meaning of the picture once the picture has been subsumed under Convention C. Of course, this conclusion is one which Gombrich would want to challenge. He wants to assert that there are many conventions essentially involved in the extraction of iconic content. I shall argue that, in any sense in which Gombrich's claim is justified, it is not incompatible with my account and that it has no tendency to establish that pictorial systems are conventional sign-systems like languages or ciphers.

Now, given that Gombrich wants to deny that pictures can be bearers of independent or autonomous truth-values, it is not surprising that he gets a bit tangled up when he tries to characterise just what it is that the realism of a depiction *consists in*. Here is what he says:

those who understand the notation [used in the depiction] will derive no false information from the drawing (p. 90).

This, of course, is hopeless. No one would derive false information from a blank sheet of paper, but such a sheet of paper is hardly the pinnacle of realistic representation. Moreover, Gombrich's definition of realism is technically inconsistent with his illusion theory. For on the illusion theory, a realistic representation is precisely one which tends to give me a false belief about the depicted object, viz, that I am seeing it now. No doubt the definition could, with suitable subtlety, be amended to avoid these gross deformities. It would still, however, need to be cast in terms of the information *derived from* the picture rather than the information *in* the picture. But a sentence does not signify the information that can be derived from it – such information is huge and potentially infinite (if one is allowed to make use of one's total information state). Instead, a sentence has a certain, possibly complex, state of affairs conventionally associated with it, as a result of the conventional assignment of meaning to its parts and of the way in which it has been constructed from these parts. This is the content of the sentence. The sentence is true if that content (state of affairs) obtains and not otherwise. Now if a sentence had to be such that one could never make use of it in the (holistic-inductive) derivation of a false belief, no sentence would ever be true. Hence, it is unreasonable to require that a realistic depiction never leads the beholder astray in his views about the depicted scenery. Surely it is easier to accept my suggestion that a picture gets its meaning (truth-conditions) thanks to a combination of natural generativity, causation and subsumption under Convention C. The result is that pictures can have a determinate truth-value quite independently of how they are used. Our definition of realism, though only in one of its dimensions (as we shall see), is simplicity itself: realism is truth in depiction.

It is worth pausing here in my argument with Gombrich to note a disagreement between my views and those of Roger Scruton.[9] Scruton has rightly criticised sundry pretentious attempts to turn various corners of the social world into elaborate sign-systems. The only excuse for the semiological fallacy of projecting sign-systems on to every aspect of reality is that it provides an opportunity for the literary critic to unleash his talent for hermeneutic overkill on such unsuspecting prey as menus, clothes and beer-mats. I thus agree with Scruton that the 'signifying' of all aspects of reality is quite unnecessary. One of Scruton's criticisms of Barthes is that there is no grammatical rule which allows one to go from the stipulated meaning of the significant parts to the meaning of the ensemble of those parts. And again, I do not doubt for a moment that Scruton has here uncovered a flaw in Barthes's project.

I wholeheartedly agree with the main thrust of Scruton's argument against semiology as a putative science of all aspects of social and cultural reality. He seems to me, however, to have made an assumption with which I cannot agree, and that is that a semantically meaningful system must have a grammar. If I am right, pictorial

---

[9] For Scruton's influential views see the essays collected in his *The Politics of Culture*, Manchester, 1981, especially essays 3, 6 and 10. I have discussed these matters in Schier 1983(c).

systems have no grammar, yet pictures can be assessed for truth-value. Furthermore, pictorial ability is generative in that once one has the ability to interpret pictures, one has access to the meaning of a potentially infinite series of visual icons. So, I do not accept it as an argument against my theory that one cannot state rules of grammar for composing the meaning of pictorial wholes from pictorial parts. This is just the wrong question to ask in the case of pictures, since the meaning of the whole is *naturally* generated from the meaning of its iconic components. Semantic generativity does not, *pace* Scruton, entail a grammar. Scruton's mistake is to suppose that the linguistic model constitutes the only possible model for a semantically meaningful system. (Indeed, I would have thought that this would be the natural initial riposte of the semiologist: that Scruton has simply foisted on him an unwelcome and unnecessarily rigid analogy between the sign-systems he claims to detect and the sign-system of a natural language.)

I detect only two arguments in Gombrich for the analogy between languages and pictorial systems which he is so anxious to press. Indeed, at one point he stresses that 'the phrase "the language of art" is more than a loose metaphor' (p. 87). The paintings of Corot and Constable are referred to as 'cryptograms' (p. 58) of the reality they depict, while it is said that Chinese pictorial art simply has a pictorial 'vocabulary' that is different from the Western vocabulary (p. 84). One argument for these bold views has already been discussed. The argument is that the beholder of a pictorial representation is necessarily beholden to a set of conventions governing the diverse systems of representation because they are selective about what they do and do not commit themselves to depicting. The correct reading of red-figure vases requires that one does not suppose they depict the figures as red. Red-figure vases can only communicate their meaning to the beholder if it is common knowledge between maker and beholder that red-figure vases do not ascribe the colour of the pottery to the depicted figure. Likewise, a stick-figure drawing of a man does not depict him as a stick or as lacking the features which are left out. Again, on Gombrich's view we must *postulate* a special convention, the beholder's knowledge of which explains the fact that he does not make stupid interpretations of stick-figure drawings.

The argument just surveyed would, if it went through, establish that Convention C is not the only convention to which the beholder is beholden when he is retrieving the iconic content from a picture. Gombrich's other argument is an argument from the *artist's* point of view. Gombrich says that 'The artist, no less than the writer, needs a vocabulary before he can embark on a "copy" of reality' (p. 87). The ability to depict reality requires that the artist should have a stock of techniques for depiction from which he can draw formulae and stereotypes for the task in hand. The analogy is between the picture-maker and the language-speaker. Just as I need a stock of vocabulary to draw upon when I construct a description of some corner of the world, so the artist needs a stock of 'formulae' to draw upon when he constructs a depiction of some section of reality. Strictly speaking, what the artist requires is not so much like a vocabulary as it is like a set of stock phrases of the kind which the orator uses for evoking various scenes in the minds of his hearers. I shall, following Gombrich, speak indifferently of pictorial 'stereotypes', 'formulae' and 'vocabulary'.

It should be emphasised here that on Gombrich's view even the artist who tries to maximise on the realism of his repertoire still requires a repertoire or vocabulary. Learning to depict the world is always a process of acquiring, by trial, error and correction, techniques for representing the myrian nuances which nature affords the human eye. Obviously, this enterprise is cumulative. The artist retains his techniques in order to use them on other occasions. Of course, if the artist is of the modern type, then he imposes on his technique a continual process of adjustment and correction.

Now my strategy for dealing with Gombrich's two arguments will be first to establish a precise notion of convention, with particular attention to the notion of a 'communicative' convention. I will then show that Convention C is a communicative convention properly so called. I will argue that, *pace* Gombrich, Convention C is in fact the only (first-order) communicative convention essential to 'pictorial' communication.

2 DEFINITION OF CONVENTION

No doubt in its standard use the word 'convention' suggests a rather hazy penumbra of meanings.[10] A conventional man is one who has no flair, someone who lacks boldness and originality of style and conception and whose habits of thought and feeling follow a predictable pattern. In this sense 'convention' carries with it the suggestion of 'conformity' as distinct from 'originality'. Now, while convention does always involve conformity, not all conformity

[10] Goodman 1968, p. 37.

involves convention. The reason is that conventional conformity is, to some degree, arbitrary. One conforms to the rule of driving on the left-hand side of the street not because one feels that such a rule is intrinsically the best solution to the problem; instead one conforms because one expects the conformity of others. Likewise, in speaking the local lingo one need have no special regard for it. What matters is that this lingo happens to be the solution which has been favoured locally. No doubt rules which start as conventions – as arbitrary selections from a class of equally plausible solutions to a problem – may come, in time, to have a 'normative' appearance. Thus, we find the classical Greek deprecating all other languages as barbaric and we find Leibniz and Herder extolling the unique metaphysical charms of the German tongue. No doubt some languages are better than others at some tasks, but this has no tendency to show that they are not arbitrary, because even when one language is better than another at a certain task, it is still possible to *conceive* of yet a third language which would do the job just as well.

Now *given* that a solution has been adopted, it may be that one ought to follow it. Given that a certain rule governing which side of the street to drive on has been adopted by a given population, one has every reason to follow the rule. Indeed, someone who drives on the wrong side of the street may be morally and legally culpable. However, failure to adopt one rule rather than another is not a matter for moral concern as long as both rules – drive on the right or drive on the left – would be equally felicitous if obeyed by all.

So the structure of a convention is,[11] roughly, this: there is a class of solutions to the problem, and these solutions are roughly equally happy; the solutions will work only if all or most people adhere to the rule; the selection of a solution from this class is arbitrary, but once a selection has been made, it is in each person's interest to conform to the rule (by and large). For example, given that a certain way of designating objects has become the rule, it is in each person's interest, when trying to communicate with members of a population following such a rule, to follow that rule himself.

We should distinguish three different kinds of rule: 'normative', 'conventional' and 'coercive'. A rule is normative for an agent if he believes he would have reason to follow that rule even if other people did not (or if he would be disposed to follow it even when other people are not). If a rule is normative, then there is reason to

---

[11] My debt to Lewis 1969 will be obvious.

prefer it to competing principles regardless of what other people are doing. People who follow such rules are traditionally said to have a conscience; more recently sociologists have come to refer to such people as 'inner directed' and Piaget speaks of the achievement of moral 'autonomy',[12] a notion which, of course, he has borrowed from Kant.

By contrast, a *convention* is a rule which is hypothetical, not categorical. The reason for bringing your conduct into line with the rule is that given that other people are following the rule, it is in your interest to do so as well. Conventions are thus based squarely on a foundation of self-interest. They should be contrasted not only with normative rules – which may of course also ultimately be based on self-interest if you believe like Plato that the just life is the only life that is good for man – but also with *coercive* rules. There may be a rule or set of rules which is such that it is in everybody's interest for everybody else to obey these rules but which is not such that it is in everybody's interest to obey the rules themselves. Of course, strictly we should say of such a rule 'It is in everybody's interest if everyone except themselves obeys the rule.' A rule of this sort creates a free-rider problem that will require the cost of disobeying the rule to be *artificially* increased.

For example, it is in everybody's interest for there to be some system of entitlement to the secure use of objects. In a small society, the individual infraction of such a rule might carry its own penalty with it. If a given infraction would tend to cause the system to break down, then such infractions would be self-correcting. However, in a complex and populous society, individual infractions of the rule might have no effect on the system as a whole. In that case, it is in everybody's interest to break the rule. But then, if everybody broke the rule, the system *would* unravel. The crucial point is, however, that the system's unravelling doesn't follow from any individual infraction. In such cases, what is required is a form of what has been called 'pre-commitment'.[13] The population needs to agree to penalise the free-rider in some way, thus in effect decreasing their own freedom to exploit the agreement by increasing the cost to the individual of an infraction.

Now it is apparent that linguistic rules are by and large of the purely conventional kind rather than the normative or coercive kind. It is in my interest to conform to the local linguistic regulations given that other people do and it is in their interest to con-

---

[12] Piaget, *The Moral Judgement of the Child*, New York, 1965.
[13] Jon Elster, *Ulysses and the Sirens*, Cambridge, 1979.

form to those regulations just because they are the established regulations.

It is because a given set of linguistic rules is an arbitrary selection from a multitude of possibilities that one must know and remember the rules which have actually been adopted by the people with whom one wishes to communicate. In particular, one must remember the meanings of the arbitrary signs which the local natives have 'chosen'[14] as the vehicles for their meaning. Now there is a crucial feature of such conventions that I will call the *mutual* (or *common*) *knowledge* condition. The point is that when I am talking to you I can understand you only if (a) I know the rules you are using and (b) I know that you know the rules that I am using and (c) I know that you know that I know the rules you are using and (d) I know that you know that I know that you know the rules I am using and so on. Each party must have this sort of iterative knowledge about the other party.

Thus, when A utters S meaning *p* to B he does so because he knows that he and B share a set of rules of grammar and vocabulary from which it follows that S is true just if *p* is the case. Each knows that the other follows this set of rules R, and it is because the other man follows R that each man himself follows R. This knowledge is also iterative indefinitely: A follows R because he knows that B follows R and he knows that B follows R because he believes that A follows R.

If we apply this notion of convention to depiction, we find that the rule that 'the naturally generated interpretation of an icon is the correct one' is a communicative convention. For as we noted, there are many possible assignments of meaning to an icon. If the user of the icon wants to convey iconically a certain meaning to the beholder, he must assume that the mutual knowledge condition obtains: that is, he adopts the rule that the naturally generated interpretation is correct because he expects the beholder will follow this rule and because he expects the beholder will expect him to be following this rule. The beholder, likewise, will follow this rule in trying to uncover what the symbol means because he supposes that the creator or user of the symbol intends such a rule to be in force. *Of course* the beholder could treat the canvas like a Rorschach blot or like cracks in a wall or faces in a cloud. But when he treats the icon as a symbol, as a representation, he treats it as a vehicle for communi-

---

[14] Conventions need not be established by explicit agreement but may evolve by trial and error, a point Hume stressed in Book III, Part II of *A Treatise of Human Nature*. Lewis 1969 makes the same point.

cating a semantic content. Now, given that the symbol could contain any of an infinity of contents, he has to ask himself which of these contents it does convey. If he interprets it in line with Convention C he does so on the supposition that this is the rule he was meant to follow by the person who made the symbol. Thus, it is a matter of convention whether a symbol is an icon at all. But given that it is, the specific interpretation is natural and not conventional.

An artist paints an apple. He paints it as bright red. Now if he wants to communicate iconically the thought that the apple is bright red, he wants to paint something such that I can naturally generate the interpretation that the symbol is of an apple and that it represents the apple as red. But, of course, if he wants me to know that this is what *he meant*, he must want me to think that the naturally generated interpretation is the correct one because of a belief on my part that he intended the naturally generated interpretation to be the correct one. If I take the 'red apple' interpretation to be the correct one for this symbol, it is because of a belief on my part that he intended the naturally generated interpretation to be correct and that he intended me to believe that it was correct on the basis of a belief that he intended me to believe that the naturally generated interpretation was the correct one.

Thus, we can roughly analyse 'S iconically means that p' along quasi-Gricean lines ('A' is the artist and 'B' designates the beholder):

A intends S to be true just if p and A intends that B should naturally generate the interpretation that S is true just if p and that B should believe that 'p' is the correct interpretation on the basis of a belief that A intended the naturally generated interpretation to be the correct one.

We can summarise all this by saying that successful iconic communication requires common knowledge between artist and beholder that they are using the rule that the naturally generated interpretation is the correct one. If such a rule is in fact in force in a population and if it is followed because of the mutual expectation that others are following it, we can call it a convention. So iconic communication requires mutual knowledge of Convention C.

Now, Convention C is a communicative convention: it governs what people mean by the use of certain symbols and thus it governs what those symbols mean. Of course, there may be conventions other than the communication Convention C at work in a particular case. Our concern is solely with such communicational conventions. Now, since a given symbol can have both iconic and non-iconic content, it is obvious that Convention C might be just one communicative convention among many applying to a given symbol. My only claim is that Convention C is the only convention essentially involved in the processing of the *iconic* content of a symbol. That other conventions may be required for the communication of the non-iconic content of such symbols is not only a fact of life but a proposition to which my theory of course commits me (since it is precisely my contention that it is *distinctive* of iconic content that Convention C is the only convention involved in the processing of such content).

3 THE ARTIST'S VOCABULARY

Now that we have a better idea of just what is at issue when we speak of the conventionality of a sign-system, I want to turn to Gombrich's arguments for the analogy between pictorial systems and linguistic systems (I shall call this the 'language analogy' for short).

I turn first to Gombrich's discussion of the artist's need for formulae and stereotypes. It is well known, of course, that painters learn at least as much from looking at man-made images of the world as they learn from the world itself. The Renaissance revolution owed a great deal of its impetus to what the Renaissance artist was able to learn from the classical heritage of image-making. Gombrich cites many amusing instances of depictions supposedly 'al vif' which are in fact just deposits of hoary pictorial stereotypes. Even the artist who strives to perfect the realism of his method by the arduous process of what Gombrich calls 'making' and 'matching' must still rely on the techniques he has picked up either from the study of other masters or from his own experiments.

Gombrich suggests that the artist's repertoire of pictorial technique is in fact equivalent to a sort of vocabulary. Yet even if the artist draws on a reserve of pictorial techniques, this by itself has no tendency to establish that this reserve is playing the role of a 'vocabulary'. Linguistic communication requires that there is common knowledge between the participants of the significance of the vocabulary; but the pictorial artist can get his message across without supposing that his audience is aware of his techniques. Linguistic communications requires common knowledge of vocabulary; pictorial communication doesn't require common knowledge of the artist's techniques. So the artist's stock of techniques simply does not amount to a vocabulary.

The artist may have a stock of techniques for depicting hands based perhaps on his knowledge of the work of some other master of hand-depiction and perhaps refined and elaborated in his own studies. From his point of view, generating new images is indeed a matter of projecting his technique for hand-depiction into novel circumstances. His studies of hands in the past will serve as necessary models which can be adapted to new circumstances. To use the happy and suggestive phrase of Lévi-Strauss, the artist is involved in a game of *bricolage*; he is able to feel his way to a new image only by using and modifying the pictorial techniques which happen to be handy. Unlike the speaker of a language, he does not have to rely on there being common knowledge of his techniques between himself and his audience. His aim is precisely to achieve a pictorial effect with his techniques, but the effect will only be pictorial if knowledge of the master's technique is inessential to the beholder's understanding of the *content* of his work. No doubt it is very life-enhancing, for beholder and match-maker alike, if the beholder is an *unsereiner* who can spot various inflections of technique. Indeed, for the aesthetic appreciation of the work, such attentions are essential; I claim only that the retrieval of the iconic content of the work does not presuppose them. That is compatible with an acknowledgement that the iconic content of a work is often, perhaps always, only a part of the aesthetic point of a work.

So, whereas common knowledge of a vocabulary is the sine qua non of verbal communication, iconic communication can get along quite nicely without such luxuries. Common knowledge of linguistic vocabulary is both active and passive; verbal communication is a production in which each party plays the active and the passive part, ideally seriatim. However, in the case of the pictorial 'vocabulary', even the *unsereiner* who is privy to the artist's habits is a long way from being able to duplicate his achievement. Knowledge of linguistic vocabulary and the necessary rules for concocting sentences from words gives you the ability both to understand other people's utterances and to make up your own.

Those who have failed to note this asymmetry between depiction and language have been led to wonder why, given the ease with which we understand images, image-making techniques develop relatively late in human history. Tom Bower asks just this question in his book on the perceptual world of the infant. He notes that language predates pictorial representation 'by several millennia in human evolution'.[15] He thinks the reason is that 'some aspects of representation are quite as abstract and conventional as mathematical symbols' (he instances differences between Western and Japanese modes of representing pictorial space). Yet the answer to his question is blazingly obvious: to have pictorial systems you need makers as well as beholders. Easy to read pictures may be, easy to make they aren't.

Of course, artists operate on many levels. When Piero depicts a dove suspended over Christ and John the Baptist in the National Gallery *Baptism*, he depicts a dove and therein represents the holy spirit. He represents the holy spirit by depicting something which is, by common knowledge between Piero and his audience, a symbol of the holy spirit. But depicting a symbol of the holy spirit isn't depicting the holy spirit, the holy spirit being as undepictable as it is unpredictable. Iconographical depiction, as we may refer to it, operates on at least two levels, the iconic and the non-iconic. An iconographical work depicts an object or situation which has a further, conventionally agreed upon, significance. It should be stressed that even at this symbolical or iconographical level, such depictions do not embed languages, for although various objects may, by convention, pick up a certain significance, there is no grammar specifying how to generate novel statements by certain combinations of symbolic elements. When Piero places a dove overhead he indicates the presence of the holy spirit. He literally depicts a dove as present, but of course he is not interested in whether there really was a dove present. Since the dove is a symbol of the holy spirit, the dove's presence is just an obvious way of depicting the holy spirit's presence. We thus interpret Piero's gesture as saying that the holy spirit was in attendance at the ceremony. How is this statement generated without a grammar?

Apparently there is a simple rule of thumb: if S depicts O and O stands (by convention) for X then if S depicts O as F it represents X as F. To be sure this is a rule which must be applied with caution – it is only a rule for generating interpretations. All interpretations generated by the rule won't necessarily be valid. Indeed, the procedure here is somewhat analogous to interpreting figures of speech. If there is a set of commonplace properties associated with some object, say the sun, then when we coin a metaphor, like 'Juliet is the sun', the way to get at the meaning of this metaphor is to try associating these commonplaces with Juliet (by substitution). Of course

[15] Bower 1977, p. 67.

this is just a procedure for generating associations; some of the associations may be pointless or bizarre. However, the better the metaphor, the greater the number of associations we should be able to transfer from one object to the other. (Goodman refers to this as 'predicate migration'.[16])

And it should be stressed that these 'associations' (or 'paraphrases' as they are sometimes called) are being tested for 'aptness' and not necessarily for literal truth. One thing we associate with the sun is that it aids the growth of plants. Does Juliet aid the growth of plants? No, that's not the point. She makes Romeo's love grow – that's the point. Obviously this involves a second substitution – of 'love' for 'plants'. It is an apt association, but not literally a true one (though there is a sexual pun lurking here that is fairly literal). Likewise, the spatial presence of the dove in the *Baptism* indicates, by substitution, the presence of the holy spirit. But of course the spirit's presence is not itself spatial. So not all of the properties of the dove in the picture are transferred to what it represents, at least not literally.[17]

It should be obvious that the fact that a mode of depiction is traditional does not entail that it is 'conventional'. The artists of the Renaissance may have looked to classical antiquity for inspiration in developing the techniques of modern pictorial representation, but from this it does not follow that they were merely conforming to the Greek modes of depiction because they were classical. They were conforming to the heritage of Apelles because they took it as normative – as an indication of the best way of trying to depict things. Classical antiquity was thought to have been doing things in the right way.

Where then does the difference lie between the 'modern' artist and his system of depiction and the traditional artist – the Egyptian, Byzantine or Kalabari artist – and his system of representation? Neither system is conventional, in the strict sense, since the styles are 'normative' in each case. Nor is the influence of tradition less pervasive in the post-Renaissance system of depiction than it is in the primitive, Egyptian or Byzantine systems. Just what, then, is the difference?

I suggest – and this is hardly a novel suggestion, since it goes back to Burckhardt – that the chief difference between the modern and the traditional artist consists in the freedom of the modern artist to

---

[16] Goodman 1968.
[17] On the more elaborate aspects of Piero's symbolism in the *Baptism* see Marilyn Aronberg Lavin's *Piero della Francesca's Baptism of Christ*, New Haven, 1982.

experiment. He also has, in the early modern period, a goal which is quite unique: he is competing with his artistic brethren in a game of trying to achieve ever more startlingly realistic effects. The upshot of this competition is to maximise the techniques for realistic depiction available to the artist. It is perhaps this attitude of competition between artists – reinforced, of course by the competition for status between their respective cities – which stimulated the rapid technical progress of the Italian Renaissance. Competition among agents who are free to experiment with various ways of maximising some value (in this case 'realism'): here we have the makings of an 'economic' theory of the Renaissance! Of course, it is not true that the goal of 'realism' was the artist's only goal or that he could pursue it unfettered. Nor, of course, was the competition strictly free, since each city had a guild which jealously guarded the rights and prerogatives of the native artisan. Nonetheless, this picture, however crude it may be, suffices to mark an important distinction between the 'traditional' artist and his 'modern' counterpart. We might sum it up this way: although both the traditional and the modern artist need and depend on traditions, the modern artist is – to an immeasurably greater degree than the traditional artist – free to choose among traditions and free to modify and break away from them if he wants. Not only is he free to do so, he is obliged to do so. In particular, an artist's dependence on tradition need not inhibit the realism of his work, so long as he is free to improve upon the traditional way of doing things and so long as he is able to refine critically his own procedures by testing them against 'the look of things'. Just as the traditional thinker maintains a relatively uncritical adherence to certain unquestionable tenets of his thought-system, so the traditional artist does not seek to modify or criticise traditional ways of representing the gods. The procedure which Gombrich has dubbed 'making' and 'matching' is alien to his method. He tries to 'match' his works with traditional works (of proven magical or ritual potency), and in so far as there is trial and error in his method, it regulates his work by holding it up to traditional prototypes, not by holding it up to nature.

What then does the 'modern' realist do? He holds his picture up to nature to see whether it captures what he wants. Now, it is a good question how precisely we should characterise this process of 'making' and 'matching'. Obviously, we need a conception of iconicity and realism in order to discuss this procedure properly. What exactly is the *test* which the artist uses on his own work? Obviously the test is, in a sense, twofold. He must test for iconicity and he must test for accuracy. Of course the artist doesn't test for these features separately, but it helps for analytic purposes to distinguish the two questions 'Have I actually succeeded in *depicting* this or that thing?' and 'Have I succeeded in depicting it *accurately*?'

Nor does the artist necessarily require that a painting should match his perceptions. He may discover that a painting, quite accidentally, gets something right which he had not noticed. There is thus an element of reflective equilibrium, in which the painting is not merely adjusted to the artist's perceptions but those perceptions may be adjusted to the painting.

Of course, it should be stressed that this merely characterises what we might call the 'technical' component of the artist's task. The aesthetic effect which he is hoping to achieve may actually require him to modify his realistic ambitions; at any rate, the aesthetic aims of the artist impose a further test on his production. It is no part of my argument that a clear perception of his 'aesthetic aims' should precede his work or that his work should be conceived as a means to some predefined aesthetic end. Just as painting can give him new eyes, and suggest previously unimagined ways of looking at things, so it can achieve undreamt of aesthetic effects. Just as painting and drawing modify the way things look to the artist, so they are bound to suggest new aesthetic opportunities. It is precisely this freedom to alter reciprocally perception, taste and symbol that characterises the modern 'system' of pictorial representation. And this freedom leads to an incredible diversity of pictorial systems and techniques within our culture – and that is yet another mark against the language analogy. For while each member of our culture is usually fluent in only one language, he is fluent in a vast variety of pictorial styles.

4 COMMITMENT AND REALISM

A picture can only light upon some aspects of reality; the rest it must consign to the shadows. No picture, however fond of its subject, can embrace all of its aspects; it cannot even apprehend every visually accessible and potentially depictable feature of the chosen object. All representations crop and detach a slice of the world and forego the rest. A picture which obeys the Albertian rules of perspective – or which approximates to such obedience – must of necessity select the angle from which it is to view a given facet of its subject; the rest it must deny itself. When Constable conjures up a cloud formation with a pencil stub he must relinquish any hope of capturing the colour which the clouds pick up from the sky. Painters such as Claude who desire to convey a sense of contrast between the foreground and the distant backdrop may do so by making a sacrifice of fidelity to local colour, bathing the foreground in warm browns and reds while showering silvery blues and greys on the distant prospect. More dramatic still is the sacrifice of all colour fidelity in red- and black-figure vases, in black-and-white photographs, and in black-and-white etching, engraving and dry point. But what such colourless icons may lose in charm they may hope to regain in tonal contrast and dramatic suggestiveness. For example, a black-and-white photograph can highlight, perhaps exaggerate, the tactile microstructure of the depicted object by emphasising just such tonal contrasts. An apple or a human body – or even a metal-bodied caravan – so depicted can become an object of lively suggestion to the tactile imagination.

So realism is no simple matter; each picture makes a highly intricate choice of features, playing up some, ignoring others. Rarely if ever are we fooled by these 'selections'. We do not suppose that when Poussin depicts a figure running out of the picture frame he is depicting the figure as cut in half. Nor do we imagine that a picture of Mount Saint Victoire taken from one side implies the absence of the other. We do not think that the child who has given us a stick-figure drawing of a bogyman necessarily means to imply that his bogy lacks all the features – face, clothes, dimensions – which he deletes from his drawing. A black-and-white photograph of Nijinsky does not – as we read it – imply that he was merely a colourless study in tonal contrasts!

Now although this may seem a harmless, even an obvious, point, it is not universally understood. For example, Daniel Dennett argues, to my mind persuasively, that mental images if they exist are internal analogues of pictures; he then argues that pictures have necessarily to be 'committal' about all potential visual aspects of what they depict. Since no internal representational system is committal to this extent, there exists no internal picture gallery. Note the mistake which Dennett makes (it is a mistake also made by some writers, such as Stephen Kosslyn,[18] who are avowed iconophiles):

If ... I were to draw a picture of [a] man I would have to go into details. I can make the picture fuzzy, or in silhouette, but unless something positive

[18] Kosslyn 1980.

163

is drawn in where the hat should be, obscuring that area, the man in the picture must either have a hat or not.[19]

From this passage we can extract the following claim:

> For any pictorial representation S and any object O and any potential visual feature F of O, if S depicts O, S must either depict O as F or depict O as not-F or depict O as having some feature N such that O's having N makes it unclear whether or not O has F.

This is at least a slight improvement on Berkeley's hoary argument against the possibility of there being a general image, against, for example, the possibility of an image of a triangle which is neither isosceles nor not isosceles. It is possible that the image is explicitly non-committal about whether the depicted triangle is isosceles or not (the triangle might be depicted *sfumato* in such a way as to make it impossible to tell just what sort of triangle it is). However, Dennett's claim is still, I think, clearly false. Dennett commits a fallacy which Wollheim has dubbed the 'figurative fallacy'.[20] He fails to reckon with the existence of abstract systems of iconic representation. Indeed, Dennett's criterion for imagery fails not only to cope with stick-drawings and abstract geometrical drawings, but fails to cope with the very fact that iconic representations are necessarily selective about what they commit themselves to depicting. A black-and-white photograph is by the nature of its medium simply non-committal about the colour of the depicted object; for every potential colour feature of the depicted object in a black-and-white photograph, the photograph neither depicts the object as having that feature nor depicts it as lacking that feature. Moreover, the object is not depicted as having some feature which makes it epistemically uncertain what colour it is. Black-and-white photography makes no claim to depict colour; it just isn't in the business of representing colour. The nature of the medium explains why it is non-committal about certain messages.[21]

Now at this point a range of responses to the selective commit-

[19] Dennett 1969, p. 135.
[20] Wollheim 1977.
[21] Dennett's intuition that a depiction is always maximally committal about the potential visual features of its depictum is ill founded. However, a depiction of O must tell you more about O's appearance than is essential to a description of O. The reason is obvious given the theory of natural generativity. If S depicts O, S must ascribe recognition-triggering properties to O. But a description can be about O even if it does not ascribe recognition-triggering properties to O. So the theory of natural generativity entails that depiction must be more committal than description needs to be. In so far as there is a grain of truth in Dennett's characterisation of imagery, it will be found in the theory of natural generativity.

ment of pictorial systems is possible. Some forms of 'selectivity' are the common property of all pictorial representations. No picture, for example, can depict more than a part of the world. Such universal form of selectivity we may safely leave out of account. It is part of the frame of knowledge which we bring to pictorial understanding that pictures can only select aspects, facets, parts of the world. Some selectivity is differential; some systems elect to commit themselves to depicting features which other systems chose to ignore. Colour photography is committal about colour, and so are some forms of realistic painting; black-and-white photography, engravings and red-figure vases are non-committal about colour. And the fact that different systems have different pictorial commitments leads to the surmise that the difference between such systems must be a matter of common knowledge; if it is not common knowledge between photographer and beholder that a black-and-white photograph of Nijinsky is non-committal about the colour of Nijinsky's buttonhole, there is a danger of misunderstanding. Likewise, the difference between the stick-drawing and a realistic painting is conventional; if the child leaves out the figure's face, we don't imagine that he is depicting the figure as faceless; if Magritte paints a man and deletes his face we take him to have depicted a faceless man, a man without qualities. Different conventions lead to different commitments. The conclusion would seem to be that there are more communicative conventions involved in pictorial 'communication' than have been dreamt of in my theory. Such, at any rate, is clearly the view of Gombrich, as we have already seen. He is not alone, however. For example Ned Block, in discussing what he calls 'the photographic fallacy' that all depictions must be committal about all the potential features of what they depict, has this to say: 'Our conventions for understanding stick figures allow them to be noncommittal with respect to clothes . . .'[22] Learning to interpret different systems of depiction requires learning the conventions governing their pictorial commitments.

First let it be said that (*pace* Block) the difference between the child's stick-drawing and the Magritte depiction of a faceless man can quite easily be explained without invoking special communicative conventions. Let us recall that a picture cannot barely depict an object as not-F. The only way to depict O as not-F is to depict O as having some F-excluding feature. Thus, one cannot depict an apple as not-green without depicting it as having some feature which

---

[22] Block 1981, p. 14. Block introduced the notion of 'commitment' which I have been using in this chapter.

excludes its being green. Now, if we turn to the child's stick-drawing of a man, we discover that he has neither depicted the man as having clothes nor depicted him as having some clothes-excluding feature. Likewise for the face. Magritte, by contrast, is committal. He depicts facelessness by depicting something else where the face should be – something which apparently excludes the face.

Unfortunately the matter cannot be left here. Perhaps, because of the peculiar properties of stick-drawings, it is clear, without appeal to conventional wisdom, what they do and do not commit themselves to depicting. But the case is more difficult with, say, a black-and-white photograph. It is easy enough to say that the photograph does not depict the object as having some colour-excluding property. The question which Gombrich and Block would still wish to press is 'How do we know this?' The trouble is that we *could* read the black-and-white in the photograph as colour-excluding properties. Indeed, in some cases this would be proper. The colour photograph of a black-and-white cube might look just like the black-and-white photograph of some other, coloured, cube. To know which is com-mittal with respect to colour, we must know the relevant conven-tion (for example, 'x is committal with respect to colour and y isn't'). The stick-figure drawing doesn't raise this question because apparently there is nothing about it which anyone would naturally read as excluding the possibility that the depicted figure is clothed.

In fact, the question we now face is not new. It is exactly the point we have already noted with regard to colour-reversed icons, namely that the colour-reversed icon, which is not *iconically* committal with respect to colour, might have a colour-normal look-alike. A colour-reversed depiction of a green tree – in which red stands for green – might resemble a colour-normal depiction of the same tree in the autumn. And surely the solution is the same: Convention C applies differentially to the features of the icon. Thus, in the case of the colour-reversed icon and the black-and-white photograph, Con-vention C does not apply to colour. In each case, one might nat-urally generate a certain colour ascription ('The tree is red' or 'The tree is black and white') and in each case it is wrong – because Con-vention C doesn't apply to the potentially colour-iconifying aspects of the depictions. It may, however, apply to aspects of the picture which iconify shape and tonal contrast. Indeed, the only difference between the colour-reversed case and the black-and-white case is that there is a further representational convention involved in the former case – the inversion convention – while there is no further representational convention involved in the latter case.

So selective pictorial commitment comes down to a selective application of Convention C. The question remains, of course, how we know whether or not to apply Convention C to a certain feature. Perhaps what is involved is a set of *second-order* conventions. I shall now enlarge on this suggestion and I hope to show that in fact not only do these second-order conventions have no tendency to enforce the language analogy, but they actually show that the language analogy breaks down at just the point where Gombrich wanted to find support for it.

Thus far I have entertained a picture of iconic interpretation as having two levels (levels which are *conceptually* distinct). One level involves the generation of an interpretation; the other involves the validation or confirmation of it. If S is a picture of O, then an ability to recognise O would suffice to give one the ability to generate the interpretation that S 'refers to' or 'is partially about' O. Such an interpretation is 'naturally generated'. In addition, there is a convention, Convention C, that says the naturally generated interpretation is the correct one. As we have seen this convention is essential. Now we are faced with the fact that Convention C may apply selectively even within the frame of a single picture. We may take our ability to generate naturally an interpretation of S as *criterial* for the application of Convention C. In other words, there is, by and large, a prima facie but defeasible assumption that the naturally generated interpretation is correct – that is, there is a presumption that Convention C is in force for our naturally generated interpretations. However, these interpretations may be negated or constrained if they would go against elements of our frame knowledge and of the knowledge which it is common knowledge is part of all men's frame knowledge.

For example, it is part of our 'background' knowledge of the world that people, flowers, churches and so on are not colourless studies in black and white. We know this without, perhaps, ever having troubled to think about it. That is why we call it 'deep background' or 'frame' knowledge. We never consciously entertain this belief, nor do we ever consciously call it into doubt. Nonetheless, such knowledge plays a crucial role in explaining our behaviour. Not only do we (tacitly) know that the world is not – by and large – black and white, we know that other people know this, we know that they know that we know it, and we know that they know that we know that they know. Thus, there is an important element of common knowledge here. Let's say that it is common background knowledge that by and large objects are not black and white.[23]

In addition to such common knowledge about the world, we enjoy a common expectation that our fellow conversationalists are being co-operative. We assume that they are fairly reasonable people who are trying to make reasonably informative and measured statements about the world. If, for example, someone says 'The issue is not all black and white', we do not take him to be uttering the banal truth that an issue can't *be* – literally – black and white. It is true enough, of course, that an issue can't be black and white. But it is too obvious. It is part of our common knowledge. So we must make the surmise that the speaker is using the words figuratively to indicate that the issue is not a simple one to decide. For similar reasons, when Romeo says 'Juliet is the sun' we know that what he has literally said is false – indeed its falsity is blazingly obvious. Knowing that it is common knowledge that Juliet is not and could not be the sun, we don't for a minute take Romeo's utterance literally.

In each case it is common knowledge that the utterance, if taken literally, would violate the rules of conversational co-operativeness, either because it is common knowledge that the statement is obviously true or because it is common knowledge that it is obviously false. If the former, it violates the imperative to be informative; if the latter it violates the imperative to tell the truth. And since this in turn is common knowledge, we filter out the noise – the obvious truth or the obvious falsehood – and search for the figurative import of the utterance.

Now I think the same point applies to drawings, engravings, black-and-white photographs and so on. Take a drawing. One could – if one were extremely naive or stupid – take the drawing by Hockney to depict the boy as though he were a set of lines. One could, that is, take the lines at 'face value'. One could take the black-and-white photograph to depict Nijinsky as black and white (and grey) all over. One *could* take a heavily outlined figure by Van Gogh to depict the man as literally having dark black bands running along the edges of his body. One *could* read a red-figure vase as ascribing the colour of the pottery to the depicted figure. But we don't do any of these things.

We are faced with a choice here, but I am not sure how much it matters which way we jump. One choice would be to say, follow-

[23] By 'common knowledge that *p*' I mean that it is widely known that *p* and that it is widely known that it is widely known that *p*.

ing Dennett (though of course transposing his view into our own terminology) that an icon depicts everything which it is possible to take it as depicting. That is, whatever we could naturally generate as the content of a picture, that picture would depict. Convention C, if it applies at all, applies indiscriminately across the canvas. However, although icons are thus all freighted with some enormously absurd literal content – a black-and-white photograph of Henry depicts him as black and white, a pencil drawing of a cloud depicts the cloud as having the pencil's colour – we don't take all of the picture's literal content seriously. We filter it out, just as we filter out the literal content of 'No man is an island' or 'Juliet is the sun.' Because it is common knowledge between photographer and beholder that Nijinsky was not black and white, we don't let the literal meaning of the photograph bother us.[24] Instead, we take the black-and-white photograph as marking tonal contrasts, shape, etc. This, of course, is what it literally does. So it is not really a case of giving a metaphorical reading of the symbol to substitute for the absurd literal reading. It is rather a case of filtering the sensible literal content from the absurd literal content.

The other choice, and the one I prefer, is to say that the content of the black-and-white photograph is constrained by our common knowledge of the world and by our common knowledge that photographer and beholder are relying on the assumption of conversational co-operativeness. Because of our common knowledge that the world is not black-and-white and because of our common knowledge that we are adhering to the maxims of conversational co-operativeness (extended to pictorial one-way communication), we take it that Convention C does not apply to the potentially colour-iconifying aspects of the black-and-white snapshot. That is, we assume that the picture is non-committal with respect to colour since if we thought otherwise we would have to suppose that the artist was either a fool or a knave.

So I think that our common knowledge of the world, plus our common knowledge of the Gricean rules of conversational co-operativeness, together generate the second-order 'conventions' which constrain the application of Convention C to various features of the picture. It follows that the pragmatics of the pictorial presentation – our assumptions about the world and our common knowledge of the world and of the rules of conversational co-ordination –

---

[24] See Grice 1961 for the original idea of conversational implicature and Grice 1975 for its application to figures of speech. Ted Cohen in 'Notes on Metaphor', *Journal of Aesthetics and Art Criticism*, 1976, 249–59 points out that a metaphor need not be false; as he says, no man *is* an island!

constrain the actual content of the picture. If this is right, then there is an important disanalogy between linguistic systems and pictorial representation.

Earlier in this chapter we had occasion to note that conventions fix the semantics of sentences by operating on their parts. Once the meaning of the part – the lexical item – is fixed, the meaning of the sentence is fixed (given the rules of grammar). In particular, Gricean rules of conversational co-ordination do not affect sentence meaning, but affect rather what we might call 'speaker's meaning'. The sentence meaning is fixed by the prearranged rules governing the meaning of the sentence parts. In pictorial systems we have a different arrangement. First, as I have already noted, the iconically significant part of an icon is always itself a whole icon (though we must take care to distinguish iconic parts or aspects from spatial parts). Thus, the analogue of the iconically significant part is in effect a whole sentence, for each iconic part of an icon iconifies a state of affairs. Each iconically significant part of an icon is, borrowing a bit of jargon from Frege, a 'saturated' symbol. That is, it has a value on its own – in particular, a truth-value. The meaning of these parts is not prearranged; though of course the artist may have a stock repertoire of such parts, the significance of these parts doesn't have to be common knowledge between maker and beholder. Precisely because, however, there is no pictorial vocabulary, no prearranged value for the parts, the value of the parts must be decided *in context*. The important fact is that (1) pictures are not decomposable into elements which have a conventionally *prearranged* significance, (2) all such parts have a truth-value and (3) the Gricean rules of co-ordination fix not merely 'maker's meaning' (to coin a term for the pictorial analogue of speaker's meaning), but also constrain the *picture's* meaning (where this is the analogue of sentence meaning). The result of this situation is that, except in rare cases, one does not have to commit to memory a specific set of instructions regarding whether a specific type of medium, style or picture is committal or not with respect to a given feature. Instead, common sense and the rules of conversational politesse should suffice to generate the second-order 'conventions' which constrain the application of Convention C to the features in a picture. In other words, if I am right, all we really need to be able to do is recognise the depicted object; from this recognitional base we generate our interpretation and the success of this interpretation in giving an account of the features of the symbol is prima facie good reason to suppose the interpretation is correct – i.e. that Convention C is in play. Now, because pictures are selective about their commitments, we need in addition some common knowledge about the word 'common' (in the sense of being both pervasive and 'reciprocal'), and we need some tacit knowledge of the Gricean rules for conversational co-operation (the artist is not a knave or a fool, and he does not take us for fools, but is trying to make some true and informative pictorial statement). This knowledge, if I am right, suffices to generate most of the 'second-order' conventions we need for constraining our interpretations of pictures. Hence, there is no sense in which there is a prearranged 'vocabulary' of pictorial representation. Pictorial interpretation is more like getting at the figurative sense behind the literal nonsense of a metaphor than like getting at the literal sense of a sentence.

It may be wondered why I refer to these second-order rules as 'conventions'. I have two reasons for doing this. First, it is in a sense arbitrary whether they apply or not. A picture which is non-committal with respect to F might have been committal with respect to F. This being so, the solution to the communicational co-ordination problems requires that there should be mutual or common knowledge between maker and beholder regarding just what second-order rule is in force. The difference between the pictorial case and the linguistic case consists in how the interpreter knows the relevant convention. In the case of the vocabulary, one must know the convention governing the meaning of the parts before interpretation can even get under way. Knowledge of the relevant conventions is necessary for the generation of an interpretation and sufficient as well. Pictures are different. Pictorial interpretation gets under way thanks to the fact that the picture manages to engage the right recognitional ability. One is entitled (*a priori*) to infer, as the best explanation of the success of one's naturally generated interpretation, that Convention C applies. Common sense and Gricean rules of conversational co-operation serve to engender the rules which constrain the selective application of Convention C. What these rules are is not known – or does not usually need to be known – beforehand. Knowledge of the relevant conventions is not necessary for interpretation to get under way, nor is it sufficient to enable the interpreter to generate the correct interpretation.

It is worth placing stress on this last point: for a linguistic system, if you know the conventions which govern the meaning of the parts and the way they are to be composed, you have sufficient credentials for interpreting the sentence's meaning. Not so in the case of the conventions relevant to pictorial interpretation. Knowledge of these would not enable you to concoct a *pictorial* interpretation in the first place – only recognitional ability can do that.

So after a deeper look at the problem of pictorial commitment, it turns out that the phenomenon of selective commitment does not at all support Gombrich's language analogy, nor does it undermine the theory of natural generativity. A deeper understanding of selective commitment requires us to abandon that analogy and look afresh at the distinctive features of pictorial representations. It turns out that our ability to distinguish the features which a picture is committed to representing is akin to our ability to detect irony, metaphor and other figures of speech and not to our ability to project interpretations of novel sentences on the basis of prearranged conventions regarding the sense of lexical items and truth-relevant modes of sentential composition. Indeed, because the second-order instructions for constraining the application of Convention C are not prearranged, but contextually generated, it is perhaps misleading to call them 'conventions' at all.

Thus far, I have treated selective commitment as a matter affecting pictorial content rather than pictorial implicature (what is 'conversationally' implied by certain forms of depiction). It is a mark of the difference between pictorial systems and linguistic systems that it should, apparently, make so little difference whether we treat 'selective commitment' as a 'semantic' or as a 'pragmatic' matter. In the end, no point of substance would be affected if we were to say that while a black-and-white photograph of Marlene Dietrich does in fact depict her (inter alia) as being black and white and certain shades in between, we do not as it happens pay any attention to this semantic 'noise'; using common sense, we filter out the noise and heed only the obviously intended or accented bits of the picture. On this view Dennett would still not be quite right in his views about pictorial commitment, since on this 'pragmatic' view of selective commitment either Convention C applies to all the potentially iconifying features of the picture or it applies to none of them; hence, all the content it is possible to 'naturally generate' properly belongs to the pictorial content of a picture to which C applies. This is not equivalent (though it is close) to Dennett's view that if S depicts O, then for every potential visual feature of O, either S is committal about F or S is explicitly non-committal about F (that is, O is depicted as having some G which makes it impossible to tell whether or not it has F). For example, the stick-figure drawing is not explicitly non-committal about the figure's clothes, but there is no tendency or possibility for us to generate naturally a misleading ascription of some clothes-excluding feature to the pictorial content of the stick-drawing. Hence, the stick-drawing is *semantically* (but inexplicitly) non-committal about the figure's clothes – and that is something Dennett's view would not allow to be possible.

5 CARICATURE

It is important to distinguish 'selective commitment' from 'caricature' (this distinction is important regardless of whether we treat selective commitment as a semantic matter or as a pragmatic nuance). There is a resemblance up to a point, but an important difference thereafter. Caricature is fully analogous to figures of speech – especially hyperbolic speech – while selective commitment is, fittingly, only partially analogous to figurative speech. Selective commitment is simply a matter of 'filtration' – of 'subtracting' the noise from the message. The remainder is pictorial content (or the 'intended' part of that content). There is no need to 'add' anything to get the point. Natural generativity does it all (in fact it does too much). Not so with caricature. Again, of course, one has to distinguish the parts of a caricature which are to be taken as committed to 'telling the truth' from those which are to be taken with a grain of salt. Naturally, these features will not necessarily be spatially decomposable, but we won't go into that again. Cruikshank's depictions of the Prince Regent are not realistic; they are caricatures. They are not, however, wholly caricatural: they obviously ascribe to him properties he has, otherwise they would not be recognisable; however, they 'exaggerate' these properties. This works because, of course, the false can imply the true. Thus, Cruikshank gives the Prince an enormous paunch and an enormous – almost steatopygous – rear end. By depicting the Prince as monstrous, he depicts him as fat. The former attribute he perhaps lacks, the latter he perhaps enjoys. Cruikshank depicts the Prince as having dimensions he does not actually have. He is not trying to deceive us; he perhaps knows it is common knowledge that no one could quite be as awful-looking as his caricature of the Prince. Well then, assuming he treats his Regency audience as neither complete fools nor thorough knaves, he must be 'getting' at something else. And of course he is: his literally false depiction 'conversationally' insinuates various attitudes towards the Prince. Pictorial metaphor, puns and irony work in a similar way. The famous drawing of Louis-Philippe depicts the King as having a pear-shaped head – indeed, it depicts him as having pearish properties in excess of those he actually had. First, it is caricature. It exaggerates his properties, but with no intent to deceive. Secondly, it is metaphor: we are invited to see the King as a pear – which literally, of course, he cannot be. But finally, it is of course a pun since 'poire' is a French commonplace for a 'fathead'. (Indeed, depicting Louis as having literally a fat head is enough to suggest that he is, figuratively, a fathead – a case of a pictorial metaphor that may be literally true.)

Caricature (along with its attendant pictorial tropes) is to be distinguished from 'selective commitment' in two respects. First, the caricaturist is clearly *committing* himself to the depiction of some properties he knows that we all know his subject doesn't have. So he is clearly committal about some properties which it is common knowledge his subject has not got. Secondly, the point of caricature goes beyond 'iconic content'. The information which serves as the basis for the naturally generated interpretation of a picture – however selectively committal – is insufficient for getting the caricaturist's point. His point is usually both 'cognitive' and 'conative'. He wants to state a fact – perhaps a fact which it is not very easy or even possible to depict, such as that the Prince Regent is a sot or that Louis-Philippe is a dolt. But naturally, his attitude is also conveyed ('poire' is hardly a neutral way of indicating someone's IQ).

Where, then, is the similarity between our ability to discriminate the commitments of a picture and our ability to detect caricature? It is just this: the information that we use (tacitly or otherwise) to detect tropical intent is the sort of information which we use when we constrain or suppress certain content ascriptions. In both cases, we utilise common knowledge of just what facts about the world are common knowledge and we make use of the assumption that the image-maker or image-user is abiding by the maxims of co-operativeness which all communication presupposes. In each case, a 'naive' interpretation is negatived because it rubs against common knowledge and the presumption of co-operativeness. In one case, we filter out the non-committed features of the depiction; in the other case, we allow that the depiction is committed to some falsehood, indeed a blazingly obvious falsehood, but we still assume that the image-maker was innocent of deceit. That is why we cast about for some implicit message.

Sometimes the 'medium' is the message. When it is, the interpretation is still reached by Gricean steps. When the 'medium' is the message, the main point of the picture is to draw attention to itself. How the painting depicts the object is more to the point than what the painting ascribes to the object, though there is no suggestion that we can easily separate these matters. Indeed, it is precisely because of the way in which a picture depicts its content that we are given the clue that the main point is not the picture's content but rather how that content is depicted – the way it has been done, the composition, the colour pigments used, the brush strokes. Let's take a Cézanne still life. We can assume that we are all acquainted with the genre of still life. We are all acquainted with how an apple looks. What then is the point of painting an apple? Precisely because the content of the picture is so commonplace, we are led to suppose that it cannot be the point of the work to communicate this content to us. To make this assumption would be to suppose that Cézanne was breaking the part of the conversational code which commands that the conversationalist should be maximally informative. If Cézanne were merely trying to be informative, his work would be meagre and ridiculous indeed. But he is not trying to be informative. He is not trying to tell us something about how apples look. He is trying to tell us something about how it is possible to depict them. He is saying 'Look, it is possible to depict them as spherical volumes, and to compose the whole set of objects in such a way as to deny the viewer entrance into the space of the picture, by raking the table and its contents up at an angle acute to the picture plane.'[25] Getting the point of Cézanne's painting requires us to see it as making a point about how still-life depiction is done and can be done.

But of course to see the way the apples are depicted is precisely to see them as depicted in a certain way – so one cannot effect a neat divorce between 'form' and 'content'. Indeed, the whole point is that we are asked to notice how it is possible to get a certain content put across. Aesthetically, what impressionism accomplishes – and perhaps pointillism even more – is a demonstration that it is possible to put the world across with (or as) a few patches or points of colour. Likewise, much of the joy of Chinese pen drawings consists precisely in noting how a scene can be evoked by just a few choice lines. We could be interested in just the semantic content of these pictures – though we couldn't be aware of that content without in some sense being aware of the pictorial vehicle itself. But we could be aware of that content without noticing certain aesthetic features of the pictorial vehicle – and this would doubtless be an impoverishment of our experience. We could also be aware, I suppose, of the material configuration of ink on paper without being aware of what

[25] For this view of Cézanne's objectives see E. Loran, *Cézanne's Composition*, Berkeley, 1943.

it depicted – though that would require a peculiar perceptual deficit. But such separations are without a doubt artificial and beside the point even when they are possible. For very often the whole point of a painting is to show that a scene can be depicted in a certain way, by a certain means, using a certain style of line or a certain repertoire of brush strokes. No doubt it is then possible for the initiate to carry the process on to a further, dandified, stage in which he sees nature as brush strokes, or cubistically or as a composition in grey or blue. But when the stylisation of nature is carried to this aesthetic pitch, the picture says not only 'Look how apples can be depicted' but 'Look how they can be seen as though they are a Cézanne still life.' Does the distinction between 'medium' and 'message' then break down? Not really, for the latter invitation is parasitic on the former since the whole point of the Whistlerian gambit is that it is possible to see nature as it has been depicted.

Realism has two dimensions. One dimension concerns truth. A depiction is iconically realistic$_1$ when its subject has all the properties it is depicted as having. Thus, caricature is not realistic$_1$ because the subject lacks some of the properties which the picture depicts him as having. Such caricature may, however, enjoy another kind of realism lacking in a spare but veridical drawing. This other sort of realism has to do with commitment. We may suggest the following as a definition of one dimension of realism (realism$_2$) with respect to F:

> S is realistic$_2$ with respect to a feature F when S depicts O, F is a potential visually recognisable feature of O, and S either depicts O as F, depicts O as lacking F (by depicting O as having some G incompatible with O's having F) *or* S depicts O as having some property H which makes it impossible to tell whether O is F or not.

It is obviously possible to be realistic$_2$ and false. Realism$_2$ involves 'maximal commitment'. The only kind of non-committalness permitted is explicit non-commitment. Thus, it can be seen that Dennett's definition or characterisation of an image was really the schema for a definition of iconic realism$_2$. His mistake was to assume that iconic representation needs to be realistic$_2$ (for every potential feature F of the depicted O).[26]

This definition of 'realism$_2$' will help to make it clear how it is

---

[26] As David Wiggins has pointed out, a definition of realism$_2$ simpliciter as distinct from realism$_2$-with-respect-to-F will require quantifying over features: S_1 is more realistic$_2$ than S_2 if it is realistic with respect to *more features* than S_2.

possible realistically to depict non-existent, imaginary or even impossible objects. The problem, of course, needs to be divided into two parts: (a) how is it possible to depict imaginary or impossible objects? and (b) how is it possible to depict them realistically? We have already tried to answer the first question. In a sense one cannot really depict non-existent objects any more than one can talk about them. One can, however, pretend to do so. One make-believedly depicts some fictional character when one creates a depiction of an F-type person – which could be true of any F-type person – but then pretends that in fact the picture is about some particular person. Thus, one might depict Prince Charming. One's picture is really – literally – a picture of *a* man having certain attributes. It is true just if there is a man having those attributes. There is no particular man who stands in a particular causal relation to that picture. However, one can pretend that the picture is about a particular man, say Prince Charming; one can pretend that there is a given man, Hercules, depicted by a series of statues telling the story of his labours. But this is just make-believe. The artist knows there is no Prince Charming, and he knows that we know it and so on. But just the same, we pretend that there is.

So a realistic depiction of a non-existent or imaginary character is really a contradiction in terms. There can't be a depiction, realistic or otherwise, of an imaginary creature. There can be a depiction of an F-type creature and we can pretend that this picture is about some particular F-type creature. A realistic make-believe depiction is simply one which is committal for a fair number of the potential visual features of an F-type creature. It is literally true just if there is someone having the properties ascribed to the man in the picture. Perhaps there is no such man, perhaps there are many such. Never mind. We pretend that there is such a man, and we pretend that this picture is about just one such man. As far as realism$_2$ is concerned, however, what matters is not truth but commitment.

Allow me to mention a puzzle – literally. Imagine that you have a jigsaw puzzle of some well-known painting, say Holbein's *Ambassadors*. Now take the completed puzzle. A series of cracks runs all over the puzzle where the various parts have been linked together. We don't take these cracks to be representationally significant at all – we just 'filter' them out. Likewise with the cracks on a painting by an old master. Of course, sometimes it is not easy to tell whether some feature is representationally significant or merely accidental. This is a different question from the question of selective commitment. Suppose the cracks cover the face of some depicted saint.

Does the picture depict his face as cracked and peeling? Of course not. This is not because the painting is non-committal – it may be obvious that it depicts him as having a flawlessly smooth and creamy complexion. These features of the vehicle are simply representationally irrelevant. Can all cases of selective commitment be understood in terms of the representational irrelevance of certain features of the representational medium?

The answer is 'No'. Take black-and-white photographs. These are non-committal about the colour of the worlds they depict. Does that mean that the black, white and grey properties of the photograph are representationally irrelevant? Of course not! These shades are the very representational stuff of the picture. So we must take care to distinguish features which are representationally irrelevant – the cracks on the face of an egg tempera painting – from those which are representationally relevant but perhaps non-committal in some respects.

9

Resemblance strikes back

1 GOODMAN'S STRICTURES ON SIMILARITY

There is a popular belief that if S – say a drawing by Whistler – depicts a butterfly, then it must necessarily resemble a butterfly, in at least some respects. As Jerry Fodor boldly puts it:

The reference of icons is mediated by similarity.
The reference of symbols is mediated by conventions.[1]

One could quibble with this admirably straightforward statement: surely icons *are* symbols of a sort and surely Fodor has somewhat exaggerated the contrast between icons and symbols whose understanding is mediated by convention. In the last two chapters I have argued at length that the real contrast between (for example) a linguistic symbol system and an iconic one does not consist in the conventional nature of the former and the non-conventional nature of the latter but in the nature of the conventions involved in each.

Nonetheless, what stands out from this passage is Fodor's claim that iconic reference is mediated by resemblance. I scrutinised this claim in chapter 1 and described its shortcomings in lurid detail, the primary one being that there does not appear to be a respect in which S resembles O for each respect in which S iconifies O. Thus, a picture of David Bowie may depict him as smiling without itself smiling or incorporating any smile-like feature. We looked at various attempts to adjust the resemblance model to reckon with this problem, but all of them seemed futile.

The breakdown of the resemblance model creates a paradox. The apparent truth that pictures resemble their depicta is challenged by reasoning which proves the contrary by appealing to equally apparent truths. Moreover, another paradox looms on the horizon regarding the status of pictures. It is evident to common sense that pictures are different from other sorts of symbols; to echo Ernest Hemingway, they *depict* what they represent. This self-evident truth funds, and is in turn reinforced by, the sense that a picture is a

[1] Fodor 1976, p. 178.

likeness of what it represents. If we are forced to see that pictorial representation cannot be mediated by resemblance, this leaves us with no understanding of what the distinctiveness of depiction could consist in. From this vulnerable position we are open to such onslaughts as Nelson Goodman mounts in the notorious opening passages of *Languages of Art*: perhaps the iconic–non-iconic distinction is spurious; and perhaps depictions do not really differ in their nature from certain other symbols which at first sight do not seem to be pictorial at all. Paradox breeds paradox. For lack of our having any clear theory of depiction to counter Goodman's arguments, we must take seriously his suggestion that pictures should be characterised in terms of syntactic density and repleteness, properties they clearly share with symbols which, pre-theoretically, we would not count as pictures.

It is this situation which funds Goodman's idea that he is founding something like a *science* of symbol-systems. Science just does tend to operate by forcing us to discard our old similarity classes and enjoining us to accept new, but counter-intuitive, classifications of the phenomena. From this perspective, those who stick to their intuition that icons just are distinctive and that this distinctiveness must somehow be captured in a way preferable to Goodman's can begin to look like reactionaries standing in the way of a putatively scientific achievement. And perhaps there is a reactionary element in much of the counter-Goodman literature, a tendency to presuppose some Dilthey-like premise, such as that the realm of meaning must be transparent to those who manipulate meaningful symbols, so if we *feel* that there is a deep difference between pictures and other sorts of symbols which Goodman would have us classify with pictures, well, we just *must* be right: there *must* be something to underwrite our sense that pictures are distinctive in a way Goodman refuses to capture.

Certainly many of the pro-resemblance arguments in the literature are of a weakness. Francis Sparshott, for example, replies to Goodman in a way that suggests he has not quite understood the real challenge to the resemblance model. Sparshott takes Goodman to be claiming that just because we can't define that resemblance which obtains between picture and depictum we should assume that there is no resemblance there.[2] If that is Goodman's argument, then he has certainly committed the so-called Socratic Fallacy of supposing that what we can't define can't be real. But this is not the real objection

[2] Sparshott 1982, p. 532.

to the resemblance model; the objection is rather that there just does not appear to be any evidence that there is a respect in which S resembles O for each respect in which S iconifies O. It is not just that we cannot define the resemblance; it is rather that when we reflect upon the matter, there appears to be no resemblance at all. So in fact intuition is far from being all on the side of the resemblance model; on the contrary, intuitions with a very strong claim on our attention suggest that the resemblance model can't be right. It is in the face of these conflicting intuitions, of this paradox if you like, that Goodman advances his proposals. If our intuitions about pictures cannot be reconciled, then so much the worse for those intuitions. Let us turn to building a genuinely explanatory theory of symbol systems instead. To be sure, that theory may entail our abandoning certain favoured classifications of symbols, but that cost is greatly outweighed by the coherence and explanatory power of our new theory.

How does this controversy look from the perspective of the theory of depiction which I have articulated in this book? At first blush it would appear that we can stand above this mêlée and see the merits and demerits of each side. Fodor and Sparshott are right in thinking there is a difference between iconic symbols *per se* and other sorts of symbols; they are probably wrong in supposing that this difference can be captured by the resemblance model. Goodman and his epigones are right to reject the claims of the resemblance model, but wrong to suppose that it is impossible to draw a theoretically significant contrast between iconic symbols and symbols of other sorts. The theory of natural generativity provides the necessary account of the distinction between iconic and non-iconic symbols, but it does not rely upon intuitions about resemblance in doing so. Consequently, from the perspective of the theory of natural generativity, the old combat between proponents and opponents of resemblance looks insignificant and faintly absurd. There are rights and wrongs on each side of the case, but neither side can ever claim victory.

But this position is not ultimately satisfactory, for it still leaves us with the first paradox: that there is a conflict between the common saw that pictures resemble their depicta and the equally apparent fact that there is by no means a respect in which S resembles O for every respect in which S depicts O. Of course, if the theoretical situation is as I have described it, then this paradox no longer really matters to the theory of depiction. It has at most a psychological significance. Just as we tend to see a configuration of marks as both duck and rabbit, so we both think that pictures resemble their depicta and realise that they can't do so; just as vision cannot reach a stable equilibrium in the first case, so intuition cannot reach a stable conclusion in the latter. But this doesn't matter: reason, in the form of an explanatory theory, has sorted things out for us.

Nonetheless, I believe the theory of natural generativity does in fact have something to say about this controversy. I want to argue that there is a sense in which pictures *do* resemble their depicta which is quite immune to the usual objections. Goodman is therefore wrong on both counts: wrong in classifying pictures with other syntactically dense and replete phenomena without regard for their peculiarity as icons and also wrong in holding that there is no clear sense in which there is a respect in which S resembles O for every respect in which S depicts O. In this dispute at least, the palm of victory can be awarded to the resemblance theory.

Let us return to Fodor's claim that 'The reference of icons is mediated by resemblance.' Arguments about the resemblance theory tend to be more drag out than knock down, but the one thing everyone will agree to is that resemblance between two things is not enough to get iconic representation going between them. Birds of a feather do not necessarily depict each other. And while resemblance is a symmetrical relation, depiction is usually asymmetrical: if X resembles Y, Y resembles X; but if S depicts O, O rarely depicts S! These points are all made by Goodman, but they establish at most that resemblance is not a sufficient condition of pictoricity: and whoever thought otherwise?

It might be thought that we could introduce the necessary asymmetry by abandoning the oversimple dichotomy suggested in the passage from Fodor. We need to wheel in communicative intentions. Thus, a picture of Churchill not only resembles Churchill; it somehow manifests its intention to resemble him. Churchill doesn't (usually?) intend to resemble his picture, but his picture is intended to resemble him. So now we have the necessary asymmetry. Of course, not everything which is intended to resemble Churchill will depict him: it must be intended that this intention (that S should resemble Churchill) should be recoverable.

Now, in fact we know that the addition of these curlicues to the resemblance model makes it more ornamental without making it a whit more functional. In chapter 1 we encountered two counter-examples to the resemblance-cum-communicative-intention model of depiction. We there imagined a child who intends his red block to be taken as representing a fire engine in virtue of its resembling that engine in point of colour and we inspected with the mind's eye a sample of Bauhaus print which was manifestly intended to stand for the Bauhaus print in virtue of its being an instance of it. Neither item is a picture of anything, yet each item satisfied the conditions of the revised resemblance model: each item resembles what it represents, the resemblance is intentional and it is intended that this intention should be appreciated.

We can reinforce this point by exploring yet another argument of Goodman's. Goodman has pointed out that paintings resemble other paintings more than they resemble what they depict.[3] While it is all very hard-nosed and literal-minded of Goodman to point this out it can't be denied that he is right. Goodman uses this point to get us thinking seriously about the notion of resemblance so that we appreciate what is involved in claiming that a picture resembles what it depicts. We begin to see that if a picture does resemble what it depicts, this resemblance cannot be of the same kind as the resemblance which obtains between one picture and another.

Now, *at a minimum*, Goodman's point establishes that icons do not iconify whatever they resemble. The primitive resemblance theory of iconic reference is doomed, since on that theory it would follow, given Goodman's axiom, that all icons were icons of each other. But perhaps by wheeling in communicative intentions we have at least staved off this grotesque conclusion. A painting of Mary isn't an icon of other paintings of Mary – however much it may resemble them – unless it is intended to be.

This rather smug reply to Goodman invites the obvious question 'What if the painting had been intended to represent the other pictures of Mary (as well as Mary)? Would it then necessarily follow that it was a depiction of those paintings?' Nothing of the sort follows at all. Perhaps the painting merely exemplifies (in Goodman's sense[4]) the Marian cycle of paintings or maybe it does include a depiction of one or more of the other Marian paintings, but thus far the analysis can't distinguish between these two situations.

Imagine a group of very hermetic artists who wish to live by – or perhaps send up – Leo Steinberg's famous *mot* that all art is about art. They set up a convention among themselves that some of their pictorial products shall represent certain of their other pictorial concoctions in virtue of certain similarities which they regard as cru-

---

[3] Goodman 1968, p. 5.   [4] *Ibid*., chapter 2, section 3.

cial. It is obvious that the emanations of this cenacle need not be icons of anything, and still less does it follow that they iconify each other.

As we know from our encounter with the resemblance theorist in chapter 1, this line of argument invites the retort that Goodman et alii are simply knocking down straw men. Nobody would put forward the bald statement that a picture resembles its depictum and leave it at that. Some further refinements are necessary. The problem with the pictures in my imaginary cenacle is simply that they do not resemble each other in the right respects. But then we have to call the resemblance theorist's bluff: just what are the respects in which an icon resembles what it iconifies? How can a flat two-dimensional surface manage to resemble the majestic corpulence of a Cyril Smith or an Orson Welles? Yet we know such surfaces to be capable of depicting these gargantuan worthies.

And this is clearly Goodman's challenge. We might call it Goodman's Fork. Either you so dilute the concept of resemblance that there is a sense in which a picture of Cyril Smith resembles Cyril Smith or you stick to a stricter notion of similarity (this stricter notion being suggested by the sense in which other pictures resemble other pictures). But if you dilute the concept it becomes so vague that nothing is explained; no clear sense can any longer be attached to the notion of a resemblance capacious enough to admit of a striking similarity between Cyril Smith and a flat, two-dimensional piece of paper. On the other hand, so long as you stick to the stricter kind of resemblance invoked in Goodman's claim – which we all intuitively accept – that a picture resembles other pictures more than it resembles what it depicts, then it will just turn out to be false that a picture of Cyril Smith resembles him.

Let me now discuss an example of what happens when you weaken the notion of resemblance. It has been suggested that the notion of resemblance we have been using is too crude. For example, Gombrich has suggested that we should abandon the claim that resemblance is symmetrical and that that would allow us to explain the fact that we see a man in a picture of him but we do not see the man as a flat, two-dimensional picture. But this sort of move is obviously open to the question 'In what sense is non-symmetrical resemblance an instance of resemblance? Hasn't Gombrich simply changed the subject?'

Here is another move. David Novitz in his excellent monograph on pictorial communication has suggested that in some sense a picture's resemblance to its depictum is not a hard, convention-independent fact.[5] Instead, picture-depictum resemblances are to some extent the product of convention: we agree to let certain marks on a flat surface resemble features of the world. It is thus perhaps just an accepted convention that the lines which describe Cyril Smith's bulk are said to resemble or be a likeness of his dimensions. Of course, the impressionists were literally correct when they said that there are no lines in nature: but by conventional agreement, we count the lines in a drawing as being equivalent to the contour of the depicted object.

It is immediately apparent that this theory simply fails to give any real role to the notion of resemblance. Of course, it says that we conventionally accept lines as being similar to contours or shapes, but it might as well have said that we simply accept by convention that lines stand for or represent shapes – the notions of a conventionally accepted interpretation of lines will do all the work done by the notion of conventionally determined resemblance classes. We can simply eliminate any reference to resemblance and there will be no loss of explanatory power.

But of course, even with the notion of resemblance left in, there is not much explanatory power in this suggestion. For one wants to ask this theory to explain why we can't just conventionally decide that verbal scratches on a piece of paper resemble what they denote. What constrains the conventional decision to regard something as resembling something else? If there is a constraint, does this constraint take the form of a resemblance which is prior to and suggestive of a convention? If it does, then of course we are left with the problem we started with, that there is no convention-independent resemblance between a picture of Cyril Smith which accounts for the former's depicting the latter. If there is no constraint at all on these conventional decisions, then we need a story that explains why we can't turn just anything into a picture by collective fiat.

If we develop Novitz's suggestion what we end up with is a theory rather like Kendall Walton's (see chapter 1, section 5), according to which pictorial interpretation is a game of visual make-believe in which there are certain conventions determining that our seeing various marks and scratches on a flat surface shall count make-believedly as our seeing the denoted objects. The problem is once again to explain what constrains the application of these rules of visual make-believe. Why can't we turn anything into a pic-

---

[5] Novitz 1977, p. 36: 'It is only because we have learned what role pictures play or can be made to play in our lives, that we find it natural to assert a resemblance between a picture and what it is of.'

ture? Moreover, as we saw, on Walton's account pictorial interpretation is very much like the interpretation of novel sentences; Walton
thus manages to miss what I regard as the crucial feature of pictorial
systems: natural generativity.

As one might then expect, it is rather difficult to see how the view
that the resemblance between picture and depictum is convention-
dependent can explain the natural generativity of pictorial interpretation. If the resemblance of picture and depictum were determined
by convention, even if only to some extent, we should need to learn
which pictorial marks were conventionally accepted as resembling
which features of the world before we could properly interpret
them. But then we should be associating pictorial marks with
object-features in rather the way we associate words with features
of the world. But this way of looking at pictorial interpretation is a
travesty. Moreover, there would be no point in saying that we were
learning conventions about what marks on a flat surface resembled
what features of the world; you might as well say that we were
learning conventions about what the marks on a flat surface represented.

2 RESEMBLANCE VINDICATED

So, heroic efforts notwithstanding, the prospects for the resemblance model look as bleak as they did in chapter 1. And yet no one
is inclined to doubt that *some* pictorial representation is supervenient
on resemblance. It is a fact adequately attested by our discussion of
colour-reversal that S can iconify O as having a certain colour C
only if S resembles O in point of its being C. It is true that we might
wish to be a bit less vague here: what degree of resemblance in point
of colour is required? Must a picture of a green apple instantiate the
depicted shade of green or just some shade of green sufficiently like
the depicted shade? What is it that establishes whether a degree of
likeness is great enough for purposes of iconification? It would seem
that even when we can confidently say that some pictorial aspect of
S is connected with resemblance, there is still a certain *vagueness* in
this notion of resemblance.

I want to claim that the theory of natural generativity can solve
the fundamental problems of the resemblance theory: it tells us what
kind of resemblance between S and O is required for S's depicting O
and it gives us some idea of the 'amount' of resemblance required
(or rather, it gives us a criterion for telling whether the resemblance
is sufficient). The respect in which S resembles its depictum O is

this: there is an overlap between the recognitional abilities triggered by S and O. This overlap is a direct consequence of the theory of natural generativity. My interpretation of S is iconic only if my ability to recognise O has become engaged in my interpretation of S. But that means that S must somehow engage or provoke my O-recognising abilities. To be sure, that is not the whole story: when I interpret S, factors other than my O-recognising abilities are involved and recognitional abilities other than those that would be called up by O are called into play. But of course these are obvious points: there is no doubt that S is *unlike* O when S depicts O – the problem has been to specify the similarities that obtain between S and its depictum. And that is what I claim the theory of natural generativity does.

The true believer in the resemblance model will not be quite satisfied with this concession. He will ask for more. Specifically, he will argue that there must be more to the resemblances between S and O than the mere fact that they trigger some of the same recognitional capacities. After all, what *explains* the fact that S and O trigger similar recognitional capacities? Surely there must be some similarities between S and O that are independent of and prior to the fact that they trigger similar recognitions. How else can these recognitional facts be explained except by citing and independently specifying these deeper similarities?

I am very dubious of this claim. Ultimately it seems to me to presuppose some homuncular theory of the mind. It is as though the resemblance theorist wishes to suggest that at some level the mind notes resemblances between picture and depictum and that it is this prior, primitive fact of a homunculus noticing similarities (which are not apparent to *us*) that explains our recognition that S depicts O. But what could be more obvious than that nothing is explained here at all? I confess that I am not subtle enough even to distinguish the claim that X notices a similarity between S and O from the claim that X recognises O-like features in S. These are so close to being the same fact that I do not see how one can be cited in explanation of the other. To say that some homuncular part of our mental apparatus notices a similarity between S and O is to say that it recognises O-like features in S.

But perhaps I have misconstrued the claim which the resemblance theorist wishes to make. It is not that some homunculus's noticing likenesses between S and O can explain my recognition of O-like features in S: this proposition has only to be understood to be rejected. Rather, the suggestion is: it must simply be a fact that S and O are alike; and we must be able to state the likeness in a way which is independent of the perceiver's recognitional capacities in such a way that these likenesses can be invoked to explain the perceiver's recognitional propensities. Once this project is carried out, we will see likeness as the deep fact in pictorial representation, natural generativity being simply the consequence of this deep fact.

Of course, it is not imperative that I commit myself on this issue one way or another, nor have I any decisive reason for rejecting the resemblance theorist's claim. What I do put forward is a doubt: I doubt that it will prove possible to give a simple, general account of the similarity between picture and depictum that does not essentially invoke the fact that S and O trigger some of the same recognitional abilities. Occasionally we may find independently specifiable similarities – such as colour – upon which recognitional similarities supervene, but this does not mean that recognitional similarities can always be reduced to or eliminated in favour of any deeper similarities. Let us suppose that for each case where there is an overlap in the recognitional abilities provoked by S and O we can eventually find other similarities which can be specified independently and which appear to co-vary with the recognitional similarities. My question is this: will we be able to say what all these separate cases have in common in virtue of which recognitional similarity supervenes upon them? Or will we simply end up with a disjunctive list: if S and O trigger similar recognitional responses, then they have this in common, or that in common, or ... etc.? The point becomes even more pressing when you ask whether a general account of iconicity – as distinct from simple pictoricity – could be given in any other terms as powerful and general as those we have provided. If not, then it would seem unlikely that we will ever be able to say what icons in general have in common with the objects they iconify other than simply the fact that there is an overlap in the recognitional abilities triggered by icon and iconified.

3 ILLUSION AND THE COGNITIVE THEORY OF PICTORIAL PERCEPTION

It must be kept in mind that S's triggering X's O-recognising ability is by no means equivalent to X's recognising O in S. When one says that X recognises a bit of Jane in John, that means that X is conscious of some properties that Jane and John have in common. But I have been at pains to argue that we need not be conscious of any specifiable properties which picture and depictum have in common.

Nonetheless, they *do* have properties in common: they provoke similar recognitional abilities. But the claim that my ability to recognise O comes into play in my interpreting S is not an introspectively verifiable claim. I do not *notice* the play of my recognitional capacities: I simply infer to their activity as part of a satisfactory theory of iconic interpretation. The main prop of this theory is the fact (argued for in chapter 5) that pictorial competence and recognitional competence co-vary. From this co-variation we have inferred a causal connection: recognitional abilities issue in pictorial competence.

The upshot is that the theory of natural generativity provides a reasonably precise account of the similarity that obtains between picture and depictum. It is not required that a picture should look like its subject in any introspectibly noticeable way. Moreover, what it is like to see S *need* not be phenomenologically similar to what it is like to see O. We are relieved therefore of the need to say in what precise degree a picture must 'look like' its depictum: it need not look like its subject at all. S and its depictum O are alike to the extent that they trigger or bring into play some of the same recognitional capacities; it is obviously not necessary to put any number on the capacities in the overlap set (the set of capacities engaged by S and O). We can say that S is similar enough to O if it is possible for someone to generate naturally an interpretation of S as being of O.

It has been a source of irritation to the resemblance theorist that sometimes resemblance, so far from promoting iconicity, interferes with it. In chapter 7 we noted of a pear decoy that the more it looks like a pear, the less the chance that it will be taken to represent one. However, if you sculpt the pear in bronze, there will be no question of mistaking it for a pear: the spectator will naturally feel inclined to take it for a pear representation. So dissimilarity is as crucial to natural generativity as similarity.

This obvious fact raises a question. Let S depict O and let X be a decoy for O. S, O and X all trigger O-recognising abilities; but in the case of S these abilities are, as it were, channelled into an interpretation of S as being of O rather than into an act of recognising S as O. What happens? Obviously my O-recognising abilities are somehow damped or checked in the case of S by other cues. S somehow signals the fact that it is not O but a symbol of O. How exactly are we to understand this process? It is here that the illusion theory will serve our turn if we spell it out carefully.

As we saw in chapter 1, the crude claim that S depicts O just if S represents O and one's seeing S gives one an illusion as of seeing O is quite ludicrous. But we did not discuss there the most obvious defect of such an account: that it provides no account of how pictorial interpretation is possible; the illusion theory entailing, indeed, that pictorial interpretation is impossible. If the proposed account of pictorial interpretation is that one pictorially interprets S when S induces an illusion as of one's seeing O, it is obvious that the theory is incoherent. For if one is to interpret S as being of O one must know that S represents O, but it is impossible to know that S represents O, or indeed that S is a representation at all, while being at the same time under the illusion that S *is* O. Consequently the illusion theory can offer no account of how pictorial interpretation is possible.

Perhaps I have been too quick to suppose that the illusion undergone in the experience of a picture involves false belief. Perhaps a picture simply gives one an experience exactly as of seeing its depictum, though one knows the experience is not veridical. But then if one knows that one is not seeing a real discobolus before one, the experience can hardly be much like one's seeing a real discus-thrower.

Nor has Sir Ernst Gombrich helped matters much by introducing the suggestion that we should understand the relation of a picture to its subject on the analogy of the relation between our seeing the duck-drawing and seeing the rabbit-drawing in the famous duck-rabbit drawing. In chapter 1 I dubbed this the alternating illusion theory, the idea being that just as one's perception of the duck-rabbit figure alternates between seeing a duck-drawing and seeing a rabbit-drawing, so one's perception of a picture of the Grand Canal alternates between seeing blobs of paint and seeing the Grand Canal.

In the first chapter I followed Richard Wollheim in arguing that Gombrich's account cannot do justice to the aesthetic value of pictorial experience, meaning by this not that Gombrich's account is to be faulted for not illuminating the value of pictorial experience but rather that it is impossible to see how, on Gombrich's view, the experience of seeing a picture of O could have any other aesthetic value than that attaching to the experience of simply seeing O. Now I want to argue that Gombrich's duck-rabbit analogy also fails to make it clear how pictorial interpretation is possible at all.

Suppose Gombrich were right that when we see a picture of a peach our experience alternates between seeing a flat, painted surface and seeing a peach in rather the way that our experience of the duck-rabbit figure alternates between seeing a rabbit-picture and seeing a duck-picture. First you see a flat surface and then you see a peach (or vice versa). You never see S simultaneously as peach and flat surface. How then do you reach the conclusion that S depicts O? Now, it is a fact that in looking at the duck-rabbit figure one does not conclude that the duck-drawing represents or depicts the rabbit-drawing or vice versa. Why, then, should anyone confronted by the alternating experience as postulated by Gombrich conclude that the flat surface represents a peach? If the inference is not drawn in the duck-rabbit case, why is it drawn when a perception as of a peach alternates with a perception as of a flat surface? Gombrich appears to lack an account of pictorial interpretation.

To be sure, the main problem with the alternating illusion account is simply that the experience of looking at a picture of a peach does not resemble the experience of looking at the duck-rabbit figure. Gombrich's account is simply not true to our experience of depiction. First, the 'duck' and 'rabbit' interpretations of the duck-rabbit drawing are equally good and non-contradictory interpretations of the same mark. The compatibility of these two interpretations is camouflaged if we speak of seeing the mark as a duck or a rabbit: obviously something can't be at once a duck and a rabbit, so these two interpretations are incompatible. However, there is nothing contradictory in a figure's being at once a duck-picture and a rabbit-picture. But there obviously is an incompatibility between S's being at once a peach and a flat surface. So the duck-rabbit analogy only seems to work because it begs the question by failing to note the difference between seeing the figure as a duck-drawing and seeing it as a duck.

Secondly, while the 'duck-picture' and 'rabbit-picture' interpretations of the duck-rabbit figure are logically compatible, they are visually incompatible: it is impossible to see the figure as being simultaneously a duck-drawing and a rabbit-drawing. If Wollheim is right, pictorial experience is just the reverse of this: while it is logically incompatible to claim that S is both a piece of painted canvas and a human being, it is possible to see S as being both a piece of canvas and a human being. If Wollheim were right, the duck-rabbit figure would be a kind of reverse image of pictorial experience.

It is evident, I think, that the alternating illusion view of pictorial experience is not one we can go very far with. But I want to argue that we can restate Gombrich's view without our having to rely on the dubious analogy with the duck-rabbit figure in quite the form in which we have been discussing it. I want to suggest that Gombrich's point is *not* (or need not be) that our experience of a picture of a peach involves an alternation between a perception of a flat surface and a perception as of a peach. Instead, Gombrich's idea is probably that just as our seeing the duck-rabbit figure involves our consciously entertaining two distinct hypotheses about the figure – that it is a rabbit-drawing and that it is a duck-drawing – so our interpreting a picture S as being of O involves our unconsciously entertaining the hypothesis that S is O and the hypothesis that S is a flat, painted surface, and so on. The rivalry between the 'duck-drawing' and the 'rabbit-drawing' interpretations of the visual evidence is inconclusive; the 'rabbit' and 'duck' interpretations seem to be equally good. However, when we see S as a picture of a peach, while we unconsciously process evidence for S's being a peach, in the end the 'peach' hypothesis loses out and we conclude that S is *really* a flat surface. The fact that we are inclined to entertain (albeit unconsciously) the 'peach' hypothesis, while it does not result in our having an illusion as of a peach, does result in our taking S to represent a peach.

So on this view, when S depicts a peach, the visual system processes cues from S, some of the cues being evidence for the presence of a round, ripe peach, and some of the cues intimating the presence of a flat, rectangular piece of painted canvas. For some reason the visual system prefers the evidence of S's being a flat, rectangular object to the evidence of its being a round peach. Nonetheless, the fact that one's visual system entertained the peach hypothesis affects one's perception of S: one sees S as a picture of a peach. So the difference between the duck-rabbit and picture-peach cases is this: in the duck-rabbit case *you* consciously entertain two different but equally good interpretations of the figure and (since the interpretations are compatible and equally good) you alternate between seeing a duck-drawing and seeing a rabbit-drawing; in the picture-peach case your visual system (or your visual homunculus if you like) entertains the conflicting 'peach' and 'flat' hypotheses; they are incompatible, so it must reach a verdict and it decides that the 'flat' hypotheses is the better grounded; the result is that you see a flat picture of a peach.

Obviously this account is not going to be uncontroversial. No doubt the feature which will attract the most scepticism is the mentalistic talk about one's visual system's 'entertaining hypotheses' and 'deciding' between them on the basis of 'evidence'. We are willy-nilly involved in just the kind of homuncular talk about which I have just been so rude in my discussion of the resemblance model.

The usual objection to the homuncular model is that it explains nothing; this charge can be based on two distinct grounds. The first reason, and perhaps the weaker, is simply that the homuncular hypothesis is not empirically sound since it postulates a process which is accessible neither to third-person observation nor to first-person introspection. By hypothesis, we are not aware of our having entertained for one moment the hypothesis that S is a peach (where S depicts a peach), so by what right are we told that this is in fact what we have done? The response to this charge is simply that it presupposes, falsely, that explanatory theories simply correlate observable events. But so long as a theory has empirically testable consequences, it is empirically kosher – even if the theory postulates unobserved explanantia.

The second objection to homuncular or mentalistic talk is simply that it fails to explain precisely what we want to explain. You do not explain *our* seeing a peach by postulating a little man who sees a peach image. But of course, no one would put forward a homuncular explanation of that degree of crudeness. Gombrich's account of pictorial perception does not explain our perceiving S as a picture of a peach by postulating a little man who perceives S as a picture of a peach. Instead, he claims to explain *our* seeing a picture of a peach by postulating a little man who processes various visual cues, rejecting some and accepting others. It isn't really necessary to suppose that this little man himself has visual experience: it is only necessary to suppose that he is a mechanism which tracks certain visual cues (input from the eyes) and who processes these cues using a certain 'programme'. Of course, how a mechanism with this programme may have evolved is another question, though one which must eventually be answered. Nonetheless, it is not at all obvious to me that Gombrich's account can be faulted for being vacuous. No doubt it contravenes the empiricist assumption that intelligence begins with experience, a homuncular or mentalist account suggesting instead that experience is a product or 'output' of intelligent activity. But what of that? A theory cannot be dismissed simply on account of its treading on the empiricist's corns.

Of course, at this point the debate begins to assume dimensions far beyond the scope of this book: we would have to look at the whole issue of the possibility of a cognitive theory of perception and we would have to engage with a whole web of issues concerning the 'top-down' and 'bottom-up' strategies in cognitive 'science', the question of innate programmes and so on. Suffice it to say that it is not obvious that homunculi have lost the day, so it is not clear that we must reject my revised version of Gombrich's illusionism.[6]

If Gombrich's account were correct, we could give a quasi-homuncular explanation of the difference between our seeing S as being a picture of O, our seeing O and our seeing some simulacrum of O(X). When we see S, our O-recognising abilities are engaged; this means that the visual system is entertaining the hypothesis that S is O. However, the visual system also finds itself entertaining cues which conflict with the O-hypothesis. When we see S as a picture of O, the little man has decided that the O-evidence is too weak to sustain the O-hypothesis. When, however, we see something as O – either O or X – that is because the visual system has found enough evidence to sustain the O-hypothesis.

It is not obvious that this homuncular explanation of the phenomena must be the right one, but it certainly looks appealing from the perspective of the theory of natural generativity. Indeed, in so far as I claim as part of my account of depiction that my O-recognising abilities are engaged by a picture of O, it is not obvious that I can avoid homuncular talk. For what does it mean to say that my O-recognising capacities have been triggered by S even though I do not take myself to be recognising S as O? Surely the 'cash value' of this claim must be equivalent to the claim that S induces me to entertain (albeit unconsciously) the O-hypothesis with respect to S.

It might seem surprising that a conceptual analysis of depiction should lead us into such murky waters. How could an analysis of depiction imply a quasi-homuncular or cognitive theory of perception? Let us review the reasoning that has brought us to this position. In chapter 3 I pointed out some interesting parallels between the causal theory of action and the natural generativity theory of pictures. The causal theory of action claims (I believe plausibly) that an act is a bodily movement which has been caused in the appropriate way by the agent's beliefs and desires. Likewise, I argued in chapter 3 that an interpretation of S is iconic or pictorial just when that interpretation has been caused (in the appropriate way) by the interpreter's ability to recognise the object which S represents. We have also noticed parallels between the causal theory of perception and the causal theory of iconic reference; a percept is about a particular object if it tracks that object, so that the percept would have been otherwise had the object been otherwise (obviously this needs refinement). Likewise, a depiction S of O tracks O in the sense that there are some features of O such that had they been otherwise, S

[6] For intimations of homunculi see Dennett 1978.

would have been otherwise. Moreover, the function of a given percept is to track an object; of course the percept itself is not designed to track its object, but it is the product of a visual system that has the evolutionary function of producing percepts which track certain features of the environment. This is analogous to a camera. The mechanism has been designed to produce symbols (photographs) that track the properties of the objects which cause or trigger the production of the photographs. A photograph is of O because there are features of O such that had these features been different, that photograph would have been different. Finally, an icon not only tracks what it represents, but iconically tracks what it represents. In other words, an icon is something the function of which is to be such that the ability to recognise the object which the icon tracks should yield the ability to determine that it is *that* object and not some other which the icon tracks. Of course, an icon will serve this particular function only if the function is made manifest. It will not be made manifest if the symbol is too much like what it symbolises, or too prone to induce an illusion as of seeing what it symbolises. So the interpreter must cotton on to the fact that S is a symbol. A picture S of O must both trigger O-recognising abilities *and* give off cues as of being something other than O. S must provoke contrary recognitional abilities.

It should be clear that the theory of natural generativity is soaked in causation. Essential to that theory are two causal claims: that an interpretation of S as being of O is iconic or pictorial in so far as it has been prompted by the interpreter's O-recognising abilities and that a picture of O is precisely something which can trigger the interpreter's O-recognising abilities. Iconic interpretation and iconicity are thus functionally defined. However, I have stressed that S's engaging my O-recognising abilities does not entail my recognising O in S or my being conscious that my O-recognising abilities have become engaged. Typically, all I am conscious of is that I am seeing a picture of O. Consequently, our causal or functional analysis of depiction seems to force upon us the conclusion that our pictorial experience is the result of prior cognitive 'processing'; and this conclusion is equivalent to the homuncularist hypothesis that there are sub-personal centres of cognitive activity in the visual system. If I am right, the analysis of depiction properly understood forces us to accept some computational or cognitive theory of mental activity. Pleasant or unpleasant, this conclusion is certainly a surprise.[7]

---

[7] My general observations here agree with the so-called 'ecological' theory of pictorial competence. See Deregowski 1980.

10

Seeing through pictures

I PICTORIAL EXPERIENCE: THE PROBLEM

It is strange, perhaps even disconcerting, to find that we have got this far in the unfolding of our story without so much as alluding to the nature of our *experience* of pictures. Now I want to broach this important topic, but more as a matter of philosophical psychology than aesthetics. To be sure, there are fascinating questions about the value of pictorial experience, but I am here concerned with a different matter. Just what do we have to add to my experience of S as a medley of colours in order to make it true that I see S as a picture of some object? In other words, what makes it true that I see S as a picture of O?

Someone may well wonder why I feel obliged to bring up a new issue at this late hour. Surely my argument is complete: I have said what pictures are by saying how we go about interpreting them. For my purposes we don't require an account of pictorial experience, however nice it would be to possess one. Indeed, surely the question 'What is it for me to see S as a picture?' is just a substitution instance of a quite general question in the philosophy of perception: 'What is it to see O as F?' In general, there is a difference between seeing (say) a rabbit and seeing something *as* a rabbit. But is there a need for a *special* account of pictorial seeing-as?

Perhaps, indeed, the answer to the question 'What is it for me to see S as a picture of O?' is really quite simple. Consider a case of someone's looking at a picture of O and failing to see it as a picture of O. A bespectacled matron enters a gallery from the cold outdoors and her glasses fog up. She sees some objects on the wall, but she doesn't see them as pictures of anything. (She may see them as pictures: but we are interested in whether she sees them as pictures of something.) Her glasses clear after a while and she sees that the red and blue objects on the wall are in fact dancing nudes by Matisse. Surely the moment when she sees these objects as pictures of Matisse nudes coincides with the moment when she would be in a position to generate naturally their correct interpretation. So the

196

analysis of pictorial experience is simple: P sees S as a picture of O at T if P is in a position at T from which she can naturally generate the 'O' interpretation of S.

This analysis needs to be spruced up a bit. Suppose P has her eyes closed as she stands before the Matisse nudes. Then it may be true that she *can* naturally interpret the paintings even though she certainly isn't now seeing them at all. So being *able* naturally to interpret S cannot be the same thing as seeing S as a picture. However, this problem is easily resolved. Let's say that P sees S as depicting O at T just if P is naturally generating the 'O'-interpretation of S at T. Now it is not a requirement on P's actually generating this interpretation that she should express it to anyone else, so I am making no claims about what P's manifest behaviour at T must be like.

Yet this analysis is also defective. I think it is by and large true that pictorial experience shadows pictorial interpretation. When I naturally interpret S as being of O, I see S as a picture of O. Yet, although pictorial interpretation and pictorial experience may be naturally co-ordinate, they surely are not identical. Pictorial interpretation is not (on my understanding) a visual experience. One pictorially interprets S when one's knowledge of S's contents is generated in a natural way. But – obviously! – there must be more to pictorial experience than simply knowing what a picture means.

We can at least imagine cases of pictorial interpretation that are not accompanied by pictorial seeing. Suppose I walk up to what I see as a blank canvas and find myself (to my surprise) inclined to say 'This canvas represents Marilyn Monroe.' Intrigued by this, I conduct a test in which I subject people to the same experience; those who are able to recognise Monroe (in photographs) find themselves spontaneously inclined to say that this canvas represents her, while those who prove unable to recognise her also prove devoid of any clue as to what the significance of this blank canvas might be. But all of the subjects report that they simply see a blank canvas. None claim to see a picture of Miss Monroe. Indeed, here's the rub: most people would agree that this canvas is *not* a picture of Miss Monroe. But it satisfies the natural generativity constraint, so on my view it ought to count as a picture! It follows that I have not yet provided a sufficient mark of pictoricity, nor will I be able to do so without offering an account of pictorial experience.

I now perceive the fallacy in my original complacency regarding what makes it true that I see S as a picture of O. It is true, of course, that 'seeing S as a picture of O' is a substitution instance of 'seeing O as F'. But from this, it has no tendency to follow that the analysis of 'seeing S as a picture of O' has no special relevance to the task of analysing depiction. The reason should be clear: while it is not a necessary truth about rabbits that they are seen as rabbits, it is an essential fact about pictures that they are seen as pictures. Yet on pain of circularity we can by no means complete our analysis by adding 'and, of course, for S to be a picture, it must be possible to see S as a picture'. For what is the content of this addition? Surely it cannot mean 'and we must see that S is something we can understand through natural generativity'. This paraphrase cannot be correct, for it appears to involve ascribing the concept of natural generativity to all those who have pictorial experience: a ridiculous notion. Possession of the concept of natural generativity cannot be a condition on the possibility of pictorial experience!

It is now evident why an analysis of depiction must contain an analysis of pictorial experience. An analysis of depiction without any reference to pictorial experience is inadequate; but on pain of circularity, some analysis of what makes pictorial experience *pictorial* must be provided.

At first blush, it appears that the analysis of pictorial experience (and hence depiction) requires some ingredient that the theory of natural generativity cannot supply. And a tempting diagnosis of this situation comes readily to mind. I have trumpeted the fact that the theory of natural generativity is a functional, non-phenomenological account of depiction. In the previous chapter, on the resemblance and illusion models of depiction, I made it quite clear that in their original incarnation these models were defective precisely because they made phenomenological claims about pictorial experience of a most implausible sort. The resemblance model in its original form, for example, claims that when S depicts O, S presents (in some sense) the appearance of O. That is: S appears like O to the perceiver. I have offered an account of S's resemblance to its depictum that involves no such phenomenological claim. It is no part of my view that where S depicts O, the experience of S resembles the experience of O in any intrinsic, qualitative way. But perhaps I have been over-hasty in entirely dismissing the phenomenology of depiction. It seems obvious that *some* account of what it is like to see S must be given before we can fully understand what it is for S to be a picture.

And although in the last chapter we saw off the phenomenal resemblance model, and also of course the phenomenal illusion model, there remains one phenomenological model of depiction that we have not eliminated: the seeing-as or seeing-in model developed in the writings of Richard Wollheim. To be sure, in chapter 1 we established that Wollheim's model could not be a self-sufficient account of pictoricity. But perhaps we must call upon the notion of seeing-as for help in delineating the nature of pictorial experience. Perhaps it is at least a necessary condition on E's being a pictorial experience that E involves seeing S as its depictum. We must now start our search for an adequate understanding of pictorial experience by canvassing Wollheim's attempts in this direction.

2 SEEING-IN

Wollheim's original analysis of pictorial experience gave pride of place to the notion of 'seeing-as'.[1] P's seeing S as a picture of O was analysed in terms of P's seeing S as O. P's seeing S as O was in turn treated as the product of two seeings-as: P's seeing S as S and P's seeing S as O. It is self-evident that this last analysis is circular, since 'seeing S as O' appears in the analysans. However, it is no part of Wollheim's project to offer a general analysis of what it is to see O as F, or in particular of what it is to see S as its depictum. Instead, Wollheim was offering an analysis of 'P sees S as a picture of O'; and it is evident that the offered analysis in terms of P's seeing S *as* O is not circular, for the notion of 'picture' does not appear in the analysans.

However, although we may not be able to fault Wollheim's analysis of pictorial experience for being circular, we may still feel that the introduction of a brute, irreducible notion of seeing S as O is a defect in the account. We may well feel that the analysis is not illuminating enough until we can say more about seeing-as.

But Wollheim has now abandoned the seeing-as model of pictorial experience in favour of what he calls the seeing-in model.[2] Evidently the seeing-in model is not just an improvement upon the seeing-as model: it is a replacement of it. Wollheim now thinks that (in general) it is just not true that we see pictures as what they depict; rather, we see their depicta *in* them. As I understand it, Wollheim's objection to his previous theory has much in common with his original objections to Gombrich's alternating illusion account of depiction. It will be recalled that on Gombrich's model our experience of a Matisse might alternate between an experience as of seeing red and blue paint and an experience as of seeing nude dancers. Wollheim objected to the idea that these two experiences alternate; instead of

---

[1] See Wollheim 1968 and Wollheim 1974.   [2] Wollheim 1980.

occurring in sequence, they temporally coincide. I see the paint at the very same time that I see the dancers.

Now, as I understand Wollheim's new account, it retains the essential simultaneous two-fold experience thesis. But it is retained in pure form. In simultaneously seeing the paint and the dancers I do not see the painted object *as* a group of dancers dancing. Instead, I *simply* have a two-fold experience as of paint and as of dancers. Why is this an improvement? I think that the problem with the seeing-as model must be that it strains credulity to suppose that one could see one and the same thing simultaneously as a patch of paint and as a group of dancers. It is this impossibility which funded Gombrich's alternating illusion model. But now Wollheim appears to have abandoned the claim that we see the paint *as* a group of dancers. Instead, we see the paint and we see the dancers and these two experiences are temporally coincident: and there's an end on it. We might put it this way: our experience as of paint coincides with our experience as of the dancers, but this experience is *not* an experience as of the paint coinciding with the dancers.[3]

It is not clear whether Wollheim would claim that my seeing the Matisse dancers in the painting can be analysed without remainder in terms of a two-fold experience as of paint and dancers. It is fairly obvious that such an analysis would be defective. I can see dancers against a painted background (cf. Bridget Riley's op-art backdrops for the ballet *Colour Moves*): but this isn't necessarily seeing them *in* the painted object against which I see them.

Of course, Wollheim could answer this objection, should he in fact wish to defend the two-fold experience model as an analysis of seeing-in. When I see the dancers *in* the Matisse, the dancers are imaginary. In general, when I see O in S, O is imaginary. O's being imaginary doesn't entail that O is not a real object – just that it is not present to my senses when I look at S. What happens if you look at me while also looking at my portrait? Well, you just have two experiences of me, and one of these experiences is imaginary.

But now let us imagine a different case. Let us imagine that I see S, S depicts you but I do not see S as a picture of you. On the contrary, I see S simply as a dark object, shrouded in shadows. However, when I look at S, I also have an experience as of seeing you. I know that I am not seeing you, and I know that you are not present: nonetheless, I have an experience as of seeing you that is simultaneous with my experience as of seeing the object which is in fact

[3] *Ibid.*

your picture. Yet I do not see this object as a picture of you – nor, I imagine, would we wish to say that I see you *in* this object (whatever that means).

This appears to be a cogent counter-example to the two-fold experience model as an *analysis* of pictorial experience. However, Wollheim might point out that it is a requirement on P's seeing O in S (on P's seeing S as a picture of O) that P should be *able* to attend simultaneously to features of O and features of S. Now, I do not know whether this constraint is in general a plausible one, but one could certainly rig up the counter-example so that it met it. Imagine that when I look at S I see a ghostly image of you. You are translucent. So I can simultaneously attend to your features and to features of the canvas (perhaps I can make out certain features of the canvas). It still does not follow that I see the object as a picture of you.

But a further ploy is available to Wollheim. He might point out, rightly, that in the case I have envisaged, I simply see the object which is in fact your picture while also having an experience as of seeing you: but I do not experience them as connected. So what we really require is (as it were) a three-fold experience: an experience as of seeing the canvas, an experience as of seeing you, and an experience as of there being certain features of the canvas which make it 'appropriate' that I should be seeing you as having certain features.[4]

Unfortunately, this analysis does not succeed. Recall the runic stone example from the first chapter. I there argued that we can imagine a tribe in which native grandsons achieve the ability to have a double experience as of seeing their grandfathers and as of seeing their grandfathers' runes. In my example, the natives see certain features of the rune as being appropriate to a given way of seeing their grandfathers. The rune is perceived as the appropriate vehicle for the seeing of one's grandfather. Now, it is clear to me that it does not follow from this description that the natives see these runes as pictures of their grandfathers. The brute fact of a double experience of S and of O, even when accompanied by seeing features of S as being appropriate to the seeing of O, does not add up to seeing S as a picture of O.

Of course, Wollheim could respond by denying that my natives really see their grandfathers *in* the appropriate runic inscriptions. He might say that I have at most established that it is impossible to give an analysis of seeing-in in terms of double or triple experiences.

---

[4] 'Appropriateness' is stressed by Wollheim 1980 (Essay V) and Wollheim 1977.

Nonetheless, it is still possible to analyse pictorial experience in terms of seeing-in. But we must realise that the double-experience model at most gives us a *hint* as to the nature of seeing-in.

For various reasons I think it would be unsatisfactory to be left with a brute, unanalysable notion of seeing-in. The most pressing danger is simply one of circularity. It is true, technically speaking, that 'P sees O in S' does not seem to be a circular account of 'P sees S as a picture of O.' But this is, I think, merely a superficial fact – the mere fact that 'picture' does not occur *explicitly* in the analysans does not really establish that there is any explanatory power in the analysis. Let us pause to ask 'In *what* does P see O?' When I see a canvas as a picture of Matisse dancers, then on Wollheim's account I see the dancers in the painting. But what is the painting? It is a *painted picture* of the dancers. Surely then we must already understand that P is seeing S as a picture when we claim that P sees O in S. It is surely *not* the case that I see the dancers in the paint or in the chalk (*what* could that mean?): I see them in the painting or in the chalk drawing.

The upshot of the argument so far is: (1) Wollheim cannot give an adequate, non-circular account of P's seeing O in S in terms of P's seeing S and P's seeing O (plus P's seeing that there are features of S which make it appropriate that he should see O); (2) Wollheim cannot give an adequate or explanatory account of pictorial experience in terms of the unanalysed notion of 'seeing-in'. In so far as one understands 'P sees O in S' this is just a fancy way of saying 'P sees S as a picture of O': the two facts are too *intimately* related to use one in the analysis of the other. Of course, I do not preclude the possibility that there might be a third sort of fact in terms of which we would analyse both seeing-in and pictorial experience.

Thus far I have overlooked one way of getting Wollheim off the hook. Could we not analyse both seeing-in and pictorial experience by judiciously combining the double-experience model with the theory of natural generativity? It is clear why the grandfather runes, for example, are not pictures: the natives do not naturally generate their interpretations of these inscriptions. Perhaps, then, pictorial experience requires some combination of naturally generated interpretation and double experience. Perhaps one could say that P sees S as a picture of O when (i) P naturally generates the O-interpretation of S and (ii) P has a two-fold experience as of seeing S and as of seeing O.

This proposal does indeed rule out all three problem cases which I have discussed in this chapter. First, it follows from this analysis that the natives do not see their grandfather runes as pictures since, although they have the appropriate double experience, they do not naturally generate their interpretations of the runes. Secondly, this analysis seems to explain why my simultaneously seeing a dark object (which in fact portrays you) and my having an experience as of seeing a ghostly version of you does not add up to my seeing the dark object as a picture of you. In this case, again, I do not generate any interpretation of the object in question so, *a fortiori,* I do not naturally generate an interpretation. Finally, this analysis would 'take care of' the case of the blank canvas which we naturally take to represent Marilyn Monroe. Although we naturally generate the 'Monroe' interpretation, we do not enjoy an experience as of Miss Monroe.

However, this analysis has a wretchedly cobbled-together look to it. What exactly is the relation between experience and interpretation on this view? It would appear that pictorial experience is just a coincidence between natural interpretation and double experience. But surely this consonance can't be a mere coincidence? Indeed, just as brute coincidence between seeing S and seeing O is not enough for seeing S as a picture of O, so brute coincidence between double experience and naturally generated interpretation is not enough for pictorial experience. For example, suppose that in the case of the ghostly image – where I am simultaneously transfixed by a diaphanous image of you and an image of a dark object which happens to be your picture – I *had* naturally generated the correct interpretation of the dark object (by whatever mechanism allowed me to achieve the natural interpretation of the blank canvas of Monroe): this would still not transform my double experience into a pictorial experience. We must sadly conclude that natural generativity alone lacks the power to transfigure a two-fold experience of S and O into an experience of S as a picture of O.

It may be wondered whether Wollheim has not actually weakened his case by shifting the burden of analysis from the notion of 'seeing-as' onto the notion of 'seeing-in'. If I see a Matisse *as* a group of dancers, I have more than a double-decker experience (of paint and dancers): I also see the work as having dancer-like features. Now by contrast, when I look at your diaphanous image while looking at the dark object which portrays you, I do not see that portrait as having an appearance like yours. Similarly, I do not see the blank Marilyn canvas as having Monroe-like features, nor do the natives in my imaginary example see the runic inscriptions as possessing grandfatherly attributes. Seeing-as would thus seem to be a stronger notion than seeing-in and a better basis for an analysis of pictorial experience.

Alas, in so far as the seeing-as model is preferable to the seeing-in model, it simply reduces to the phenomenal resemblance model. For seeing S as having O-like features means seeing visible similarities between S and O: and we have already concluded that we cannot in fact find such visible similarities for each respect in which S depicts O. Consequently, the strong notion of seeing-as inherits all the defects inherent in the resemblance model.

It is now appropriate to step back and ask 'What went wrong with Wollheim's theory? What is wrong with the omnibus-experience model of pictorial experience?' The problem is that the double-experience model cannot explain the articulation or structure of pictorial experience. When I see S as a picture of O, my experience has a content with a certain *structure*: S is a picture of O. It is not possible to explain this structure in terms of experiences which simply have as their objects the same elements – S and O – as my pictorial experience. In other words, in pictorial experience, I see S and O as related in a certain way, by the 'picture'-relation. But the simple coincidence of 'seeing S' and 'seeing O' cannot amount necessarily to an experience as of their being related in a certain way. The 'seeing-as' model is superior to the brute omnibus-experience model because it at least attempts to respect the structure of pictorial experience. It is suggested that an experience as of S's bearing the 'picture'-relation to O can be explained in terms of (or is equivalent to) an experience as of seeing S as bearing various resemblance-relations to O. When Wollheim requires that one should not only see S and 'see' O, but also see the appropriateness of certain features of S to one's seeing O as having certain features, this requirement again is intended to create an analysis which respects (or models) the structure of pictorial experience. However, this analysis fails simply because the notion of 'appropriateness' is not sufficiently defined. Certainly my native grandsons see the runic inscriptions, and certain aspects thereof, as appropriate to the particular ways in which they envisage their dead kindred: yet *ex hypothesi* their experiences are not *pictorial*. The seeing-as model provides a more explicit suggestion of what 'appropriateness' might amount to: similarity. Yet we know that in fact the similarity account is false. So Wollheim's account seems to be stuck either with not enough structure or with the wrong kind of structure.

Why did the attempt to combine the natural generativity account with the double-experience account fail? Simply because the mere fact that an omnibus experience E is accompanied by a natural interpretation has no tendency to establish that E has the structure of pictorial experience. Whatever explanation of pictorial experience we arrive at, it must have the effect of placing some kind of *constraint* on the structure of the experience. The claim must have the general form: an experience E with structure S will also have the structure of being an experience as of x's being a picture of y.

Now we know that natural generativity by itself is not enough to impose the necessary structure. The natural generativity constraint is simply not experiential or visual enough to do the job; and the seeing-in or omnibus-experience model, while it is explicitly visual, is not capable of imposing the right structure. So must we start again from scratch? Can nothing of our previous work be used in providing an account of pictorial experience? Remember: the problem of pictorial experience is one which *must* be solved by an adequate theory of depiction, for pictures must be seen as pictures and we must analyse 'seeing S as a picture' in a way which does not make essential use of the concept of a picture.

Obviously any analysis of pictorial experience must also respect another fact: that that experience has a certain significance, that such an experience involves my knowing the significance of the artifact in question. Seeing something as a picture involves my seeing it as having a certain content, as being accurate only if there are certain objects that have certain properties. Consequently, pictorial experience is explicitly *interpretative* in nature. Seeing S as a picture of O entails or involves knowing what S means. It is reasonable to conclude, therefore, that the correct account of pictorial experience cannot be entirely estranged from a proper account of how pictures are interpreted.

3 PICTORIAL EXPERIENCE: THE SOLUTION

Let us return once again to the magic blank canvas that we find ourselves willy-nilly inclined to take for a representation of Marilyn Monroe. What immediately stares us in the face is: a blank canvas. Nothing in our *conscious visual experience* of the canvas corresponds to or matches the representational features I ascribe to it. That is: there is nothing about my conscious visual experience such that had that item been different, my interpretation of the canvas would have been different. This suggests that the crucial requirement on pictorial experience is that items of a naturally generated interpretation should co-vary with or track specific items in the 'contents' of my visual consciousness. Let us try to put this constraint more precisely:

P's conscious visual experience E is an experience as of S's being a picture of O as F_1 . . . F just if: E is an experience as of colours or marks on the surface of S and for every representational content P ascribes to S of the form 'O is F_k': (1) There is some feature of P's visual experience as of the colours or marks on S's surface which 'mirrors' this content ascription so that either (i) the experience would have been different had the content ascription been different or (ii) the content ascription would have been different had the experience been different; and (2) the interpretation in question (A represents O as F_k) is naturally generated.

It seems to me that this definition of pictorial experience has several features that are worth noting. First, it must be stressed that the reference to *conscious* visual experience is ineliminable. When I interpret the magic white canvas of Miss Monroe, it may well be (it must be!) that I am receiving subliminal visual cues that somehow trigger my Monroe-recognising abilities. However, it is impossible for these cues to be made directly present to visual consciousness in the example I have imagined. That is why I can never experience the canvas as a picture of Miss Monroe. I confess that I have no idea of how to go about explaining or analysing the difference between conscious and sub-conscious visual awareness: for my purposes I must simply help myself to this distinction.

Secondly, it is a consequence of my definition that pictorial experience can be mistaken or inappropriate in various ways. If, for example, S is not a picture but is instead something like a picture (for example, the scarab-marks discussed in chapter 7), if I see S as a picture my experience is mistaken (just as it would be a mistake to see a squirrel as a rabbit). Moreover, even if S is a picture, I can see it as depicting things which in fact it doesn't. It seems to me a good feature of my account of pictorial experience that it allows us to assess such experiences as correct or incorrect. Nor is the mistake *simply* a matter of a mistaken interpretation. If I naturally generate an incorrect interpretation of the blank Monroe canvas – one which, say, differs from the interpretations offered by others – it would be ridiculous to impugn my experience. I have not incorrectly seen the canvas as representing Monroe in a certain way – because I have not seen it as representing Monroe at all. I can impugn my experience of S only if that experience reflects or mirrors the mistaken interpretation.

The relation of 'mirroring' is a third point to stress. In requiring that P's experience of S should mirror his interpretations of S, I do not commit myself on the question of whether the experience is responsible for the interpretation or the interpretation for the experience. It seems to me that there is good reason to cast the definition of pictorial experience in this non-committal mould: who can doubt that sometimes, primitive facts about experience shape our interpretations of S while that interpretation also affects our experience?

It is also crucial to mark the importance of the natural generativity constraint. An experience will count as seeing S as a picture of O only if it mirrors a *naturally generated* interpretation of S. Obviously, only by requiring the natural generation of the reflected interpretation can we mark the difference between seeing S as a picture and simply seeing S as a meaningful symbol. No doubt, our experience of sentences and other symbolic artifacts co-varies with our interpretations of them, but those interpretations are not naturally generated.

It is, I think, a fact that the difference between seeing the magic white canvas of Miss Monroe and a Warhol collage of Monroe is not fully captured by our explicit analysis of pictorial experience. For example, when I look at the Warhol collage, I am not *surprised* to find myself interpreting it as a picture of Monroe; but when I face the blank canvas and nonetheless say that it represents Monroe I am *surprised* that I feel this inclination. However, it seems to me that this difference is purely accidental. If I become accustomed to such magic canvases I will no longer be surprised by my inclination to interpret them. You may say 'You can perceptually discriminate those objects which are likely to yield pictorial experiences from those which won't prior to interpreting them; but you could never tell whether a canvas was going to be "magic" in advance of actually asking yourself whether there is any particular interpretation of it you feel inclined to offer.' I suppose this does point to a difference between pictures and magic canvases, but again it doesn't seem to indicate the existence of some crucial or essential feature of pictorial experience that I have as yet failed to capture in the web of theory.

I take it that my account of pictorial experience lacks the phenomenological constraint which Wollheim's two-fold experience model imposes. On Wollheim's view, when I see a picture as of O I have an experience as of seeing O. I have not made any essential use of this notion at all in my account of pictorial experience. Consequently, in so far as both 'seeing-as' and 'seeing-in' at least imply the occurrence of a double experience, they imply something not required by an adequate account of pictorial experience – if my account *is* adequate. Now, when I see a picture of Miss Monroe, it is far from obvious that my experience of the picture is pervaded by an experience as of seeing Miss Monroe. Indeed, the postulation of such an experience seems to me without any warrant whatsoever. The most that could ever have been said for the positing of such a double experience is that it helped to explain something crucial about pictorial experience. But then, if we can explain pictorial experience without reference to such a duplex experience, Wollheim's account must succumb to Occam's Razor.

4 THE END OF 'SEEING-IN'

Of course, it is impossible to prove that there is no aspect of pictorial experience that is explicable only by invoking the notion of 'seeing-in'. It has been suggested to me that perhaps a fully correct account of our intuitions concerning colour-reversed symbols would require us to stipulate that a picture is a fully iconic representation of O as F only if we can see an O which has F in it.[5]

On my account of depiction, if we can naturally interpret S as representing an O that is F, S depicts O as F, provided S was intended to represent O as F *and* provided that S was created with the intention that its correct interpretation should be accessible to anyone who could recognise that something was O and that something was an F-type thing. Now, it seems to be possible to imagine an S that satisfies these constraints but is not a picture of O as F.

Imagine people who are innately equipped to make the right interpretation of colour-reversed symbols; they know that red on the picture surface stands for green in the object and that green on the picture surface stands for red in the object. Confronted with a colour-reversed symbol, they naturally generate the correct interpretation. They know that the symbol we would naturally take to be a picture of a green tree is really a representation of a red tree. But since the colour-reversed symbol of a green tree does not depict it as green, and since these people can naturally generate the 'green' interpretation of the colour-reversed symbol, it follows that natural generativity is not an adequate mark of pictoricity. We may assume that the colour-reversed symbols are manufactured by colour-inverts for other colour-inverts. They are made with the intention

---

[5] The possibility of such an objection was put to me by Malcolm Budd. Budd also forced me to see the importance of giving an account of pictorial experience.

that their contents should be naturally interpretable. All my conditions for a symbol's pictoricity seem to be satisfied: and yet these symbols surely are not pictures of green trees.

Now here we seem to have a problem ideally suited to the double-experience model. *Surely* the reason we would not wish to count the colour-inverted symbols of green trees as pictures of green trees is that we do not have an experience as of seeing a green tree when we look at them: instead we see (as it were) a red tree. Even the innately colour-inverted do not see the symbols as green trees. They see them as red trees but then apply the inversion rule 'If S is a picture of x and S is red, then S represents x as green.' So perhaps the double-experience model really does serve a useful purpose: at least it helps to explain why the innate colour-inverts do not see a red picture of O as depicting O as green.

I do not believe that the innate colour-inverts are in fact naturally generating their colour interpretations. Their interpretations are, of course, natural in the sense of being the result of an innate disposition to give twisted colour interpretations; but these interpretations are not natural in the proper sense. It has not been asserted that their interpretation of S as representing a green tree emanates from an ability to recognise trees plus an ability to recognise green things plus simple initiation into the practice of depiction. In fact, it seems to me that the only way to make sense of the idea of innate colour-inverts is to suppose that they have a wired-in rule that tells them to give twisted colour interpretations of pictures. The only difference between innate colour-inverts and artificial colour-inverts is that the former possess innately the rules which the latter have to learn. The fact that the rule is innate does not matter; the very fact that such a rule plays an essential role in the inverts' interpretation shows that their interpretations are not recognitionally generated but depend, essentially, on this special rule.

It might be asked why we must suppose the innate colour-inverts to have an innate inversion rule. Let us suppose that they are just wired in such a way that red pictures engage their green-recognising capacities. Does this supposition *really* make sense? Let us suppose that these inverts can make the same colour discriminations we can. They can see that a red picture is more like a red tomato than like a green tomato. How could a red object engage a green-recognising capacity? Surely such a capacity would have to be defective if it were systematically engaged by red pictures. I am not sure I would still call it a green-recognising capacity. I would perhaps think that in fact these people were operating with the concept 'green*' where x

209

is green★ just if x is green and not a picture or x is a picture and red. It is obvious that this capacity is not a colour-recognising capacity at all, since whether or not something is 'green★' depends not only on its colour but on whether or not it is a picture.

Here it might be suggested that perhaps natural generativity is language-relative. Suppose my colour inverts do operate the concept 'green★' as I have suggested. Given their innate propensity to take red pictures as symbols of green things, they would naturally say that a red picture of a tomato represented the tomato as green★. But clearly the red picture also engages their green★-recognising abilities. So surely it must follow that they have naturally generated the green★ interpretation. But then it would follow – given that natural generativity entails pictoricity – that these pictures do depict green★ tomatoes. But surely, since they are red, these pictures cannot depict green★ tomatoes – for green★ tomatoes are green.

But this objection from language relativity is no good. It is indeed true that when a colour invert meets a green★ canvas he says that it represents a green★ object; it is also true that the canvas engages his green★-recognising capacities. But it is not true that his interpretation is naturally generated. The reason is clear. The ability to recognise green★ things (green objects that are not pictures and red objects that are) is not solely responsible for his interpretation of a given canvas as representing a green★ object. The green★ interpretation of a green★ canvas also involves the colour-inversion rule that red pictures shall stand for green objects. Of course, where the depicted object is not a picture, this rule means that green★ pictures stand for green★ objects. But on the supposition that our colour inverts discriminate colours in the way we do, it follows that this rule is a colour-inversion rule for them; the fact that 'green★ represents green★' is an inversion rule is simply concealed by the strange meaning these people attach to green★. If one is clear-headed, one can see that these people are not naturally generating their ascriptions of colour-content to their inverted symbols.

What emerges from this argument is the importance of my claim that we pictorially interpret S as being a picture of an O that is F only when S engages our O- and F-recognising abilities so that our interpretation of S is the result of their having been engaged or triggered by S. The colour-invert, whether innate or artificial, whether operating bent predicates like 'green★' or straight ones like 'green' and 'red', does not recognitionally generate his colour interpretations. Some rule for decoding colour-inverted symbols must be wired or dinned into him.

Indeed, we should note that the innate colour-invert is faced with a handicap when he confronts non-inverted symbols. Surely an innate invert – one who is innately designed so that he has to generate the inverted interpretation – would generate incorrect interpretations of colour-normal symbols. The colour-invert might be designed less rigidly; perhaps he is just designed so that he would naturally tend to give the inverted interpretation. In this event he might learn the colour-normal rules, just as we have to learn the colour-inverted rules: but he would never be able to generate naturally the correct interpretation either of colour-inverted symbols or of colour-normal ones. He can interpret the inverted symbols only because of his innately wired-in inversion rule and he would only be able to interpret the colour-normal symbols by learning a rule which negatives or overrides his innate propensity to propose twisted colour-interpretations. Whether he is interpreting inverted or normal symbols, the innate invert needs to know more rules than the non-invert. In general, it is evident that the information cost of interpreting inverted symbols is greater than the information cost of interpreting non-inverted symbols – provided one is not an innate colour-invert. Being an *innate* invert increases the cost of interpreting colour-normal symbols without reducing the cost of interpreting colour-inverted symbols.

It is worth stressing that the information cost differential only shows up on a global scale. In 'On Drawing an Object'[6] Richard Wollheim suggested that one difference between the colour-inverted scheme and the colour-normal scheme was that the decoding of an inverted symbol requires an *inference* while interpreting a normal symbol does not. Now, I take it that Wollheim did not suppose a colour-invert would always have to reach his interpretations via specific inferences; it is possible that the invert could become just as familiar with his code as we are with our language: interpreting inverted symbols would become 'second nature' to him. However, we could still represent his knowledge in the form of an inference. The inference might go like this:

(1) If S is red and S depicts x, S represents x as green.
(2) S is red and S depicts x.
So: (3) S represents x as green.

But we could also represent the natural generator's interpretation as a form of *modus ponens*:

[6] Wollheim 1974.

(1)* If S is naturally interpretable as being an O that is F, S
represents O as F.
(Convention C)
(2)* S is naturally interpretable as representing an O that is
F.
So: (3)* S represents O as F.

Each interpretation can be represented as a form of *modus ponens*; if
one simply looks at the information used in one inerpretation, it
might seem that the two interpretations have the same information
cost. However, matters change if you consider what global competence in a colour-reversed system would require: it would require
knowledge of several colour-inversion conventions *plus* all the usual
recognitional abilities. By contrast, knowledge of Convention C
and the relevant recognitional abilities will endow you with competence in the completely iconic system. If one looks at these interpretative inferences locally, it just seems that the iconic systems
simply invoke a different convention from the non-iconic systems;
but viewed globally, one sees that iconic systems only require Convention C – and one also realises that the role of Convention C in
iconic interpretation is quite unlike the role of conventions in non-
iconic systems. Knowledge of Convention C is not *content-specific*: it
does not give you by itself knowledge of the meaning of any icon or
part thereof; linguistic conventions, by contrast, tell you the meaning of parts of sentences.

In general, the theory of natural generativity offers an adequate
account of our intuitions regarding colour-reversal. We have found
no need to rely on either of Wollheim's suggestions regarding
colour-reversal; it is not true that deciphering colour-reversed symbols requires inference, and even though we can represent this
decoding as inferential, particular colour-inverted inferences
require no more premises than colour-normal inferences. The difference only appears at the global level. Moreover, I have not found
it necessary to rely on the double-experience model of pictorial experience to explain why it is that the innate colour-inverts do not see
a red canvas *as* a picture of a green object. I conclude that we have
been given no reason to accept the postulation of a double experience in pictorial perception. More constructively, I have proposed
that a visual experience of S is a pictorial experience if it specifically
reflects or shadows the perceiver's naturally generated interpretation of S. Without specifying the specific structure of a pictorial experience E, I have simply said that its structure must track the

structure of the naturally generated interpretation of S. Tracking or mirroring involves more than an isomorphism; it is not enough that there should be a feature of E corresponding to each feature of the naturally generated interpretation. It is required that aspects of experience and interpretation should co-vary: had the experience been otherwise, the interpretation would have been different and had the interpretation been different, the experience would have looked different.

5 MENTAL IMAGES

We may now succinctly state the complete definition of a picture: S is a picture if we can recognitionally generate knowledge of S's meaning, provided that we can see S as a picture. Let us call S a quasi-picture if it satisfies the first half of this definition but not the second. Our imaginary magic canvas of Miss Monroe would be a quasi-picture. Are there any actual quasi-pictures?

It seems to me that if – and this is a big 'if' – there are mental images, then it is likely that they are quasi-pictures. As Dennett, Kosslyn, Block[7] and others have stressed, if there are mental images, they must be like pictures in some definable way. There is no reason for postulating mental images unless we have grounds for positing internal picture-like representations. Unfortunately, all attempts to say what mental images would be like have foundered on the lack of an adequate analysis of depiction. Moreover, it is not introspectively obvious that we have experiences as of seeing mental pictures. In other words, there are no contents of our consciousness which we see as mental pictures. But if we take mental images to be quasi-pictures we no longer need to suppose that mental images are experienced as pictures. After all, the magic canvas of Miss Monroe was (would have been) a quasi-picture: but we do not (would not) experience it as a picture of Miss Monroe or of anything else. So we could say that a mental image would be an internal quasi-picture, that is, a form of internal representation such that the subject would have access to the information it contains just provided that he were able to recognise visually the objects and properties represented. It is not necessary that there should be anything it is like to have access to such pictorially encoded information; indeed, it is not even necessary to be conscious of them as pictures – it is not necessary to visualise mental images. But this

[7] Dennett 1969 and Dennett 1978; Kosslyn 1980; Block 1981.

result is just what we want. We do not want to say that when I visualise a discobolus, I visualise a mental image of a discobolus: I just visualise the discobolus. Nonetheless, it might be argued that my ability to visualise the discobolus is a function of my accessing information that is stored in quasi-pictorial form.

Of course, since mental images are quasi-pictures and quasi-pictures in turn are defined as symbols interpretable on the basis of relevant recognitional ability, it follows that the notion of a mental image cannot be used in the analysis of the notion of recognition. Nonetheless, it may be wondered whether this analysis establishes that mental images can never be used to explain someone's recognitional ability. May it not be that my encoding a mental image of a discus-thrower is what enables me to recognise discus-throwers? The answer again is clearly negative. For the information from a quasi-picture is only accessible as *pictorial* information to those who already have the ability to recognise the objects encoded in the quasi-picture. A picture can be *pictorially* interpreted only by someone who already has the relevant recognitional ability.

This point can be clarified by considering *public* pictures. It is certainly true that I can teach you how to recognise Sergio by showing you a picture of Sergio. But two facts are noteworthy. First, the picture was produced by someone who can already recognise Sergio. Secondly, this picture endows you with the ability to recognise Sergio – to recognise that a certain person is the one called 'Sergio', for example – only if someone who possesses the relevant recognitional ability tells you that this picture represents Sergio. Pictures can only generate novel recognitional abilities because of their *publicity*: they are created by others and they are interpreted for us by others. It is clear that a mental image cannot, like a public image, form the basis of a novel recognitional ability.

If I am right, mental images are recognitionally inert: they cannot affect new recognitional abilities. We may put the point in the form of a dilemma. In so far as there is reason to postulate that P has a mental quasi-picture of O, there must be reason to suppose that P has some internal representational token which she interprets on the basis of her ability to recognise O. If she does not already have the ability to recognise O, there can be no reason for ascribing a mental image of O to her: for then she would not have the ability to interpret the internal token pictorially. So if we suppose S is P's mental quasi-picture of O, we must suppose that P accesses the information encoded in S on the basis of a prior ability to recognise O. If we deny the prior ability, we must deny that P can have pictorial access

214

to S. Either way, mental images cannot both function as pictures and be used to explain recognitional ability. Of course, to prove that mental images cannot explain recognitional ability is not to show that they have no function in one's mental economy.

The non-publicity of mental images creates another problem. I have said that a picture S represents O only if it is intended to do so, only if it is made by someone who intends (1) that S should represent O, (2) that the O-interpretation of S should be naturally producible and (3) that this intention (and all other relevant communicative intentions) should be known. But as mental images are not created, and as they are not instruments of communication, it is unclear how they can achieve their significance; the Gricean mechanism helps explain the meaning of public or manifest images: what explains the meaning of *internal* images?

It may help to compare mental quasi-pictures to the photographs produced by a camera that continues to produce pictures even though no one is operating it. I have said that photographs achieve their semantic status by a different route from that taken by paintings, drawings and etchings. One cannot plausibly say that a photograph S depicts O only if someone intended S to represent O, for it may well be that no one had any hand in the production of S, and even if someone intentionally took the photograph, it may well turn out that they were quite unaware of what its pictorial content would be. However, we can say in general that a photograph is produced by a mechanism (a camera) such that the creator and user of the mechanism intend that the mechanism should create representational tokens that are naturally interpretable as being of the objects which in fact 'cause' the photograph. An object 'causes' a photograph in so far as that photograph tracks features of that object's appearance. In general, it is also intended that those who look at photographs should be aware of these intentions. Now, we have still had to bring notions of purpose and intention into the account of how a photograph achieves content or semantic significance. Clearly such notions cannot play a role in the explanation of how mental quasi-tokens get their significance. Nor is it clear what can play this role. The most likely form of explanation would be some argument for there being a mechanism in the brain that has evolved through natural selection because of its ability to create and store tokens such that these tokens track various features of the world and such that the mind knows what features are tracked by these tokens in virtue of its ability to recognise the features tracked.

I am not at all sure how or whether such an account could be made to work in detail. However, I would at least hazard the suggestion that there could be a reason for such a mode of information storage to evolve in creatures with a certain recognitional ability. Such tokens would not explain recognitional ability, but they might just serve as a useful way of storing certain facts. In particular, I have argued that the information costs of interpreting iconic symbols is generally lower than the information costs incurred in non-iconic interpretation. However, it is far from clear to me that we could ever have good reason to posit mental images or any other form of internal representation.

Are not mental quasi-pictures, as I have described them, dispensable? It appears likely that anything we could explain by positing mental images could be explained by simply invoking the relevant recognitional ability. After all, if we posit the mental images, we willy-nilly posit the recognitional abilities associated with the ability to interpret pictorially or 'access' it. So if we can use the recognitional ability alone to explain what we use the mental image to explain, we should dispense with the mental image. So in general the challenge which the iconophile must answer is this: 'What is the point of positing an internal quasi-picture of O as something over and above the visual ability to recognise O?'

Suppose that I am having a daydream of walking through Florence. I try to visualise my first walk in the Boboli Gardens. I visualise the back of the Pitti Palace, certain statues in the gardens and the famous Venus in the Grotticella. I may ask myself 'How do I know that I have visualised the right gardens? How do I know that I have not strayed (as it were) into the garden at Fontainebleau?' Isn't it just this: I am confident that I have the ability to tell the difference between the two gardens? I can test this ability publicly. Others agree with me when I point to a picture and say 'That's the grotto at Fontainebleau, not the one in the Boboli.' I am sure that this ability carries over to my visualisings: if I am able to recognise Primaticcio's grotto when confronted with it, directly or through pictures, I shall be able to tell whether I am visualising it. My ability to interpret my visualising seems to be of a piece with my ability to recognise the objects visualised. And this strongly suggests that my visualisings just *are* quasi-pictures; from which, please note that it does not follow that I experience my visual imaginings *as pictures*. It is just that I treat them as though they played the causal or functional role played by quasi-pictures. I have access to the contents of my visualisings, and accordingly can assess their success, because I can visually recognise the objects visualised.

216

On this view, mental images just are what I am interpreting and understanding when I construe my own visualisings: yet I am not aware of them as pictures. I come to think of them as quasi-pictures only when I reflect upon what I must be doing in interpreting these visualisings and when I reflect on the similarity between the constraints on pictorial understanding and the constraints on my knowledge of the contents of my own visualisings.

What I would emphatically wish to reject is the thought that one can *explain* my ability to recognise the success of a visualising in terms of mental images. I certainly think that no explanatory mileage whatsoever can be got out of the supposition that some homunculus within me compares my visualising with some mental image of what is to be visualised and then informs me of whether I have got it right or wrong. It is well known that there are insuperable objections to any such picture: how does the homunculus know that he has correctly interpreted the mental image? If, for example, we suppose that he has an image of the Boboli which he compares with my visualisation in order to determine whether I am really visualising the Boboli, we must ask how he knows that his image is indeed an image of the Boboli. Surely the answer is: he has the ability to recognise the Boboli and it is this which allows him to interpret the image in question (otherwise, as we have seen, his interpretation of the image would not be pictorial in the relevant sense). But then, if he can recognise the Boboli and he can apply this ability to judging whether his image of the Boboli is accurate, he could have applied this ability directly to my visualising. So on my view we have good reason to think that there are mental images: our visualisations precisely lead us to this conclusion. But it is evident that these images are not themselves explanatory of any cognitive or recognitional ability. They fall on the side of things which require explanation rather than on the side of things which can be used in providing explanations.

It may seem strange that I have spoken of 'interpreting' our visualisings. But it can't be doubted that we do interpret them – for we have a conception of what we are visualising and that is just like knowing what something depicts or what a sentence says. The intentionality or directedness of visual imagination is something admitted on all hands. What is clear is that this cognitive ability to interpret our visual images or imaginings cannot in any way be *explained* in terms of visual images.

Perhaps we can clinch the point by imagining a case where I hear some words running through my head. Now I may well be unable to interpret these words even though I can recognise the objects which in fact they signify. Perhaps the words are in Russian or some other language wholly unknown to me. How they came to be in my head is irrelevant. The point is this: surely visual recognitional ability is not enough for me to know what these imagined words mean. By contrast, so long as I can recognise the Boboli, so long as I can recognise the famous Bologna statue of Venus in the Grotticella, I can know whether or not I am visualising the Boboli and the statue of Venus or whether I am in fact visualising something entirely different. But once we establish that there are mental images, we discover that this is really a rather unexciting truth – and that all the explanatory work remains to be done.

References

Aarsleff, Hans, 1982, *From Locke to Saussure: Essays on the Study of Language and Intellectual History*, London

Alpers, Svetlana, 1983, *The Art of Describing: Dutch Art in the Seventeenth Century*, London

Barish, Jonas, 1981, *The Anti-Theatrical Prejudice*, Berkeley

Bennett, Jonathan, 1976, *Linguistic Behaviour*, Cambridge

Block, Ned (ed.), 1981, *Imagery*, London

Bower, Tom, 1977, *The Perceptual World of the Infant*, Glasgow

Chomsky, Noam, 1957, *Syntactic Structures*, The Hague
  1965, *Aspects of a Theory of Syntax*, Cambridge, Mass.

Craig, E. J., 1975, 'The Problem of Necessary Truth', in Simon Blackburn (ed.), *Meaning, Reference and Necessity*, Cambridge

Danto, Arthur, 1981, *The Transfiguration of the Commonplace*, Cambridge, Mass.

Davidson, Donald, 1967, 'Truth and Meaning', *Synthese*, 17, 304–23
  1968–9, 'On Saying That', *Synthese*, 19, 130–46
  1979, 'What Metaphors Mean', in S. Saks (ed.), *On Metaphor*, Chicago
  1984, *Inquiries into Truth and Interpretation*, Oxford

Dennett, D. C. 1969, *Content and Consciousness*, London
  1978, *Brainstorms*, Vermont

Deregowski, J. B., 1980, *Illusions, Patterns and Pictures: A Cross-Cultural Perspective*, London

Evans, G. and McDowell, J. (eds.), 1976, *Truth and Meaning*, Oxford

Fodor, J. A., 1976, *The Language of Thought*, Sussex

Foucault, Michel, 1970, *The Order of Things*, New York

Geach, P. T., 1967, 'Intentional Identity', *Journal of Philosophy*, 64, 627–32

Gombrich, E. H., 1960, *Art and Illusion*, Princeton
  1963, *Meditations on a Hobby Horse*, London

Gombrich, E. H. and Kris, E., 1940, *Caricature*, London

Gombrich, E. H., Hochberg, J., and Black, M., 1972, *Art, Perception and Reality*, Baltimore

Goodman, Nelson, 1966, *The Structure of Appearance*, Indiana
  1968, *Languages of Art*, Indiana
  1972, *Problems and Projects*, Indiana
  1973, *Fact, Fiction and Forecast*, 3rd edn, Indiana
  1978, *Ways of Worldmaking*, Sussex

Gregory, R. L., 1966, *Eye and Brain*, New York
    1970, *The Intelligent Eye*, New York
    1974, *Concepts and Mechanisms of Perception*, London
Gregory, R. L., and Gombrich, E. H. (eds.), 1973, *Illusion in Nature and Art*, London
Grice, Paul, 1957, 'Meaning', *Philosophical Review*, 66, 377–88
    1961, 'The Causal Theory of Perception', *Proceedings of the Aristotelian Society Supplementary Volume*
    1975, 'Logic and Conversation', in Davidson and Harman (eds.), *The Logic of Grammar*, Encino, California
Hagen, M. (ed.), 1980, *The Perception of Pictures*, Vol. 1, London
Holt, E. G., 1957, *A Documentary History of Art*, Vol. 1, New York
Kim, Jaegwon, 1969, 'Events and their Descriptions', in Rescher (ed.), *Essays in Honor of Carl Hempel*, Dordrecht
    1973, 'Causation, Nomic Subsumption and the Concept of an Event', *Journal of Philosophy*, 70, 217–36
    1976, 'Events as Property Exemplifications', in Brand and Walton (eds.), *Action Theory*, Dordrecht
Kosslyn, S. M., 1980, *Image and Mind*, Cambridge, Mass.
Kripke, Saul, 1980, *Naming and Necessity*, Oxford
Kris, E. and Kurz, O., 1979, *Legend, Myth and Magic in the Image of the Artist*, New Haven
Langer, S. K., 1942, *Philosophy in a New Key*, Cambridge, Mass.
Lewis, David, 1969, *Convention*, Cambridge, Mass.
Novitz, David, 1977, *Pictures and their use in Communication*, The Hague
Panofsky, Erwin, 1954, *Galileo as a Critic of the Arts*, The Hague
    1959, 'Style and Medium in the Motion Pictures', in Mast (ed.), *Film Theory and Criticism*, 1974, Oxford
    1964, *Tomb Sculpture: Its Changing Aspects from Egypt to Bernini*, London
Perkins, D., 1981, *The Mind's Best Work*, Cambridge, Mass.
Pirenne, M. H., 1970, *Optics, Painting and Photography*, Cambridge
Sampson, G., 1980, *Making Sense*, Oxford
Sartre, Jean-Paul, 1948, *The Psychology of Imagination*, New York
Saussure, F. de, 1966, *Course in General Linguistics*, New York
Scheffler, I., 1979, *Beyond the Letter*, London
Schier, F., 1983(a), 'Michel Foucault's *This is not a pipe*', *New York Times Book Review*, 22 January
    1983(b), 'Arthur Danto's *Transfiguration of the Commonplace*', *Times Literary Supplement*, 4 February
    1983(c), 'Roland Barthes's *The Fashion System*', *The New York Times Book Review*, 24 July
Sellars, Wilfrid, 1963, *Science, Perception and Reality*, London
Simon, Herbert, 1969, *Sciences of the Artificial*, Cambridge, Mass.
Sparshott, F., 1982, *The Theory of the Arts*, Princeton
Steinberg, Leo, 1972, *Other Criteria*, Oxford

Thomas, Keith, 1971, *Religion and the Decline of Magic*, London
  1983, *Man and the Natural World*, London
Walton, Kendall, 1973, 'Pictures and Make-Believe', *Philosophical Review*,
  82, 283–319
Wollheim, Richard, 1968, *Art and its Objects*, New York
  1972, 'Style Now', in B. Smith (ed.), *Concerning Contemporary Art*, 1974,
  Oxford
  1974, *On Art and the Mind*, Cambridge, Mass.
  1977, 'Representation: The Philosophical Contribution to Psychology',
  Critical Inquiry, 709–23
  1980, *Art and its Objects*, Cambridge (second edition)

Index of names

Index of subjects